Preaching
with BOLD
Assurance

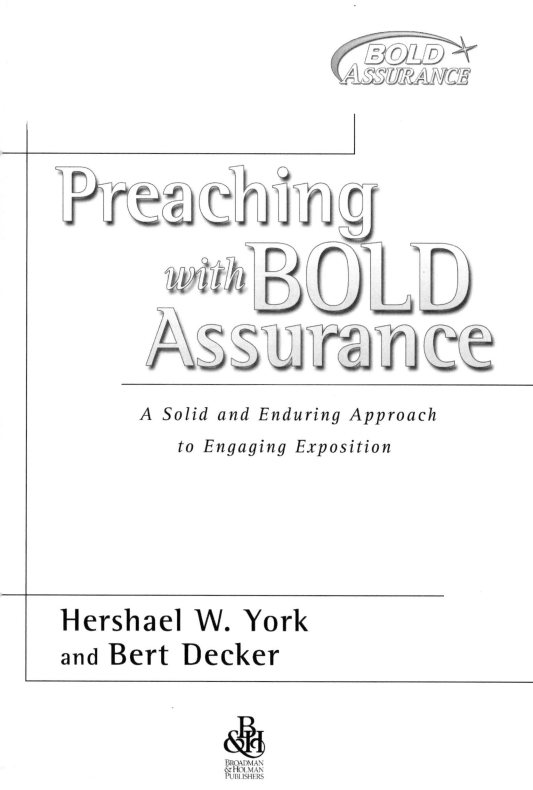

BOLD ASSURANCE

Preaching *with* BOLD Assurance

A Solid and Enduring Approach
to Engaging Exposition

Hershael W. York
and Bert Decker

BROADMAN
&HOLMAN
PUBLISHERS

NASHVILLE, TENNESSEE

13-digit ISBN: 978-0-8054-2623-6
10-digit ISBN: 0-8054-2623-X

Published by Broadman & Holman Publishers,
Nashville, Tennessee

Dewey Decimal Classification: 251
Subject Heading: PREACHING

Unless otherwise noted, Scripture quotations are from the Holy Bible, New International Version, copyright © 1973, 1978, 1984 by International Bible Society. Scripture quotations marked NASB are from the New American Standard Bible, © the Lockman Foundation, 1960, 1962, 1963, 1968, 1971, 1972, 1973, 1975, 1977; used by permission. All italic in biblical text has been added by the authors.

05 06 07 08 09   10 9 8 7 6 5 4 3

For Wallace York, my father, mentor, pastor, brother and friend,
who first gave me a love for preaching and preachers.
—Hershael York

For Dru Scott Decker, beloved wife, author, speaker, discipler,
and a Proverbs 31 woman.
—Bert Decker

Contents

Introduction

Those who proclaim the Word of God are a very busy lot. Most preachers are pastors whose preaching is one of many jobs he must routinely perform. Time for study has to be squeezed between budget meetings, hospital visits, staff retreats, crises, correspondence, funerals and family duties. Sermon building is often little more than a frantic cut and paste from others' sermons in books, tapes, or the Internet and may even border on outright plagiarism. With so many demands and so little time, preachers seldom go the next step and give any serious forethought to how they will actually *deliver* the sermons they have glued together. As a result, stunted pastors preach small sermons to spiritual pygmies—and they don't even do it *well*.

Preaching with Bold Assurance issues a challenge to pastors and preachers everywhere to take up the mantle of the preaching ministry and to proclaim boldly the Word of God in a way that will reflect accurately the meaning of the text, challenge the lives of the listeners, and engage them so that they *actually hear and can implement* what they have heard. This book will not make preaching easy, for such an awesome task was never intended to be so, but it will aid the preacher in mastering the multitasking that preaching demands. Following the principles of this book can make your time *much more effective* and productive so that your energy is increased by the bold assurance that you gain from rightly dividing the Word, developing the sermon, and delivering the message.

Bold Assurance is an exciting communication concept that builds speaking skills and confidence with God-given principles. In our first book, *Speaking with Bold Assurance,* we wrote for Christian laity and leaders alike. The reception the book received and the testimonials we have heard have confirmed our convictions and our approach. Teachers, laypeople, litigators, legislators, and preachers have confirmed that the principles of Bold Assurance work. But we have also been asked how to apply those principles *specifically* to preaching. This book is the step-by-step application to preaching of Bold Assurance principles.

As you read the following pages, you need to know a few things up front. First, this book unashamedly advocates an

> *"For God did not give us a spirit of timidity, but a spirit of power, of love and of self-discipline."*
> 2 TIMOTHY 1:7

expository model of preaching. In other words, we believe that the power of preaching lies in the inspired text of Scripture and that the preacher must preach the text with the same basic intent as that of the author. God used real people to write his Word, and they spoke to real issues. The Bible is as relevant today as it ever was, but the modern preacher has to show that relevance by explaining the meaning and leading listeners to apply it to their immediate contexts. Preaching expositionally does not necessitate a particular format, however. The preacher may discover many ways to explain the meaning and accurately apply the text, but the shape and direction of the sermon will be dictated by the meaning of the passage and not vice versa.

Second, we believe that merely explaining the text is not a sufficient model for a preacher to follow. Not only must his *sermon* explain the text and lead in practical application, but his *delivery* must also engage and grip his audience by the power of his conviction, passion, and warmth. We do not have to choose between biblical accuracy and oratorical skill. We strive to preach a biblical sermon with all of the preaching tools at our disposal.

Third, while many fine books on preaching are readily available, we are confident that we have something helpful and unique to add. We combine an uncompromising commitment to exposition of the sacred Scriptures with a determination to communicate it in an engaging way that challenges a contemporary audience to respond. We combine decades of experience from two worlds that meet in the pulpit. One of us is a respected pastor, professor, and homiletician with a doctorate in New Testament and Greek, the other a leader in the field of oral communications and an innovator in public speaking. Together, we share our convictions and knowledge of the three elements that intersect in the act of preaching: text, sermon, and delivery. Our prayer is that preachers will never choose between being either biblical or effective but learn that they can and *must* be both.

Hershael W. York actually wrote most of this manuscript in consultation with and building on the delivery principles of Bert Decker. Decker's oral communication theories and York's years of pastoral and classroom experience are a strong combination. But the book is written by a preacher for preachers, so the personal examples and experiences told in the first person singular are from Hershael.

> *"...for the Lord will be your confidence."*
> PROVERBS 3:26

Our purpose, therefore, is to provide conviction about the *why* and instruction about the *how* so that preachers who read this book and implement its strategies will learn the sheer delight of preaching and, as a result, will see the Holy Spirit grip the hearts of hearers by the faithful preaching of the Word.

If you read and follow the potent principles that are in this book, you will learn to:

- Understand the meaning of the biblical text
- Determine the main point and application of a passage
- Create and organize ideas
- Think on the perceptual level
- Enhance your credibility
- Overcome stage fright
- Preach persuasively
- Keep an audience attentive and involved
- Make your point
- Think on your feet
- Avoid being intimidated

- Communicate with authority
- Illustrate sermons well

The result of preaching God's Word with proven and practical skills to increase your speaking effectiveness is *preaching with bold assurance.* As you commit yourself to communicating His truth, be prepared to experience God using you more powerfully and more frequently than ever before. And, as a result, may God be glorified and the Kingdom expanded as pulpits blaze with conviction and truth!

> "Now go; I will help you speak and will teach you what to say."
> EXODUS 4:12

Part I
The Text

CHAPTER I
The Privilege of Preaching

The burden of the Word of the Lord . . . The fire in my bones . . . The inexorable, relentless, irrepressible calling to preach the Word of God in a manner worthy of the God who calls.

I recall times when I have been preaching when God simply moved in and took over. I fail to comprehend it myself, let alone explain it to anyone else. The closest analogy I can use is that it is like standing outside of myself, watching myself preach, knowing that God is speaking through me in an incredible way. I used to think that those moments came almost randomly, that God seemed almost capricious. But after years of preaching and observation of myself and others, I realize that those times occur when I am *most saturated with the Scripture* I am preaching, convinced of its meaning, emboldened by its power, secure in its application. I feel no strain, no duplicity, no regrets that I have not spent enough time with the Lord and the text he has given.

But I also remember the other times—the times when the burden of preaching crushed me because I was not sufficiently aware of or convicted by the sermon I preached. Feeling the weight of preaching to people who came to hear a word from God, I felt weak and afraid because I knew I had not paid sufficient attention to the text. Even if I did understand the text, I had not thought carefully how best to relate it to people. I relied on my past training rather than a current walk with God. Spending much time in the urgent matters of ministry, I knew I had failed the essential task of spending time with him and his Word. Though I built a sermon, I did not give consideration to the *best* way to connect with my congregation. I settled merely to explain the text, as though giving a history lesson, rather than to challenge my listeners to conform their lives more to the image of Christ as a result of its meaning. My delivery denied the very power of the God I was supposedly proclaiming.

Such moments feel like swimming upstream in a river of Jell-O. When my anemic sermon finally reached a merciful conclusion, I felt like apologizing to everyone who sat through such a pitiful presentation of God's powerful Word. My wife, usually a great encourager, would sit beside me in silence on the drive home, unable to deny what we both knew to be true.

Preaching well is a huge commitment. So why would anyone want to bear such a burden? Why put yourself through weekly agony with the potential for public humiliation? Any preacher *knows* the answer: because speaking as God's representative, an agent of change and salvation, is the greatest and highest privilege in the world. Whatever study it may demand, whatever sacrifice it may require, whatever effort it may entail is eclipsed and forgotten in the sight of lives touched by God and changed by the gospel.

PREACHING IS ALIVE AND WELL!

While preaching requires hard work, sweat and toil are not virtues in themselves. Our efforts have to be *effective*. The carpenter who drives every nail in with a hammer is not necessarily any more a craftsman than the one who uses a pneumatic hammer that can drive a nail with the pull of a trigger. And the one who does it the old-fashioned way is not necessarily a good carpenter just because he takes more time. In the same way, we are wise to be willing to do whatever is necessary to preach well, because the Lord demands it and our people deserve it. But what if we can discover and master tools that will help us be more effective with our

> *If the ax is dull and its edge unsharpened, more strength is needed but skill will bring success.*
> ECCLESIASTES 10:10

study, our sermon, and our skill in delivery? A commitment to excellence means that we desire effectiveness and not only effort.

Since effectiveness in communicating God's Word is our goal, we can find no greater means of sharing the truth than through the medium of preaching. While many have challenged preaching's usefulness and branded it as outdated and ineffective, preaching still remains God's primary means of ministering the Scriptures to his people. Oral communication is the most personal and powerful way to connect with others.

The largest and most successful ministries in the world have one thing in common: they are led by communicators. The great revivals and movements throughout Christian history are almost always ignited by God's use of a communicator: a bold, impassioned man of conviction who has a heart to share God's Word with people. Augustine, Martin Luther, John Knox, Jonathan Edwards, D. L. Moody, and Billy Graham each exhibited a fire of passion and a heart of conviction. But that proves true not only of well-known preachers who touched masses, but also of the men who serve in small communities and country churches. One rarely finds a poor communicator who succeeds as a pastor, even in a small setting. While a pastor can overcome to some extent poor preaching skills by his work ethic and people skills, why would he settle to do so? The best way to get people involved in a church is to give them something worth hearing at every service. When church members start inviting people to come to church because they want their friends to hear their pastor, church growth is enhanced.

> Preach the Word; be prepared in season and out of season; correct, rebuke and encourage— with great patience and careful instruction.
> 2 TIMOTHY 4:2

Frankly, no one wants to come to a boring church service. People need to be engaged and challenged. They want to feel a connection with the preacher and with the Word he proclaims. They are accustomed to television, movies, and entertainers, and few will sit still for a dry thirty-minute homily. The solution is not, as some have suggested, to turn worship services into entertainment—or even infotainment; the answer lies in passionate preaching of *propositional truth*.

While some preachers shrink from preaching propositional truth, they fail to understand the needs and the motives of their parishioners. One reason people come to church is that they desperately need to hear a word from God. Their lives are often unhappy as they struggle with issues of work, family, divorce, remarriage, blended families, aging, health, ethics, sex, lifestyles, and finances. When they come to church, they want and need to hear ultimate truth. They want to know what God says about how to work out whatever issues they are facing. While many preachers may be committed to providing answers to their pressing questions, if those answers are presented in a tiresome, tedious, and uninspiring way, we can hardly be surprised when the listeners do not feel that the answers are valid.

If we want our hearers to feel compelled to apply the truth, they need to hear the truth presented in a compelling manner. We must not content our-selves with content alone, but we must also preach to the audience in a way that connects with their lives.

The Great Need of the Day

This is the challenge of biblical preaching today. The needs of people have not changed since the Bible was completed. They are still born into a sinful world, separated from God, in need of salvation. They still struggle with "the cravings of sinful man, the lust of his eyes and the boasting of what he has and does" (1 John 2:16)—which are the same temptations that Eve faced in the Garden of Eden when she "saw that the fruit of the tree was good for food and pleas-ing to the eye, and also desirable for gaining wisdom" (Gen. 3:6). Thousands of years later, our temptations and struggles may take on a different form, but at their core they are still the same struggles as those presented in Scripture. So people still need to hear God's "teaching, rebuking, correcting and training in righteousness" (2 Tim. 3:16), but they also need to hear it in the way that best communicates and demonstrates the Bible's relevance. Further, they need to be shown how to *apply* the truth that has been presented.

What we are suggesting is engaging exposition. While some preachers who call themselves expositors may accurately depict the meaning of the text when they preach, if they are monotonous and dull, they will have few hearers and fewer still who get excited about God's Word. Our job is more than just explaining the text. Our job is to make it vibrant, fresh, and accessible.

When I first came to The Southern Baptist Theological Seminary as a preaching professor, the seminary administration issued a press release and made much of the fact that I was committed to an expository model of preaching. Within weeks I received a letter from a man who criticized exposition by saying that it "does not lend itself to illustrations, and is usually an expounding of the Word without any relation to life; it becomes dry, even boring, without the windows of illustrations that complement and undergird the good news. Expository preaching does not challenge the mind or the emotions, is essentially simplistic, teaching very little of the larger, cosmic sweep of the gospel to all of life."

When I responded to his letter, I wrote, "Your objections are not to expository preaching at all. You object to *bad* preaching. If one of my students preached a sermon such as you describe, he simply would not pass my class." I went on to describe what exposition really is and how it can be done well. To his credit, he wrote back and apologized and admitted that he had only heard expository preaching criticized. Furthermore, he had the unfortunate experience of hearing a person preach poorly and then claim that he was an expositor.

Expository preaching does indeed explain the text, but it also must answer the great epistemological question: *so what?* When a man of God stands in the pulpit and proclaims the Word with passion, conviction, and emotion, his audience will truly hear the content of the message. Only when they actually hear it can they act on it. Making that emotional connection with the message forces a decision: will I accept and apply the truth of this text, or reject and refuse it?

The Attendant Power of the Holy Spirit

In a word, the ingredient of preaching that we long for is *power*—not the power of education, as important as that may be. We cannot be content with the power of rhetorical skill, either, even though we certainly want to work hard to grow in those areas, too. The power we want is that which can only be attributed to the Holy Spirit as he grips our hearts with the Word and compels us to preach to others the truth that has so captivated us.

The power of the Holy Spirit cannot be manufactured. We do not offer a recipe for spiritual power that comes when we follow steps A, B, and C.

Spiritual power comes only when we saturate ourselves with the Word, surrender ourselves to God's will, and discipline ourselves in God's way.

Even then, the power of God manifests itself in different ways. Sometimes the power of God falls like rain in a place, and we see obvious and tangible results as the lost are converted and the saved find conviction and comfort in the Word. At other times, though, the power of God is much more quiet, more subtle, but no less potent. Men become better husbands. Employees manifest a Christian work ethic. Students realize the importance of dedicating their minds to a Christian worldview.

But these changes, whether explosive or subdued, are the work of the Spirit and the result of God's use of human preaching. We do not claim that if a preacher studies enough or delivers his sermon well enough that the Spirit of God will always attend his preaching with dramatic results. But we are confident in observing that the more a man of God gives himself to this sacred task—the more committed he is to an accurate exposition of the text and a passionate presentation of the sermon—the more frequently and dynamically the Holy Spirit seems to work through him. In the same way that the more we witness the more we see a sovereign God save people, we can say that the more consumed we are with preaching the Word effectively, the more our preaching has an effect. Although we cannot take credit for the power and presence of the Holy Spirit, we can usually take the blame for his absence.

> Do you not know that in a race all the runners run, but only one gets the prize? Run in such a way as to get the prize.
> 1 CORINTHIANS 9:24

So like Paul we do not rely on the wisdom of man for our power, but like the great apostle we also seek to persuade men. And with a reliance on the Spirit and a commitment to excellence in our preaching, we avoid no subject, fear no reaction, and seek no glory but Christ's.

THE POWER OF THE HOLY SPIRIT AND PREPARATION

Although God is sovereign and can work through anyone he chooses to use, he clearly uses those who are most committed to preparation, study, and hard work. If we want to have a real demonstration of the power of the Holy Spirit in our lives, ministries, and sermons, we cannot simply do nothing while hoping that God decides to use us. We strive and agonize in our study and commitment to our calling so that we are always at God's complete disposal.

> *I have become all things to all men so that by all possible means I might save some. I do all this for the sake of the gospel, that I may share in its blessings.*
> 1 CORINTHIANS 9:22–23

Our preparation, our diligence to study, our commitment to be better communicators does not discount the power of the Spirit, but instead *expects* it. Because we really believe that God can and will use us, we prepare the text, the sermon, and our own delivery skills so we are fit vessels for God to use.

Someone frequently objects that God does not need our abilities in order to use us. He can use the most unskilled and ignorant preacher. Although there is more than a nugget of truth in that statement, it is also not a reason to ignore important skills and leave them undeveloped. We have known preachers who were living in sin whom God used anyway, but that is not an excuse for us to live in sin. We have known preachers who preached sermons that were almost heretical—and still someone trusted Christ. But this does not mean that sound doctrine is unimportant. God once spoke through a donkey (see Num. 22:21–30), but that hardly serves as a model of ministry.

The history of preaching leaves an undeniable body of evidence that God uses men who are committed to the Word, to holiness, and to the power of preaching. God anoints such men and speaks through them to save the lost and to edify and rally the saints. To this end we should master every available means to improve our knowledge of the Word, our ability to craft biblical sermons, and our skill at connecting with an audience.

We can imagine no greater spiritual blessing than to be used by God to bring people to Christ and to encourage and instruct his church. Biblical preaching is an opportunity to meet a great need in the lives of people who most need to know God, so our commitment ought to reflect our belief in the power and potential of preaching.

CHAPTER 2
The Goal of Preaching

No one else knew the secret that Nathan held in his heart and mind the day he walked into the presence of King David and began to tell him a story of injustice. Listening intently, David's emotions were touched as he heard the old prophet of God relate the tale of a wealthy landowner and shepherd who stole his neighbor's only sheep in order to serve it to his guest. The tenderhearted king began to boil within and to crimson visibly, incensed at the selfishness and injustice of the rich man who would steal his neighbor's one precious lamb.

Then the prophet thrust in the verbal dagger: "You are the man!" (2 Sam. 12:7). He proceeded to expose David's adultery with Bathsheba and subsequent murder of her husband, Uriah. Trapped by his own sense of justice and righteous indignation that had arisen during Nathan's story, David immediately repented. And the beauty of that repentance has served as a guide for millions of believers who have found solace and direction in Psalm 51 during a time of confession and restoration.

But imagine instead a different scene. Imagine that Nathan used a different tactic. What if he had just walked into the court of the king and openly accused him of adultery and murder? David would perhaps have responded in a confrontational way. After all, his word was law, and he had absolute power. Not only might he have rejected the call to repentance; he might have ordered the prophet's execution!

The wisdom of drawing David in *emotionally* was the key. Nathan undoubtedly could have imparted the *information* to David in a more concise manner. He also could have spoken with him in a more confrontational manner. He certainly could have told him in a more concrete manner. Yet he spoke first to his heart in order to get the information through to his head. Making the emotional connection with David was instrumental in getting David to *act* on Nathan's rebuke rather than just to hear it.

FILLING HEADS OR CHANGING LIVES

If you get nothing else from this book, understand this: sermons are not about just imparting information. They should be custom-built to change lives. We don't want to fill their heads; we want the proclamation of the Word to grip their souls and motivate them to conform to the will of God. Our approach to the Bible and to preaching, therefore, has *application* as its ultimate goal. Application is what makes the Bible come alive and makes sermons practical.

Visit any bookstore, and you will always find a sizeable group of people in the advice, self-help, and do-it-yourself sections of the bookstore. The *New York Times* nonfiction best-seller list became so dominated by self-help books that they now have their own category, "Hardcover Advice," that is replete with the books Americans turn to in order to learn more about managing their lives. In a world of moral meltdown, family failure, social chaos, terrorism, and economic uncertainty, people want to know *how* as well as *what*.

But too often this understanding escapes busy pastors. Even though our own schedules are dominated by people hurting with marital strife, ethical dilemmas, financial foolishness, and sexual sin, we pride ourselves on the hours we spend preparing a sermon on the identity of the 144,000 in Revelation chapter 7! We would rather preach a sermon on whatever pet doctrine we like (or dislike) than to show our people *how* to do the hard work of applying the Bible in their lives and social contexts. Let's face it: it is much easier to preach a sermon on the typology of the tabernacle than on how to let Christ live through you when you are trapped in a bad marriage.

Two Errors of Preaching

So we settle for something less than biblical truth applied to contemporary life. In fact, preachers tend to fall into one of two errors. If every road has two ditches, it really doesn't matter which one you fall into; either way, you are off track.

Error #1. On the one hand we may preach factoid sermons. We become modern Matthew Henrys in miniature, faithfully attempting verse-by-verse exposition, thoroughly exegeting the text, smugly explaining how many gallons are in a firkin and how many furlongs are in a mile and the relative value of a drachma in U.S. dollars. We clarify the concept of a bond slave and the laws of levirate marriage, and convince ourselves that merely *explaining* the text *to* a modern audience is the same thing as showing its relevance *for* a modern audience.

Such a sermon is what I call a sermon that even the devil agrees with. Preachers resort to outlines filled with generic categories like the *purpose,* the *problem,* the *process;* the *method,* the *man,* and the *message;* the *cause,* the *condition,* the *conclusion;* Jesus was the *sent one,* the *scorned one,* the *saving one.* But outlines that just break down the passage into summary statements do not urge any action on the listener. Hence, these are sermons that even the devil can agree with! They rely on a cognitive appreciation of the facts revealed in the text.

In his epistle James rebukes his readers for such thinking: "You believe that there is one God. Good! Even the demons believe that—and shudder" (James 2:19). In other words, merely *knowing* the truth is something even the devil can do. Does Satan not believe that there is one God? Does he not know the mystery of the Trinity better than us? Satan surely recognizes that Jesus is God's Son. Since he knows God personally, no one can doubt the devil's direct knowledge of these things. The difference is that Satan never *acts* on the truth. Do we really want our congregations to settle for a knowledge without action?

James goes on to chide his audience for their insistence that mere faith—simply believing the facts—is enough. James explains that Abraham had to *act* on his faith. If head knowledge of the facts of the gospel is not sufficient to take a person to heaven, does it not follow that *preaching* facts will not be sufficient to urge people to act on their knowledge? Just as James insisted that we must have a faith that works, so we insist that a sermon without application is dead, too! If James could urge his readers to act on the truth they knew, then so should we!

Make no mistake about it: our sermons should clearly explain the meaning of the text. When appropriate, the preacher ought to explain how much a drachma is worth or the identity of the 144,000. He just shouldn't stop there and think he has really preached.

Several years ago I had a student in my preaching class who was very resistant to my approach to preaching. Like many others, he was convinced that it was the preacher's job just to preach the biblical facts and let the Holy Spirit do the rest. We talked over lunch one day as he respectfully told me of his disagreement. He shared with me that he had already been a pastor for fourteen years and that he was convinced that if people only knew the content of the Bible well enough, they would act on it in ways revealed to them by the Spirit.

I nodded to let him know I was hearing him, and then I went through my regular list of questions designed to challenge his thinking. "Why does the Holy Spirit need you to explain the text if he doesn't need you to apply it? Couldn't he illumine their minds without you? And what if you have someone in your church smarter than you; do they really need you? Can't they just figure out the content for themselves?" But then I asked him the one question that goes beyond theory: "How is your approach working? Are your people accurately and adequately applying the Scripture to their lives? Do you see them growing in their conformity to Christ?"

My question was met by stunned silence, and then he quickly went back to his objections. We finished our lunch, and I really didn't think much more about it until later in the semester when he asked to speak to me once more. This time his attitude was completely different.

For months this young pastor had preached his heart out about evangelism. He had preached nearly every passage in the Bible that demonstrated the need for evangelism, the way God blesses it, and how the Holy Spirit uses it. He was convinced that he had done everything he could to teach his people about the necessity of sharing the gospel with others. Then, following his series of sermons on evangelism, at the very next business meeting of the church, he introduced a program to train members how to share their faith. Feeling that they would be ready to act on what they had learned, he asked the church to vote to approve and implement the program. He was stunned when the very people who had sat through his exhaustive series on evangelism voted down his initiative.

Their failure to act on his preaching shook the young man to the core of his beliefs about preaching. Confident that he had truly shown them the biblical mandate, he was hurt and bewildered when they rejected it. So he told me, "I said, 'I'm going to try this York's way,' and from that point on I began to focus not only on *content* but on *application*. In every sermon I would preach the truth of the text and then confront them with a decision whether or not they would obey the command or the implications of the text."

With a smile of delight on his face, he then related to me how the very first time he did it, the response was amazing. "People began to compliment my preaching and to ask me what had gotten into me. What's more, we began to see real response in the invitation and in their lives during the week. Wives called me to tell me that their husbands were changing. Deacons began to serve in more helpful ways. It was amazing, and it was immediate. Then I had to admit that the reason they had never done anything was that I never *told* them to do anything with the authority of Scripture. I would preach doctrine but never relate it to life. I would tell them what Paul did, but I never told them that meant they had to do it too."

Error #2. If one great failure of preaching is giving content without application, the other great blunder of preaching is being only emotional in our presentation, making an emotional connection that is devoid of biblical truth. This kind of preaching often allows the listener to draw his or her own conclusions. Under such preaching people may be moved, but seldom are they changed. When preachers mistake emotion for the work of the Spirit, they undermine the authority and intent of Scripture. As essential as emotion is in the task of preaching, one dare not divorce it from biblical content and sound application. A preacher can dramatically relate the story of the crucifixion, for example, but if he only makes people sorry that Jesus suffered so horribly, he may as well be talking about a dog getting hit by a car on a busy highway. It is not merely the event that matters but the *meaning* of that event.

If some preachers choke their people to death on spiritual meat, other preachers starve their congregations on spiritual cotton candy. They do not feed, nourish, and grow their people in the Word and in obedience to Christ. They may be articulate, well read, and relevant. They may build a sizeable congregation, but they will not build a church that is serious about the Word of God.

The goal of our preaching should be *engaging exposition.* The preacher of the Word should not settle for being a commentator or a communicator. His passion must be to preach the Word in such a way that he accurately teaches the meaning of the text and leads his audience to discover its implications for their life situations so that they respond in obedience and become more like Christ as a result.

Inductive preaching has many advocates. They propose that the sermon should be preached in such a way that the listener is encouraged to infer the meaning and application of the text. Several famous preachers and professors of preaching insist that this is the way we should preach. They even insist that this is the way Jesus preached, as though that settled the issue for us.

But the biblical prophets always preached otherwise. Let's go back to the biblical example of Nathan's confrontation with David. What if Nathan had told David the story, watched him grow enraged at the obvious injustice inherent in his tale, and then left him to think about it. Does anyone seriously think that the story would have had more effect on David than when Nathan stuck out his weathered old finger in the face of his indignant king and said, "You are the man!"? The prophets often got in the faces of their listeners and seldom left them to wonder about how to apply what they were saying.

Don't Try to Preach Like Jesus

Frankly, we are never told to preach like Jesus and probably shouldn't try.

While that sentence may shock and make you wonder why we would make such a strange statement, allow me to explain. Certainly we should emulate many elements of Jesus' preaching: his passion, his high view of Scripture, his confrontation and application, and his tendency to force a decision of acceptance or rejection. But on the other hand, we must admit that Jesus, as the sovereign Creator of this universe, had intents, information, and abilities that we do not have.

Let's look at an example from his personal witnessing, and then we'll look at his preaching. In John 4, Jesus told the disciples that he had to do what no Jews of his day would do: he had to go through Samaria. They did not know (nor could they) that he had a divine appointment with a woman at Jacob's Well. When Jesus got to Samaria, he stopped by the well at midday and found this woman drawing water by herself, rather than early in the day with the rest of the women of the town. As Jesus proceeded to talk with her, not only did he confront her with his own claims to be the Messiah, but he also began to name her sins. He told her how many husbands she had had and also that the man she was currently with was not even her husband!

Now, first of all, none of us can know such intimate details about the sins of people we just met, and even if we could, it probably would not be best to use such knowledge! After all, we are sinners just like they. So should we witness to others because Jesus witnessed? Absolutely! Should we follow his methodology? No! We can find certain elements in his witness that must be in ours, but we can also find elements that are the sole province of the Son of God and cannot be emulated.

The same is true of Jesus' preaching, particularly his preaching in parables. First of all, Jesus had no single methodology of preaching parables. Sometimes they were short, other times much more extended. Sometimes he clearly explained them, and other times he offered no explanation at all, simply an admonition that whoever had ears to ear, let them hear. We might wonder why Jesus did that, but the Bible provides us with the answer. After preaching the parable of the sower, Jesus concluded with, "He who has ears to hear, let him hear" (Mark 4:9). But then, afterward, his closest disciples asked him about the meaning of the parable. He answered them, "The secret of the kingdom of God has been given to you. But to those on the outside everything is said in parables so that, 'they may be ever seeing but never perceiving, and ever hearing but never understanding; *otherwise they might turn and be forgiven!*'" (Mark 4:11–12, emphasis added). It might give us pause, but the text clearly states that Jesus' sovereign purpose was to keep some of his listeners in the dark. It was all part of God's plan to culminate in Jesus' crucifixion and resurrection.

Frankly, that is not a burden that we can ever bear nor do we want to! So when some preachers defend their inductive method of preaching, letting the listener draw his or her own conclusions, I always wonder if they are also so bold as to claim the same purpose of Jesus. Would we say that we preached a sermon with an inductive method so that some people listening would not repent and be forgiven? If we cannot claim his stated purpose as our model, then perhaps neither should we follow his methodology simply because he used it. So while our preaching might indeed have inductive *elements*, we really cannot shy away from the fact that the preaching of the prophets and apostles was almost exclusively deductive and directly applicational.

What Do You Want Out of Your Preaching?

While it is a good thing to preach a great sermon, our goal should never be great sermons. The object of our preaching is to see God change the lives of our listeners by the Word that is preached. The sermon is merely God's means (and therefore ours) to the ends of his purposes. Like the prophets and the apostles, we preach for a *decision*, not merely for information.

Paul told Timothy, "All Scripture is God-breathed and is useful for teaching, rebuking, correcting and training in righteousness" (2 Tim. 3:16). Of the four purposes of Scripture listed, only one is informational and three are directly applicational and exhortative. Our preaching, therefore, should be neither deluged with data, nor should it engage in mere emotionalism. Rather, it should use both information and emotion in order to encourage and inspire obedience.

CHAPTER 3
The Commitments Expositors Must Make

While many preachers will stand in a pulpit this Sunday, few who would call themselves expositors will. Fewer still will be the number of preachers who actually *are* expositional in their preaching. Expository preaching is not for everyone, because it is the most demanding and challenging way to preach. On the other hand, this kind of preaching is what God uses to change lives more than any other kind, because a person cannot preach expository messages unless he is saturated with the Word of God. And the more our sermons are dependent on the inspired text, the more inherent power they will have.

But every preacher must decide whether he really wants to be an expositor. A true expositor of the Word will have to make some commitments up front. Before he ever opens his Bible to study, he will need to make some commitments about his task. Before he ever stands behind a pulpit, he must be convinced of certain elements of preaching.[1]

A COMMITMENT TO THE TRUTH OF THE TEXT

Preachers who are not convinced of the inspiration of the text will have no interest in telling others what it says. While not every preacher who holds a high view of Scripture is an expositor, it seems inconceivable that one who is committed to exposition would not do so as a result of his belief that the biblical text is the perfect revelation of God.

A doctor prescribes a medicine because of her belief in its efficacy. Her intent is to help the patient get well. Every procedure she initiates, every prescription she writes, and every therapy she recommends has that goal in mind. She prescribes the treatment because she believes it has the power to make the patient well.

In the same way, the expositor preaches the Word because he believes it can help his listeners. He also believes that *only* the Word can provide the kind of benefit that people really need. Other resources may prove helpful, but they cannot meet the deepest need of a person's life: a restored relationship with God through Jesus Christ. A message that comes from any source other than the Word of God will fail to supply the listeners with the true source of salvation. Preaching on financial management may prove popular and even helpful, but it will only help people have more wealth to leave behind when they die. A series of sermons on having a happy family may indeed teach people better interpersonal skills at home, but if that is *all* they get, then their happy family on earth will be the only happiness they ever know throughout eternity. Homilies on ecology may exhort listeners to be good stewards of creation, but without the message of the gospel they can only make the earth a better place from which to go to hell.

A high view of Scripture means that the Bible *is* what God says, and what God says is what we must say when we preach. If a preacher mounts the pulpit with a conviction of the truth and sufficiency of the Word of God, his preaching will be marked by passion and power. A high view of Scripture is the *sine qua non* of exposition.

A Commitment to the Profitability of *All* Scripture

Beyond a conviction about the truth of the Bible, anyone who would be an expositor must also be convinced of the *totality* of God's revelation. While many preachers may hold the Bible in high esteem, going so far as to use words like "inerrant" or "infallible," the vast majority of them are not truly convinced that every part of the Bible has merit and impact for today.

Most preachers agree with Paul's words to Timothy, "All Scripture is God-breathed and is useful for teaching, rebuking, correcting and training in righteousness, so that the man of God may be thoroughly equipped for every good work" (2 Tim. 3:16–17). But one would not know this by examining the preaching calendar of some preachers for several years. They may pay lip service to a belief in the inspiration of all of the Bible, but their preaching belies their true suspicions. By skipping over books or passages that are difficult or seem dated, they plant the suggestion in the minds of their churches that the Bible is a buffet from which one may pick and choose what suits him or her.

Each successive commitment gets more difficult to hold and to practice. Some, no doubt, will think this commitment too restrictive. Can't we be expositors and still be selective in what passages we exposit? If by "selective" we mean that we can ignore Ecclesiastes or the Minor Prophets or the genealogies or the lengthy descriptions of war and killing that is found in the Bible, the answer is a definitive "no."

Learn now a principle that will be repeated in this book and that should haunt every moment spent in study and in the pulpit: *the way you handle the Word in the pulpit is the way your people will handle the Word in their lives.* In other words, if you don't preach the difficult passages when you come to them, if you skip over something just because it seems hard for a modern audience to comprehend, then you are teaching them to do the same. And, to be frank, we live in an age and a culture that struggles with the very nature of the blood atonement of Christ itself. If we ignore passages and themes of Scripture because we think they are hard for a contemporary audience to appreciate, then we might as well excise the main theme of God's Word.

On the other hand, if every time you stand in a pulpit you *always* relate the meaning and application of a text, then that is what the people in the pews will do, too. And when you encounter texts that are challenging because they seem mundane or politically incorrect, if you do the difficult task of teaching what this passage says about God and how this knowledge should affect our lives, then your people will approach the Bible the same way. Every time they read it, they will automatically ask themselves what it means, what it says about God, and how they can apply it. And when that starts to happen in a church, God works in a mighty way.

No one part of the Bible is more inspired than any other part. The Old Testament is just as inspired as the New. Ecclesiastes is every bit as much the Word of God as the Book of Romans. The inscripturated words of Paul are as authoritative as the words of Jesus. Some confuse this statement with asserting that Paul was, in his person, as authoritative as Jesus, and that is certainly not true. But when Paul, under the inspiration of the Holy Spirit, wrote words into which God breathed and intended to be preserved in His Word, he had as much authority as the words of the Sermon on the Mount. Ultimately, every word of the Bible is from God and, therefore, authoritative. Just as Jesus was both human and divine and yet without sin, so is God's Word the marvelous revelation of God presented in human terms and written by human authors, yet without error. For this reason, we ought to preach the *whole* Bible.

When I was preaching through the book of Joshua in my church, I was enthralled by the action of the spies, Rahab, the march around Jericho, the sin of Achan, and even the deceit of the Gibeonites. But when I got to those middle chapters in which the defeat of the kings and the cities are recorded and the mass killings that are the substance of war are told in detail, I understood what a challenge it was to get a modern congregation to understand how the Israelites could be justified in wiping out entire civilizations, including women and children. Furthermore, God directly ordered them to do it.

One Sunday, after I preached on the last narrative text with any plot, just before I got into one of those difficult sections, a member came to me after the service and said, "I am anxious to see what you do with next week's passage!" That one sentence told me that he not only *expected* to hear his pastor explain those verses; he *needed* his pastor to do so. What a disservice I would have rendered had I not then done the hard work required to teach what that part of Joshua says about God's sovereignty and ownership of all of his creation, including human life. I also was able to show them how these civilizations had heard, like Rahab, of the God of the Israelites and had ample time to repent, but they did not. The passage taught both God's sovereignty and man's responsibility.

I was curious to see how the member who had the question would respond to my sermon. Sure enough, after the service he came to me, but instead of commenting on what he had just heard he said, "Now I want to see what you do with the division of the land in chapters 14–21!"

———

Admittedly, even though all Scripture is equally inspired, it is not all equally profitable. In other words, you will find a lot more spiritual nourishment in Romans 8:28 than in the list of returning exiles in Nehemiah chapter 7. They are both the Word of God, but God did not pour equal amounts of beneficial material in them. That is why we may sometimes be able to take large blocks of Scripture and preach the one central truth that is revealed in it, while at other times we may spend several sermons in a single verse or small passage. But the true expositor will nonetheless make it his goal to preach the whole Word of God, lashing his sermons to the text and refusing to skip over passages that are difficult to explain.

A COMMITMENT TO THE NATURE OF PREACHING

Once we are settled on the truth of the Word and the profitability of all of the Word, we then must arrive at a consequent view of what preaching is. Preaching is not just building a sermon, telling stories, inspiring an audience, or giving a speech. If the Bible is the Word of God, then preaching is *speaking God's words.* The purpose of preaching is to lay bare the meaning of a passage, to present its application, and to show its relevance to the audience. With such a reliance on the text rather than on personal opinion or human thought, the preacher can say with confidence, "Thus saith the Lord!" In other words, when our sermons arise from the text, based on sound hermeneutical and exegetical methods, we can call men and women everywhere to obey the admonitions of the text, to believe its prophetic word, to accept its directions for the home, and to trust its word of salvation.

While we clearly want our audience to discover this meaning and inculcate it into their lives, our primary goal has to be faithfully explaining it. Any decision they may make based on a deficient explanation of Scripture will probably be a deficient decision as well. We cannot make a direct application, we cannot call on them to repent, we cannot urge them to take action, if we have not first accurately explained the text.

We want this point to be clear in the minds of our readers, because much of this book is devoted to helping preachers make an emotional connection through good delivery style. Other parts focus on making good applications that confront people and demand a response. While we make no apology for advocating those aspects of preaching, we never want anyone to think that those elements alone are sufficient for preaching. We speak God's words *only* to the degree that we accurately reflect the meaning of the text. If our exegesis is in error, then our application will be as well, and our delivery is rendered irrelevant. Faithfulness to the text is the foundation for everything else in this book and in our sermons.

Haddon Robinson defined preaching in this way: "Expository preaching is the communication of a biblical concept derived from and transmitted through an historical, grammatical, literary study of a passage in its context, which the Holy Spirit first makes vital in the personality of the preacher, and then through him applies accurately to the experience of the congregation. As a result the congregation has an experience with God through the accurate application of the Word energized by the Holy Spirit which conforms them more to the image of Christ."[2]

This is an excellent definition because it reminds us that preaching is not from within the preacher, but it emanates from the text *through* the preacher. We cannot be content with serving as sermon builders on the one hand, or mere toastmasters on the other. We preach the Word to men and women, and we first let it grip our minds and hearts. Many times we have been preparing a text when the Holy Spirit began to trouble us and to show us the sin and flaws in our own lives and characters. As we let God do something *to us,* he prepares to do something *through us* as his Word is preached.

A COMMITMENT TO THINKING

As we proceed through our commitments that expositors must make, we are struck with the fact that preaching is not an easy task. A lifetime of study, preparation, and experience can make us more proficient. This book as well as others can make preaching *easier,* but they can never make it *easy.* When asked how long it takes to prepare a sermon, a wise preacher will respond, "My whole life!" Indeed, we pour everything of ourselves into our preaching.

This means we cannot be lazy in our thinking. If we are to be *effective,* and not just *busy,* then we must settle once and for all that we are willing to do some clear, hard thinking about our preaching. This thought process will take three different paths.

The first area we must think about is *what the Scripture means.* In other words, we must do the necessary work of applying hermeneutical and exegetical processes to discern the meaning of the text. These are further explained in the following chapter, but suffice it now to say that we need to discover the original meaning and intent of the passage. Meaning is not arbitrary, nor is it intentionally hidden. We can be certain that the author had an intended meaning and that he wanted his readers to know it. The biggest part of our early preparation, therefore, is thinking about the meaning of the passage.

The second sphere of thought is about *how the passage applies.* No knowledge of the Bible is or should remain purely academic. God does not inform us merely to fill our heads with useless knowledge. Every revelation of himself and of his truth is for the purpose of conforming us more to the image of Jesus Christ. So when we preach, we should never have a cognitive goal as our final objective. We don't just want people to *know* the truth; we want them to *act* on the truth.

Certain texts of the Bible are easier to apply than others. James's epistle, for instance, is very easy to apply because it is written with straight imperative statements such as, "Consider it pure joy, my brothers, whenever you face trials of many kinds" (James 1:2). He begins the body of his epistle with a command, and he hardly falls into any other format throughout the entire book. Making application from that is easy, because the application springs directly from the author's own pen.

Narrative passages, however, and didactic passages with lengthy doctrinal discussions are quite a bit more difficult. Because of this, many preachers forget the real purpose of preaching and simply leave application out of the sermon. If they are preaching an Old Testament narrative, for instance, like the story of David and Bathsheba, they are satisfied to just tell the story. Their only real goal in preaching that sermon is to acquaint their listeners with the biblical tale. They may assume that the story speaks for itself and that the conclusion (Don't commit adultery!) is so obvious that it hardly needs emphasis, or they may actually *want* their audience to discover this truth for themselves. But remember, we should never preach the event, but the *meaning* of the event.

The same is true for those didactic and doctrinal passages in the New Testament. Ephesians chapters 1 and 2 collectively serve as a good example of a heavily doctrinal passage. Preachers are often content to interpret the passage without making application. This is one reason why many voices in the Christian community decry doctrinal sermons: they are reacting against dogma without duty. We do well to remember that the Book of Ephesians, like all the other epistles, was written as a single unit to be read aloud in one sitting. The heavy pragmatic emphasis that Paul gives at the end of the epistle was in no way divorced from the deep doctrine at the beginning of the letter. We would do well to keep that doctrine always tied to the deeds of the Christian faith, too.

As we prepare to preach, therefore, we must constantly be asking ourselves what the lives of our listeners will look like if they truly listen and live in the light of this truth. If they believe that we are predestined to be conformed to the image of Christ (Rom. 8:29), how should they think, live, and behave? What impact should the truth they heard on Sunday morning have on their Monday morning, Thursday afternoon, or Saturday night? Once we can see that in our minds, then we urge them to live that way as a result of their belief.

The third matter of which we must think is hardly discussed at all in preaching books or circles, but those who give attention to it are the ones whose preaching connects and has tremendous effect. We must also commit to thinking about *how people perceive.* In other words, we have to think about the way people think!

I believe the Golden Rule: Do unto others as you would have them do unto you. My problem does not lie in my belief, but in the way I put it into practice in my life.

Recently my son, Seth, was taking a trip, and I packed a cooler with drinks and goodies for him to take. He expressed great appreciation, but when he returned home a week later, he still had many of the things I had bought for him to take. When I began to probe why, it became evident—to my embarrassment and my family's amusement—that I had packed his cooler with the things that *I* liked, not the things that he would enjoy eating.

I had fulfilled the letter of the Golden Rule: I had done for my son what I would *love* for someone to do for me. But I somehow fell short of the real intent of that principal. Because what I truly would want done for myself is for someone to learn the things I enjoy and do *that*, not necessarily what he would like himself.

The focus of our preaching often fails to make that extra step as well. We don't take the time to think about *the way our audience* perceives, about how they process information. Instead, we just assume they enjoy the things we do, that they think the way we think. When we fail to think on the perceptual level, the conceptual level fails to excite anyone either. Good preaching takes both.

Frankly, it is hard to think about thinking. It feels like thinking about breathing, so we don't do it much. Yet this is an important step because not everybody processes information the same way. The hooks that work in some regions or cultures may not set well in others.

I was once preaching in a country whose sensibilities and empathies are very different from that of the United States. I was speaking in a marriage retreat setting, and in order to make the point that couples should sometimes do impractical things for one another, I told the story of O. Henry's *The Gift of the Magi.* It relates the tale of a poverty-stricken wife who sold her beautiful, luxurious hair to buy a watch chain for her husband, while at the same time the husband sold his heirloom watch to buy fancy combs for his wife's glorious hair. The story is a real tear-jerker in the United States, but when I related that story in Brazil, everyone at the retreat began laughing uproariously. They thought it was *funny*.

While one might expect such differences between countries, rural people react very differently to stories and sermons than do urban people. Folks who live in the North don't have the same perceptions as people in the South. White churches and black churches will have different ways of learning the same truth.

And the preacher who ignores these variations will do so to his own peril. While the truth of the text does not and will never change, the *method* of relaying that truth is constantly changing with location and audience. A wise preacher learns early how to exegete his audience as well as his text, not that he might change his message, but that he might deliver it in the most effective manner possible.

When I was pastoring I saw Dr. D. James Kennedy preach on tithing in a creative manner that I adapted and used for my congregation, too. I have always believed that no church of at least middle-class members should ever be in need of money. If members only tithed, the church would have plenty for missions, for its own programs, and for salaries. Early in my pastorate I was forced to recognize that our people just weren't very giving.

Normally our worship time consisted of two groups of worship songs punctuated by a pastoral prayer and greeting, but on this particular day I had secretly informed our worship leader that my sermon would start after the first block of songs, though he was not to tell anyone and was to prepare the worship service as normal. After we sang a few songs I led in a prayer and then I apologized to any visitors we had for what I was about to say. "I have to deal with a church family matter," I said, "and I know that might make some of you uncomfortable, but it must be done." I drew a deep breath and with a pained look I said, "It has come to my attention that a sizeable amount of money is missing from the church. I am not sure who has it, but I can say in all honesty before God that your pastor is not guilty of any wrongdoing in the matter. I did not steal the Lord's money."

By this time, the sanctuary was deathly quiet. People were stunned and silent. I continued, "I am also convinced that no one on this staff is guilty in the matter as I have spoken with all of them, but the fact remains that we are missing a lot of money." Drawing out and heightening the tension, I spoke in tones of disgust that anyone could steal from the Lord. Choruses of "Amen!" began to ring through the building.

Finally, when I was ready, I quietly said, "The money we are missing is,not money that you gave and then someone else stole. (Pause) The money we are missing is the money that God told you to give . . . and you never gave." There was about a three-second delay, and then, in chorus a gasp followed by chuckles which quickly became loud laughter.

But here was the moment I had planned for. I had anticipated their response, right down to the laugh. Now I was ready to drive the point home in a way that *really* connects. "And I can tell by your laughter," I said leaning directly into the microphone, speaking almost in a whisper, "that you think it is less of a sin. But that is not what God says . . ." Then I proceeded to preach from Malachi chapter 3 about what God thinks of those who rob him.

Our offerings jumped up over 40 percent and *never* went back down. For the first time people began to think about God's opinion of their giving. No doubt I could have imparted the same information in another way, but figuring out a way to say it that would grip their hearts and minds was far more effective than just dumping the information on them.

The way we present truth involves thinking not only on the conceptual level about the truth we present, but also on the perceptual level about the way our audience will best hear us. Thinking about the meaning of the text and how it applies demands a mental discipline that we cannot preach without.

A COMMITMENT TO REFLECTING AUTHORIAL INTENT

Our fifth and final commitment is the dividing line between the hard-core, committed expositor and the expositor of convenience. This commitment means that we are never welcome to preach a meaning from a text other than the one the author had or that was shown elsewhere in Scripture that referred to that text. We limit ourselves to authorial intent because we believe that words have real meaning.

This commitment bears some explanation and justification. What this means is that many common methods of preaching have to be thrown out the window. Many traditions of preaching find some catch phrase in the Bible and then extrapolate from that some truth that may indeed be true— but it has nothing to do with the text.

Examples of such preaching would be preaching a sermon on the Holy Spirit from 1 Samuel 3:3: "The lamp of God had not yet gone out, and Samuel was lying down in the temple of the LORD, where the ark of God was." It is easy to make the lamp like the Holy Spirit and to preach a sermon about doing something before God's light goes out, but that is hardly the meaning of the text. Another example would be to preach a message about the necessity of developing a vision for the future from Joel 2:28: "And afterward, I will pour out my Spirit on all people. Your sons and daughters will prophesy, your old men will dream dreams, your young men will see visions." As desperately as some churches need to develop a vision, that has nothing to do with Joel's prophecy.

The difficulty with making this commitment is that such sermons are often *good!* We have heard sermons that were true, that made a real connection with the congregation, and that were very applicational and practical in nature. They are often preached by men who have a very solid systematic theology, so they do not necessarily say anything that is biblically wrong. Yet, unfortunately, the sermon still has nothing to do with the intended meaning of the Scripture. This makes such pithy, phrase-centered sermons particularly tempting, because they are often done well by creative and doctrinally centered preachers (like Charles Spurgeon). But that does not make them right for several reasons.

Picture biblical truth like a mighty stream. It is moving one direction, and in the middle of the stream runs a channel in which the water runs swiftest and deepest. When we preach the text with the same intent as the author, even addressing the same kind of problem or audience as the biblical writer did, we preach with the force and depth of the main channel. Our sermons have maximum flow. But if we take a verse out of its context, we find ourselves standing in the water, as we are within the scope of biblical revelation. But we are in shallow water and do not experience the natural force of the text. The preacher will experience the greatest anointing of the Holy Spirit and the greatest effectiveness possible when he places himself squarely within the confines of the biblical author's intent.

Making this commitment means that we cannot preach a sermon from John chapter 4 on the necessity of personal witnessing if we do not believe that the author's intent when he wrote it was to urge us to be gospel witnesses. We cannot preach on the eight laws of leadership from the Sermon on the Mount unless we truly believe that the author intended to give us eight laws of leadership.

Frankly, this may rob us of some cherished and time-worn sermons, but do we really want to settle for emotion and creativity if it is bereft of biblical truth? Surely we can and must find a way to be within the scope of the passage and also be creative and gripping.

One final word about authorial intent bears explanation. Many Bible scholars deny that anyone can know an author's intent because one cannot get inside the head of another person, especially if that person is dead. Can we really know what Paul meant in Ephesians if he is not here to explain himself? Some go so far as to assert that it is impossible to know *anyone's* intent by reading their writings.

The answers to this objection are numerous and obvious, but our first response is to wonder why people who don't believe in authorial intent write books! How do they expect anyone to know what they wrote—and why try anyway? Furthermore, our entire civilization is built on the notion that words have an agreed-on meaning, and that the meaning of a word is revealed by its context. All the scholars who attack the notion of authorial intent have mortgages and contracts, each of which is dependent on all parties involved understanding and agreeing to the meaning of the contract. We simply are not free to tell the bank that our understanding of the mortgage is that we don't have to make a payment every month. That contract has an actual meaning, and it will be enforced in a court of law if we fail to perform its obligations—no matter what our interpretation may be.

Clearly, every passage in the Bible had an intended meaning when the author wrote it, and that meaning has not changed. Its applicability or the way it works out in life may have changed, but its meaning is the same as the day it was written. The ritual or dietary laws of the Old Testament, for example, do not have the force they once had because they have been abrogated in Scripture, but the meaning is still what it always was. While we may have to show a complete meaning as revealed in other Scriptures to be true to the whole meaning of Scripture, we can and must understand the author's original intent and let that be our guide. Then, as we compare that text with other texts, we can arrive at its force and place in God's revelation of himself.

If we are convinced of these things and willing to make these five commitments, then we are ready to get down to the business of understanding the text and building the sermon.

CHAPTER 4
Approaching the Text

The worst way to spend a Saturday evening is swimming in flop sweat in a desperate and panicked search for something to preach. The richness and vastness of the Bible does not lend itself to a rushed and frantic Saturday search for poignancy. Good preaching will come only through planning, preparation, and intention.

In fact, preaching well demands that we master three elements: the text, the sermon, and the delivery. We cannot state forcefully enough that *nothing else matters* if we do not understand the text correctly in the first place. On any given Sunday, pulpits will be filled by three kinds of preachers.

The first kind is really convinced of the Word and is driven by strong convictions and commitment to the authority of the Word. He *knows* the Bible. But when he stands to preach, the sermon falls mostly on deaf ears because he cannot say it well. While his belief system is correct, and even his sermon may be well constructed, he has such a dull delivery that people easily tune him out and don't get much of what he says.

The second kind of preacher is not very biblical, perhaps, but he is a natural in the pulpit. He is engaging, inspirational, and even entertaining, and people love to hear him. But when he is finished, no one can really articulate the content of his sermon or what changes it demands in the listeners' lives. Like cotton candy, he leaves his audience with a sweet taste, but nothing to chew on and no nutritional value.

But the third category of preacher combines strong convictions about the Word with a delivery that keeps his congregation tuned to his every word. Not only does he have something to say; he says it *well*. His sermon arises from the text, but he builds it in such a way that it heightens interest and drives home the practical application. That is the kind of preacher we want to be, that we *must* be. Our people deserve that kind of communication. The gospel demands that kind of communication.

So we must keep this goal in mind at every step of the process. This is what we are after. We will settle for nothing less than preaching to change the lives of our listeners, and we will work at every element of our preaching so that we are completely at God's disposal. While God is not limited and can use anyone he wants, the observable reality is that God *usually* uses individuals who work to make themselves available to him through the gifts he gives them. After all, God once used a burning bush to speak to Moses, but that is not his *usual* way, so we had better not count on him doing it in our case!

This book is about sermon preparation and preaching, but let us be clear at the outset: *nothing can or will happen apart from prayer and the Holy Spirit.* The most brilliant expositor will accomplish nothing apart from the Spirit's gracious work through him and in the hearts and minds of his listeners. The most eloquent speaker will be able to *move* hearts, but he cannot *change* them. Every step of our study must be saturated with prayer and our own sense of complete dependence on God. Though we do not apologize for hard work, deep study, and intense preparation, we must never think that our own commitment is the source of power. God alone deserves the glory for calling us to commitment and for using our study.

A Suggested Approach to Exposition

Expository preaching is defined not by a style nor by a particular methodology, but by the end result of explaining and applying the meaning of the text. *Expository preaching is any kind of preaching that shows people the meaning of a biblical text and leads them to apply it to their lives.* Contrary to some popular notions of expository preaching, that does not necessarily mean working through a passage verse-by-verse. A one-sermon overview of a book can be expository, provided it teaches the author's intent and purpose in writing that book and the impact it should make on our lives. By the same token, one might do an expository series, spending months in a book of the Bible, carefully digesting each verse and its significance.

Furthermore, an expository sermon could take on many forms. One might do a sermon on the parable of the lost sheep in the dramatic persona of the shepherd. In the same chapter, one could preach on the story of the prodigal son from the point of view of the older brother (who is, after all, the real point of that parable!). So long as the author's intended meaning, purpose, and application are maintained, the precise form of the sermon is a function of the preacher's personality and the expectations of the culture.

While we will speak more of sermonic form later, the main point we assert here is that discerning and sharing the meaning of the text is the foundational task of preaching. Nothing of eternal value can happen in the lives of the listeners unless the preacher has been faithful to that task. While we may debate stylistic preferences and homiletic niceties, the meaning of the Scripture is paramount.

Just as we do not claim that only one style of preaching is expository, neither do we claim that a pastor has to preach book by book or chapter by chapter. On the other hand, years of experience and observation indicate that this is the *best* way to get people acquainted with the Bible and to equip them with a strategic grasp of the Scriptures. Preaching through books or sections of the Bible, alternating between the testaments and forms of biblical literature, is essential to helping people comprehend the totality of God's revelation of himself and his salvation.

People need to know the warp and the woof of the poetic literature of the Old Testament just as they need to know something about the New Testament epistles. To understand the Bible, they need a basic comprehension of the historical books and the prophetic books of the Old Testament. They should be able to articulate a basic time line of biblical history, appreciating the order of the major events of the Bible, like creation, flood, calling of

Abraham, the move of Jacob and his sons to Egypt and subsequent captivity and exodus, the conquest of Canaan, the establishment of the kingdom of Israel, the division of the kingdom and its subsequent decline, the exile, the restoration to the land, the intertestamental period, the arrival of John the Baptist, the life of Christ, the events of Acts, the missionary journeys of Paul, and the writings of John in the final days of the apostolic period.

Helping people learn so much about the Bible takes time and intention. Succeeding requires, first, deliberate planning of a preaching calendar and, second, longevity in a pastorate. Frankly, each of these helps the other happen.

Part I: Planning to Preach

A pastor's strategy for preaching, therefore, should take the congregation's need to know the Scriptures into account. He might, for instance, plan a series preaching through the Minor Prophets, preaching a single sermon overview of each of the books for twelve weeks. On the other hand, he may spend a year working through a Pauline epistle. So long as he is limiting himself to the author's intent and making application to contemporary life, he is being expositional.

While an expositor may not be locked into any single style of preaching the text, he needs a systematic approach to preaching the Bible that acquaints the congregation with the integrity of biblical revelation. One of the best ways to accomplish that is to preach passage-by-passage through a book of the Bible. For the sake of illustration, let's assume that we are going to preach through a single book of the Bible such as 1 Corinthians.

Read the text many times. The best way to prepare to preach a book of the Bible is to fall in love with it by reading it several times and in several translations. Choose accurate translations to really understand the author's meaning, and include a paraphrase or a highly interpretive translation or two because, though they may not render exactly the meaning of a text, they often capture the emotion of an author better than a woodenly literal English translation. After reading the book four or five times, one begins to catch the natural divisions of the document like a craftsman sees the grain in a piece of wood. An author's style begins to become apparent. Discourse markers stand out and call attention to units of thought.

Determine the preachable units within the book or section. While reading the book once again, make a list of each *preachable unit*—a passage that recognizes the natural divisions of the author, yet acknowledges time constraints that a preacher must respect. Natural divisions must never be ignored, but they sometimes must be further divided or, on the other hand, combined. In 1 Corinthians, for example, it would be foolish to preach the first half of chapter 5, which is about disciplining a member in sin, and then the following week to preach the remainder of the chapter together with the first half of chapter 6, which is about a different subject altogether. If possible, the preacher should preach chapter 5 as a single unit. If he feels that he cannot do it justice in a single sermon, he should by no means combine part of it with a different subject simply because one follows the other.

Finding the right unit for preaching is probably more difficult in the Old Testament, especially in those passages in which the author makes just one main point, but he takes pages and pages to do it. The divisions of the land in Joshua chapters 13–21 serve as an appropriate example for our consideration. The care God took to see that each tribe received an allotment and that it was surveyed properly says something important about God, about social justice, about the preservation of wealth from one generation to the next, and about his ideal for human society. The care with which the author records precise landmarks and instructions about the division of the land is not by accident. But these main truths are revealed in the *totality* of that division, not necessarily in the minute details.

While there may be some salient details that emerge in this particular text—the cities of refuge, Caleb's portion, God's special treatment of the Levites—it is probably not possible to preach a meaningful sermon on the geographical location of the northern boundary between Judah and Benjamin as it passed through the Adummim gorge (Josh. 15:7). This is one of those passages in the Bible that is equally *inspired* but not equally *profitable*. Yet, taken as a whole, one can still mine riches for instruction about God and application in churches, homes, and society today. In such a case we might elect to preach the meaning of that lengthy passage in one sermon, foregoing reading it all aloud or commenting on every verse. We need not fear that we have done the Scripture a disservice. Frankly, that is the only way a preacher could, in a normal lifespan, ever preach through the Bible. Coupled with encouragement to church members to read through the Bible every year or, at the very least to read the book under study, a pastor can succeed in instilling the Word in their lives.

In the New Testament, however, we face a different kind of struggle. Especially in the epistles, one can easily get bogged down and spend so much time in a single book or section that church members fail to see the big picture. It would be like an art critic who specializes on the intricacies of the Mona Lisa's nose and nothing else. Nearly every book of the New Testament is a well that will not run dry, and one could spend months in even the smallest books (and some *do!*). The preacher has to strike a balance between paying too little attention to the text to do it justice (because he fears preaching the same book for too long) and spending too much time in a single book (because he fears missing *anything* of value). Too little time in a passage betrays the wealth of Scripture, while too much time ignores the totality of Scripture.

Preaching through a major book of the Bible may seem like a daunting task. Some pastors fear that their people will not be able to stay interested and engaged for a long series. Consequently, they seldom walk their people through an author's development of thought and argument so they can see for themselves the true and full meaning of the book.

We have three responses to this fear. First, *people will stay interested and engaged as long as the preacher makes it interesting and engaging.* In other words, the burden is on *you.* Why is it any harder to make fifty sermons through the Book of Romans interesting than to make fifty sermons through ten different smaller series interesting? You are responsible for keeping the congregation engaged, and that takes thought, planning, and execution. Every sermon you preach, whether part of a series or not, has to be well constructed, well illustrated, and passionately delivered.

Second, *longer books can often be broken down into sectional series.*

Preaching through the Book of Romans does not simply have to be "The Book of Romans," but rather a series on "Why Man Needs God" (chapters 1–3) followed by "How Faith Works" (chapters 4–6), "How to Defeat Sin" (chapters 7–8), "God's Great Plan" (chapters 9–11), and "What a Christian Looks Like" (chapters 12–16). One can be creative and still remain faithful to the author's intent.

Finally, *don't underestimate your people or the Word.* Christians have a supernatural desire for the nourishment of the Word. Furthermore, they have the Holy Spirit who creates a hunger within them and bears witness to the things of God. The Bible is the most exciting book in the history of the world. The perennial best-seller of all books, the basis for much of Western art and literature, the fountain of wisdom that millions have turned to for centuries, the Bible can hold the attention of modern listeners. Neither the relevance nor the attraction of the Word is in question. The only factor that might cause listeners to turn from it is the preacher—and that is why you are reading this book! You don't want to be the weak link!

So as you read through the book to determine the preachable units, simply make a running list on a sheet of paper. Remember, this is not carved in stone. You may later find that a particular passage is so rich that you need two sermons to do it justice, or you may find that you need to combine two into one. That can be adjusted later, but for now you need a good idea of the length of the series and the breakdown of the book. A breakdown of the first nine chapters of 1 Corinthians, for example, might look like this:

1:1–9
1:10–17
1:18–25
1:26–31
2:1–5
2:6–16
3:1–9
3:10–17
3:18–4:21
5:1–13

6:1–11
6:12–20
7:1–9
7:10–24
7:25–40
8:1–13
9:1–14
9:15–23
9:24–27

In determining where to begin and end a unit, we used three criteria. First, *grammar and literary device* is the most obvious clue. We should never end a sermon in the middle of an author's sentence. Some of Paul's lengthy sentences may be an exception, but even then we are not free to divorce the part from the whole. Within the author's writing he gives us clues to the division of the text by his use of logical connectors, repetition, conjunctions, and variation. We will say more about this later in the book, but even at this early stage of analyzing the passage we should notice them.

The second clue to dividing the text is *theme*. Hebrews chapter 11, for example, is clearly about faith. The author's repeated use of "by faith" to introduce a subject is a literary device that provides a clue, but so is the overall theme of faith. The shift of theme in chapter 12 indicates that the previous section is closed and the author is building on it, but he is clearly moving on. Our sermon, therefore, should probably not try to tackle two different themes. While they may certainly be connected, they are still distinct.

Finally, *time* is a very real criterion we must use in determining the length of the passage. Most pastors must stay within certain reasonable time constraints. So while Hebrews chapter 11 is clearly an integral unit, one could probably not preach all forty verses of Hebrews 11 with its cast of characters and martyrs from the Old Testament and do it justice in a thirty-minute sermon.

Label the main theme of each preaching unit. Haddon Robinson introduced "the big idea" into the preaching vernacular in his excellent book, *Biblical Preaching: The Development and Delivery of Expository*

Messages.[3] His argument is that every sermon should have one central theme around which it is organized and that is the main theme of the text. We concur, but we don't believe the preacher should necessarily wait until actually preparing the sermon to figure out what that main theme is. After you determine the units that you can preach, go back through the list and label each one with the dominant theme of the passage. What is the main point being made by the author?

Beware that you do not just list the *event* or the *form* of writing that the author uses. For instance, if you are preaching through Joshua, and you want to label chapter 6, you don't call it "The Defeat of Jericho." That is just the event, not the meaning. Preaching relates the purpose that the author had in mind. Ask yourself what is the lesson to learn, what is the sin to avoid, what is the promise to claim? Joshua 6 might properly be labeled, "The Victory of Faith" or "The Reward of Obedience." The author is not just telling us a story; he is telling us a story that exhorts us to obey as Joshua and the Israelites did. The story encourages us to have complete faith in God's promises and to act on those promises. *That* is the meaning of the event.

Returning to our example of 1 Corinthians chapters 1–9, we might find it easy to simply label our first division "Paul's Greeting," but that would fall short of the importance of this text. First, that is not its meaning, but merely its placement in the book. But even more importantly, these opening verses carry much more importance than a friendly "howdy." Read them carefully:

> Paul, called to be an apostle of Christ Jesus by the will of God, and our brother Sosthenes, To the church of God in Corinth, to those sanctified in Christ Jesus and called to be holy, together with all those everywhere who call on the name of our Lord Jesus Christ—their Lord and ours: Grace and peace to you from God our Father and the Lord Jesus Christ. I always thank God for you because of his grace given you in Christ Jesus. For in him you have been enriched in every way—in all your speaking and in all your knowledge—because our testimony about Christ was

confirmed in you. Therefore you do not lack any spiritual gift as you eagerly wait for our Lord Jesus Christ to be revealed. He will keep you strong to the end, so that you will be blameless on the day of our Lord Jesus Christ. God, who has called you into fellowship with his Son Jesus Christ our Lord, is faithful. (1 Cor. 1:1–9)

Certainly Paul greets his readers, but he does far more than that. Having read through the book several times we know that Paul later issues several sharp rebukes about their sins. He has to deal with divisions, incest, lawsuits, fornication, gossip, perverted views of sex, idolatry, abuse of spiritual gifts, and doubts about the resurrection. Knowing that, we may be shocked to find that Paul's first comment to them is that they are "sanctified in Christ Jesus" and "called to be holy." He comments about the grace of God that is given them and rejoices that they will be preserved "blameless on the day of our Lord Jesus Christ." We know that Paul has to rebuke them for their misuse of spiritual gifts and the childish way they pride themselves in them, yet he thanks God for their gifts, particularly their "speaking" and "knowledge." He goes so far as to say that they "do not lack any spiritual gift."

To label this passage as Paul's greeting would miss the subtlety and wisdom that the apostle demonstrates as he nimbly lays out threads of discussion for later use. Weaving through it all, however, is this one dominant theme that God set them apart, called them to be holy, and will keep them blameless to the end. In other words, Paul is reminding them of the reality and the goal of their sanctification in Christ. The main point, therefore, would be their sanctification. Go back to your list of preachable units and write beside 1:1–9 the theme, "sanctification." In the same way, go through every division and write the main theme beside the text, so you finally have a list that looks something like this:

1:1–9	Sanctification
1:10–17	Dealing with Divisions
1:18–25	The Wisdom of God in the Gospel
1:26–31	The People God Uses

2:1–5	The Power of Paul's Preaching
2:6–16	The Spirit's Work in the Gospel
3:1–9	Christian Immaturity
3:10–17	How to Leave a Legacy
3:18–4:21	The Temptation to Please Everyone
5:1–13	Church Discipline
6:1–11	Conflict Resolution
6:12–20	Dealing with Sexual Temptation
7:1–9	Sex and Marriage
7:10–24	Honoring God in Spite of Circumstances
7:25–40	Sex and Being Single
8:1–13	Christian Liberty
9:1–14	Surrendering Our Rights
9:15–23	Preaching the Gospel, Reaching the Lost
9:24–27	Self-discipline

Now you have a strong acquaintance with the text and the major themes, which is an excellent way to begin to formulate ideas and preaching strategies. Although you are not yet at the stage of building the sermon, you will find that this stage is one of the most creative of the entire process. As you read through the text, the Holy Spirit begins to make it live in your heart and resonate in your mind. Needs of your congregation that the text addresses will come to mind as well as illustrations, stories, and points for application. Jot them down because the next step gives you a method of storing them for later use.

Organize for sermon development. Now get a box of manila folders that you can use, one folder for each division of text. Write on the tab the passage and the theme. In our previous example of the first nine chapters of 1 Corinthians we would have nineteen folders labeled. After you are finished, put them in a drawer that is close at hand, preferably one in your desk, because you will want easy access to them over the course of the next weeks and months. As ideas for outlines, illustrations, and supporting material come to your mind, you can jot them down and put them in the folder. Knowing the themes that you will be dealing with heightens your awareness, creativity, and interest in those subjects.

Reading the newspaper one morning, you may encounter an article about the high incidence of divorce among couples who lived together prior to marriage. Clip it out and put it in the folder labeled "7:1–9: Sex and Marriage." Reading a magazine article you come across a story about a Christian sect that still adheres to the Old Testament dietary laws, so you cut that out and slip it in the "8:1–13: Christian Liberty" folder. Listening to a sermon on the radio, you hear a great illustration about evangelism which you know will fit well with Paul's emphasis on becoming all things to all men, so you jot it down and insert it in "9:15–23: Preaching the Gospel, Reaching the Lost."

You find that you evaluate every article you read, every humorous story someone tells you, and every news bit on television for how it might fit into your preaching schedule. By the time you actually start preparing those sermons, you just might have a wealth of material and ideas because you have been thinking about those texts and themes and looking for material for months. This method enables you to keep your mind focused on the whole of the book you are preaching instead of only the next sermon.

With current technology it is also possible to do all of this work electronically on a computer, but you will probably need a scanner for optimal use and best results. You can easily label computer folders with each text, and then place scanned documents or date files into the appropriate folders. Some programs can capture web sites, too, and import them into your folders.

Diagram the passage. At the heart of much bad preaching is little planning and much procrastination. If you want to preach well, you need to know your passage inside and out. Study it often and let it rest in your mind and grip your heart. Last-minute study and sermon building is a recipe for disaster. Even if you are one of those rare individuals who can actually pull it off to some degree without anyone else knowing the difference, *you* know it and God knows. You cannot say that you gave the Lord or your people your best. Not only does that simply feel lousy, but you will be judged by the Lord who gave you the gifts you squandered.

Reading the book of the Bible many times as you decided how to divide it for sermons is a great first step. The subsequent thought you give it while searching for illustrations and supporting material is helpful, too. But nothing will make the text breathe and reveal its heart like diagramming the passage. While this step is a bit more technical in nature and not necessarily essential—thousands of faithful expositors have never diagrammed a biblical text—it will prove itself one of the most fruitful efforts any expositor can endeavor. Nothing else reveals the author's thoughts quite as clearly as physically showing the relationships of clauses and words. This section is a bit technical, so if this method of understanding the text is not your cup of tea, just skip on to the next part of this chapter and read part I of chapter 5 very carefully. Our feelings won't be hurt, and you can still preach great sermons.

On the other hand, if you want to get inside the author's mind and understand more precisely what he was saying, go through the hard work and repeated practice of learning to diagram the text before you begin to build the sermon. A textual diagram is not like the grammatical diagrams that you learned in ninth-grade English. Rather, a textual diagram reveals the hierarchical structure of the passage.[4] An author reveals his main thoughts through his choice of verbs, modifiers, and objects. To get a feel for what we are talking about, let's look at this simple sentence:

Going to the store yesterday I briefly saw a big, brown dog bite an old man who was passing him on a bicycle on the ankle.

This sentence has several verb forms, but there is only one main verb. It has several nouns, but only one subject. The first thing we want to look for, then, is the subject and verb, followed closely by an object or a predicate nominative. The subject we locate is "I" and the verb is "saw." The direct object is "dog." But the sentence has several phrases that modify either a verb or a noun. When we diagram, we want to establish the subject, the verb, and the object, and then we want to show what modifies what. By physically tying the modifiers to what they describe, we come up with a simple diagram of the sentence that looks like this:

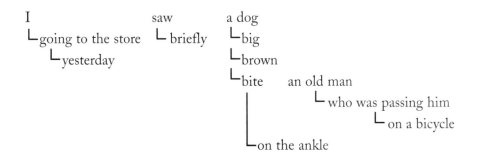

Notice that the subject, verb, and object go on the same line, showing the bare skeleton of the sentence that frames everything else that appears. Every other word of that sentence somehow hangs on one of those words, whether directly or indirectly. You may notice as well that the words that modify "dog" are not the same kinds of words nor do they carry equal weight in the sentence. "Big" and "brown" are simple adjectives that further portray the dog for us, while "bite" is a verb in the dependent clause of which "dog" is the subject. So the two adjectives answer questions about the dog's appearance, while the verb answers a question about his action. "An old man" is the direct object in the dependent clause, but also serves as the subject of a participle, "was passing," which has its own prepositional phrase, "on a bicycle." By placing the words on the page, physically connected to one another, we can easily see the structure and relative importance of each clause and word.

This sentence is simple enough, but now let's look at a literal English translation of Philippians 2:1–8.

> If you have any comfort in Christ, if some encouragement of love, if any fellowship of the spirit, if any bowels and mercies, fulfill my joy in order that you think the same thing, having the same love, one-souled, thinking the one thing, not at all according to selfish ambition or vain pride, but in humility each one considering others exceeding themselves, not everyone looking out for his own possessions, but also for the possessions of others. Let this mind be among you which was also in Christ Jesus, who, though being in the form of God did not consider

PHILIPPIANS 2:1-8

1) Εἴ τις οὖν παράκλησις ἐν Χριστῷ,
   εἴ τις παραμύθιον ἀγάπης,
   εἴ τις κοινωνία πνεύματος,
   εἴ τις σπλάγχνα καὶ
      οἰκτιρμοί

2) Πληρώσατέ μου τὴν χαρὰν
   ⌐ ἵνα τὸ αὐτὸ φρονῆτε
   └ τὴν αὐτὴν ἀγάπην ἔχοντες
   └ σύμψυχοι
   └ τὸ ἓν φρονοῦντες

3)   μηδὲν κατ' ἐπιθείαν
   μηδὲ κατὰ κενοδοξίαν
   └ ἀλλὰ τῇ ταπεινοφροσύνῃ
   └ ἀλλήλους ἡγούμενοι ὑπερέχοντας ἑαυτῶν

4)   └ μὴ τὰ ἑαυτῶν ἕκαστος σκοποῦντες
   └ ἀλλὰ καὶ τὰ ἑτέρων ἕκαστοι.

5)   └ Τοῦτο φρονεῖτε ἐν ὑμῖν
     └ ὃ καὶ ἐν Χριστῷ Ἰησοῦ,

PHILIPPIANS 2:1-8

1) If there be therefore any consolation in Christ,
   if any comfort of love,
   if any fellowship of the Spirit,
   if any bowels and
              mercies,

2) Fulfil ye my joy,
   └ that ye be likeminded,
   └ having the same love,
   └ *being* of one accord,
   └ of one mind.

3) └ *Let* nothing *be done* through strife
      or vainglory;
      └ but in lowliness of mind
      └ let each esteem other better than themselves.

4) └ Look not every man on his own things,
      └ but every man also on the things of others.

5) └ Let this mind be in you,
      └ which was also in Christ Jesus:

6)

7)

8)

ὅς
ἐν μορφῇ θεοῦ ὑπάρχων
οὐχ ἁρπαγμὸν ἡγήσατο
τὸ εἶναι ἴσα θεῷ,
ἀλλὰ ἑαυτὸν ἐκένωσεν
μορφὴν δούλου λαβών,
ἐν ὁμοιώματι ἀνθρώπων γενόμενος·
καὶ σχήματι εὑρεθεὶς ὡς ἄνθρωπος
ἐταπείνωσεν ἑαυτὸν
γενόμενος ὑπήκοος μέχρι θανάτου
θανάτου δὲ σταυροῦ.

6)
    └ Who
  └ being in the form of God,
  └ thought it not robbery
    └ to be equal with God:

7)
  └ But made himself of no reputation,
    └ and took upon him the form of a servant
    └ and was made in the likeness of men:

8)
  ┌ And being found in fashion as a man,
  └ he humbled himself,
    └ and became obedient unto death,
      └ even the death of the cross.

equality with God something to be grasped, but emptied himself taking the form of a slave, being in human likeness and being found in appearance as a man he humbled himself becoming obedient to the point of death, even the death of a cross.[5]

Reading those verses from Philippians chapter 2, we might say that the main thought is to be like Christ, but the diagram reveals that Paul is doing more than just telling the Philippians to have the mind of Christ. The striking feature of the diagram is that the main verb which governs the entire passage is "fulfill," and everything else in the passage hangs on that. The four "if" statements which introduce a conditional sentence hang on the verb "fulfill," but so does Paul's characteristic explanation of the form that this action will take. In other words, Paul is saying, "If you want to make me happy, here is what you can do—be minded like Christ." The Philippians wanted to help Paul while he was imprisoned, so after assuring them that he was alright (in chapter 1), Paul then took advantage of that personal relationship that he had with them in order to get them to do the right thing.

Furthermore, notice that everything that Paul said about Christ hangs on the relative pronoun "who." Many preachers have preached some of the rich Christological truth of this passage, but if that is not related to the main verb of the passage and Paul's ultimate admonition that we have that same mind, then we have missed the main point. Rich as it may be, the Christology of the passage is not its main point. How do we know that? Because the verb tells us that the main point is to make Paul's joy full by having unity in the church, and that unity can only be attained by taking on the mind of Christ. So we should preach that text the same way that Paul wrote it, rather than to divorce it from its context.

While the purpose of this book is not to teach a methodology for diagramming, we encourage further study and practice to learn how to diagram. If this is too technical or difficult, you can certainly still understand the meaning of the text without it, but the diagram just makes it so very plain to see. We know and have seen how very beneficial this is for the preachers who will take the time and effort to learn how to do it. Happily, the more you do it the easier it gets. We have dozens of testimonials from colleagues and former students whom we have urged to diagram passages before building the sermon that testify that this may be the single most beneficial step in preparation. It deepens your understanding of and intimacy with the text. And when you know the text well, your confidence level is high, and that translates into passionate preaching with bold assurance.

If possible, the pastor who has learned Greek and Hebrew should diagram the passages in the original language. That is, after all, why a minister takes the time and makes the sacrifice to go to college or seminary and learn the languages God chose for the Bible. While knowing the original languages is by no means necessary to understanding the Bible, everyone agrees that being able to read the text for oneself without lexicons and concordances is not only thrilling, but yields a greater understanding of the Scriptures. If you choose to diagram the passage in an English translation, we must warn you that the translations that are easiest to read are poorest for diagramming. The more woodenly literal the translation, the closer it reflects the structure of the original text. The King James Version is usually the best for diagramming and seeing the underlying structure.

To see what we are talking about, compare the literal translation of Philippians 2:1–8 above with a modern translation and see how differently they diagram. Hardly any of them would keep "fulfill" as the only main verb. For ease of reading, they usually break longer sentences into shorter ones. This is fine for reading and getting the author's sense, but it won't work for discerning the author's structure, so that is why we recommend the original language or a literal translation.

Even those of us who are committed to diagramming know, however, that not every passage really needs to be diagrammed. Epistolary passages, lengthy discourses, and prophetic texts almost always need to be diagrammed. But straightforward narrative texts, proverbs, or short pithy sayings like the Beatitudes seldom reveal any more nuance in the diagram than is apparent on the page. Remember that diagramming is your servant, not your master, so use it well; but do not think that the diagram is the object of your study.

PART II: MINING THE MEANING

You could be the greatest Greek exegete in the world and be adept at diagramming every passage in the Bible, but if you cannot *communicate* the truth of God's Word, then you will fail as a preacher. And if you understand every nuance and implication of the text, but you cannot package it in a way that the people understand, then all your work serves only to fill your head, but it will change no hearts.

If you want to truly understand the text *and* find the way to preach it with an applicational emphasis, then you must look for and discern three things about every passage you study: the *context, content,* and *concern* of the text.[6]

Distinguish the Context

Words have no inherent meaning, no more than the letters of an alphabet have meaning. The letter "R," for instance, means nothing standing alone. We have to combine it with other letters to approach a meaning, but if we combine it with the letters "U" and "N," it still does not necessarily mean anything. The word "run" only means something when we place it in a *context*. It has no inherent meaning, only meaning that we agree on in a cultural setting, and that is revealed through its usage. So when you read the word "run," what, exactly, do you think it means? Does it refer to what a river does, what a nose does, what a woman's hose do, what athletes in a race do, what a politician does, what a car engine does, or what a pool shark does to the table? The word only takes on meaning and significance when placed within a context.

But what context is enough for meaning? In other words, what is the basic unit of thought? We have shown that it is definitely not a single word, but we must admit also that it is not the sentence. A sentence alone can be insufficient to reveal true meaning. Suppose you walked into a room and heard someone utter some horrible words about Jews. You might be incensed and think that person is a horrible racist. But what if you learn that the person who is speaking is a college professor teaching a lesson about the rise of anti-Semitism in Europe before World War II, and you realize that he was quoting the words of the young Adolph Hitler. Far from endorsing those words, the professor was denouncing them. You heard a complete sentence come out of his mouth, but you did not understand the context; therefore, you missed the meaning.

The basic unit of thought, therefore, is the paragraph. To truly comprehend the sense of words, you must have sufficient context to insure that you have the intended meaning of those words *in their context.* When it comes to understanding literature, especially the Scriptures, context is everything. Divorced from context, the words of the Bible can be—and unfortunately often are—twisted and perverted to justify all kinds of evil. Ripping verses out of their context and assigning them a meaning that the author did not intend is doing violence to the Scripture and is an affront to the Word of God. We could easily take the verse about Judas that "he went away and hanged himself" (Matt. 27:5), then we could quote the words of Jesus from Luke 10:37, "Go and do likewise," and follow it up with another quote from Jesus, "What you are about to do, do quickly" (John 13:28). By ignoring contexts and putting together verses that weren't originally connected, we can come up with a diabolical instruction!

That is precisely the way cults, errant sects, and manipulative preachers work. They ignore context and pervert the Scriptures to come up with a basis for their own preferences. An expositor, however, limits himself to the authorial intent, and he knows that the only way one can know the author's intent is to go by the context.

Context is a clear indicator of meaning. In everyday life, context is so compelling that even if someone misuses a word, we usually know what they meant anyway. One pastor we know once wrote an article in the church paper on the difficult subject of divorce and remarriage. He was dealing with the passages known as the "exception clauses," which spell out the times when divorce is allowed. What he said in the article, however, was very different. He wrote, "The Bible gives two conditions under which adultery is permissible." Somehow the mistake made it past proofreaders and into the church paper. While he took a lot of teasing and good-natured ridicule about it, no one took the statement at face value. The context of the article (and even of his life) was so clear—the topic was divorce and remarriage, after all—that everyone who read the article and noticed the mistake knew exactly what had happened.

If context is that strong when one makes a mistake, how much stronger is it when our words are chosen well and accurately? And that is why an expositor pays such close attention to the context. But the context involves more than just the surrounding words. In fact, we must consider at least three kinds of context.

Know the historical context. Some parts of the Bible just won't make sense if you don't seek to understand what is happening historically in the passage. A basic understanding of the sweep of biblical history is essential for the preacher as well as for the congregation. Part of the historical context is *geographical*. Where does the story take place? We may need to learn where the author was when he wrote the letter. Where were the recipients of the letter? Depending on the book or its place in history, the geographical context may be essential to understanding the text. Psalm 137, for instance, is a psalm written as a lament by Jewish exiles in Babylon who were missing their homeland. The psalm makes little sense if we don't understand that setting.

John 4 records the story of Jesus' appearance to the Samaritan woman, and demonstrates the way Jesus shattered cultural prejudices. We can't know the depth of Jewish prejudice against the Samaritans until we realize just how far out of their way they would walk to avoid going through Samaria, the most direct route. Old Testament narratives can seem lifeless until one understands something about the geographical locations of the events. Jesus' journey from Galilee to Jerusalem may seem insignificant until one realizes the distance that he traveled on foot. Paul's journeys and epistles resonate with a greater vibrancy when we get an understanding of the geographical details. The Book of Acts is even organized around the geographical progress of the gospel.

There may be *specific historical factors* as well that lead us closer to understanding the text. This would include any background events or factors that contribute to the meaning. Imagine preaching the Book of Esther, for example, if you do not explain that the story takes place in Persia, where many of the Israelites were in captivity and completely at the mercy of the Persian king. The New Testament would hardly make sense at all if one were ignorant of the Roman occupation of Israel. The events surrounding the birth of Jesus are more thrilling when one understands the historical facts about Augustus and Herod.

Similarly, part of the historical context is *cultural detail* and factors that explain the meaning of stories, events, or teachings. Since our culture is often so removed from the ancient Near East, bridging this gap becomes an extremely important function of an expositor. Modern Western readers may find it difficult to relate to an ancient agrarian patriarchal society, so preachers have to take the time to help their listeners get inside the world of the Scriptures, often leaving their twenty-first century sensibilities behind them.

For example, when Jesus encountered the woman at the well in John chapter 4, she was drawing water in the heat of the day, and she was alone. Relating to a society in which women did the hard labor of carrying gallons of water on their heads may run against contemporary ideas. But in John chapter 4, the woman was not drawing water with the other women, who would have done that task early in the morning before the sun got too hot. They usually met at the well not only to get water, but also to learn the latest news and to steal a few moments with friends before diving into the rest of the day's chores. *This* Samaritan woman, however, apparently was not welcome to come to the well when the other women came. Jesus tells us why as the narrative progresses. She was a loose woman, the kind other women didn't like. Knowledge of the cultural details clues us into the woman's loneliness, sinfulness, and readiness to trust Christ. The change in her life and her witness to her neighbors are highlighted when we understand the culture.

The marriage at Cana, Roman crucifixions, the place of the Areopagus in Athenian politics and philosophy—all of these are examples of cultural factors that are important to understanding the meaning of a biblical passage. While no historical context may be more difficult to learn, surely no context is more central to the author's meaning, particularly since we live in a culture so radically different from the one we see in the Bible.

Closely akin to the cultural context is the *religious* context. Since most of the Bible concerns either false religion or true worship, a certain understanding of the religions mentioned in the sixty-six canonical books is necessary. Whether Baal, Dagon, or Zeus, the false gods and religions of the ancient world play a significant role that is often crucial for comprehension. Not only the gods themselves, but the customs associated with the religions of the Bible are integral to a complete understanding. Much of the Old Testament is dedicated to establishing and explaining Jewish religious practices. Most people don't know what phylacteries are, so Jesus' rebuke of the Pharisees will make little sense without some explanation. The Sabbath laws, a constant source of dispute during Jesus' ministry, have to be explained as well. The repeated references to the "high places" in the Old Testament are additional examples of religious historical context that would alter the meaning of a passage unless correctly understood.

Know the textual context. Every verse in the Bible is related to those around it and serves a function in a much larger argument or narrative. John 3:16, for example, is perhaps the most beloved verse in the Bible and is usually quoted by itself. While we can understand its basic meaning hearing it alone, we can understand it far better when we see it in the context of the larger story of Jesus' encounter with Nicodemus. John was commenting on Jesus' revelation of himself to Nicodemus by explaining the reason Jesus came.

Textual context has at least two aspects that an expositor must consider. The first is the *progress of revelation* and the second is the context of the *specific book*. By "progress of revelation" we take into account that, although every verse in the Bible was given by God as a part of the whole Bible, the whole Bible was not given at one time. So when some books were written, the inspired author was moved by the Spirit of God to write about a particular subject, but the human author did not understand all that God *eventually* revealed about that subject. Job, for instance, had some idea of the resurrection because he wrote "And after my skin has been destroyed, yet in my flesh I will see God; I myself will see him with my own eyes—I, and not another. How my heart yearns within me!" (Job 19:26–27).

This does not mean, however, that Job understood everything about the resurrection that Paul tells us in 1 Corinthians 15. We cannot read more into an author's meaning than he actually intended, so we must be familiar with the place of the text in the grand sweep of God's revelation in the Word. We must not attribute a greater understanding of a subject to a particular author than he himself revealed, although it may sometimes be acceptable to point listeners to a later text in which God revealed more on the subject.

In the same way, the passage that we study has a particular function in the specific book of the Bible in which it is located. Separated from its place in the argument or the narrative, a text may seem to mean something other than what the author intended, sometimes even the opposite. Jesus himself told parables that seem to praise someone of unsavory character, like a steward who cheated his master. He might even seem to compare God to an unjust judge who has to be nagged into doing the right thing.

The larger context, however, reveals that Jesus used parables of *contrast*, by which he argued that if one thing is true in a fallen world, *how much more* does this principle work with God. If a cheating steward knows the value of money, *how much more* should the children of the kingdom understand it? If an unjust judge, who does not want to do the right thing, will respond to repeated requests, *how much more* will a loving heavenly Father, who is inclined to do good for his children, respond to the petitions of those he loves?

Similarly, some of Paul's strong statements about the nature of grace and the inability of the law in Romans or Galatians may seem to deny holiness—

unless one reads the rest of those letters in which he answers the objections that his strong view of grace raises. Much of the Book of Ecclesiastes has to be read in light of its conclusion. Taken by itself, the majority of the book would seem depressing or even hopeless, so its relation to the rest of the book has to be explained. If one were to quote from a speech of Eliphaz in the Book of Job, one might actually advocate something that is diametrically opposed to the book's real meaning. The speeches of Job's friends have to be taken in their context with the understanding that they really don't know what they are talking about. Their role in the drama is to articulate a false view of suffering and even of God, which God himself dispels when he finally appears.

In the same way that a passage has a relation to the rest of the book and its meaning is thereby affected, so each book holds a relation to the rest of the Bible. That relationship to the other books of the Bible also is essential to interpreting the passage. Nowhere is that more true than in the Old Testament, especially the Pentateuch and the passages of the law. If a preacher attempts to preach Old Testament law, for instance, without accurately understanding how it was either fulfilled or abrogated in Christ, he will lay burdens on people that God does not intend for them to carry. In the same way, Old Testament prophecies that have been fulfilled in the New Testament are incomplete if the preacher ignores their fulfillment and relationship to the rest of the Scripture. It would border on nonsense for a preacher to preach a messianic prophecy from the Old Testament without informing the congregation that God fulfilled his word through the coming of Jesus.

Know the literary context. While both historical and textual contexts may go well beyond the immediate passage in view, the literary context is the most immediate context that the preacher must examine. Even apart from the Bible, we read different kinds of literature with different presuppositions about its meaning and the nature of what it says. A scientific report on the nature of fog, for instance, creates in us a very different expectation than the opening line of Carl Sandburg's poem, "The fog comes in on little cat feet." Reading a meteorological report makes us look for fact and information, while the poem clues us to expect emotion and evocative imagery. If a meteorological report says that fog forms at 100 percent humidity when the air cools to the dewpoint, we would take that at face value as *fact*. Reading Sandburg's poem, however, no one of average intelligence would think for a moment that the fog has literal feet, much less those of a cat. We intuitively know that the author is using the language of *imagery* to suggest an image and a feeling that is evocative of fog.

To move to biblical interpretation, we can see how this principle works when we contrast the reading of a narrative passage and a poetic text. John 21 records the story of Jesus' encounter with Peter, relating the details of Jesus' appearance to him and the other disciples in Galilee. Jesus appeared to the hapless fisherman and suggested they cast their empty nets on the other side of the boat. Following his suggestion, verse 11 records that they caught 153 large fish. Now here is the question: *how many large fish did they really catch?*

Bible-believing preachers will resolutely answer that they caught *exactly* 153 large fish. While they may or may not have caught others that they did not number, the count of *large* fish is precise: 153. The number is not a round number, but a distinctly peculiar number. It has the unmistakable ring of truth, suggesting that someone counted and noted the specific number of "keepers" they caught (as any good fisherman would!). Furthermore, the number occurs in a *story*—a narrative text that nowhere indicates it should be taken figuratively, allegorically, or as myth. A narrative text presented as actual events should be taken in precisely that way. We accept, then, that their nets were filled with 153 large fish, not 152 or 154. The text is clear.

But what about poetry? Would we apply the same standards of interpretation to a poetic statement like Psalm 50:9–10 in which God speaks and says, "I have no need of a bull from your stall or of goats from your pens, for every animal of the forest is mine, and *the cattle on a thousand hills*" (emphasis added)? When the psalmist writes these words as though spoken by the Lord, are we to conclude that God owns the cattle on *exactly*

1,000 hills—not 999 or 1,001? Of course not. We understand both intuitively and from the text itself that the real meaning of the verse is that God owns *everything*.

Our point, then, is that the *form of writing* affects our understanding of its meaning. Apocalyptic literature is filled with symbolism that must be properly interpreted. Prophecies, too, often use figurative language. Forms of writing include discourse, narrative, poetry, hymns, songs, parable, and other literary conventions that authors used to convey meaning.

One special note is in order regarding the form of biblical proverbs. Although one book of the Bible bears that name, we are speaking specifically of the form itself. A proverb is a generally observed truth—but not a *universal* truth. The Book of Proverbs is *not* the book of *promises,* as though they provide a divinely guaranteed and foolproof way of avoiding poverty, calamity, and disappointment. Proverbs are generally observable truths that serve as guidelines for wise behavior and success in various areas of life, but they are not *universal* truths. Much of Proverbs, for instance, is about being industrious and obtaining wealth, but not every industrious Christian in the world has the opportunity to gain wealth. Some may do everything right and according to wisdom of Proverbs, and then lose everything in an economic collapse or tragedy that is beyond their control.

Proverbs 26:4 states: "Do not answer a fool according to his folly, or you will be like him yourself." The very next verse reads: "Answer a fool according to his folly, or he will be wise in his own eyes" (Prov. 26:5). If these verses were universal truths, they would be contradictory, but since they are general truths, their meaning changes. Taken together, the writer is saying that we must apply discernment and wisdom in choosing which way to deal with foolish people.

To further illustrate, verse 27 of the same chapter reads: "If a man digs a pit, he will fall into it; if a man rolls a stone, it will roll back on him." No thinking person could possibly take that verse to mean that *every* time anyone on the planet earth digs a pit he will invariably fall into it. Instead, that is the author's creative way of telling us that we are often ensnared in the very schemes we devise to trap or harm others. Our treachery often turns on us.

Yet Proverbs 22:6 is often preached as though it were a divine guarantee of godly children given to those parents who rear their children just right: "Train a child in the way he should go, and when he is old he will not turn from it." Although the author suggests that good parenting *generally* produces children who follow the Lord, he does not *promise* that there is a foolproof recipe for rearing children. If that were true, parents would be to blame for every sin of their adult children. But such is not the case. After all, God is the best parent of all, and just look what his children do!

Just as the form of writing within a given book is crucial for discerning the meaning, the *genre of the book* is likewise crucial. Form describes distinct types of writing within any one book, while genre is the term applied to the category of literature to which the book itself belongs. While Bible scholars may debate terminology and the precise categories of genre, the basic genre of the Bible are *history, epistle, gospel, apocalyptic,* and *wisdom.* These different kinds of literature determine the way we read them. For instance, we do not read about the woman running into the desert in Revelation 12:6 with the same expectation of meaning as when we read about the woman at the well in John 4. The one, we suspect, is a symbol; the other we know to be a literal woman. Similarly, we do not read a gospel the same way we read an epistle. One is descriptive, the other generally exhortative.

Bear in mind that a particular book, such as a gospel, may have several different forms within it. Matthew's Gospel, for instance, obviously belongs to the genre of gospel, but within it we can find narrative, discourse, and apocalyptic discourse. Acts is a history, yet we find discourses, narrative, prophecies, and poetry within it. Ezekiel contains apocalyptic, prophecy, narrative, and discourse. Paul incorporates hymns, poetry, narrative, discourse, exhortation, and didactic forms in his epistles. Our understanding of meaning changes with the forms and with the genre. The preacher, therefore, must have a thorough appreciation of each author's choice of form and genre in order to fully understand his meaning.[7]

Determine the Content

Once we understand the various contexts that inform the meaning of the text, we can begin to move toward understanding of the content that the passage carries. That content is not recognized by simply looking up the words in a dictionary or concordance, however. In fact, we need to analyze the text in at least three ways that help us distill all of its substance.[8]

Structural analysis. With the possible exception of the collection of wisdom in the Book of Proverbs, no biblical author wrote in a stream of consciousness style with disjointed, haphazard thoughts. Even in Proverbs, however, one may often discover a thematic arrangement and development of thought, especially in certain parts of the book. In general, the books of the Bible are written in a logical order that develops a particular argument, narrative, theme, instruction, or any combination of these categories. Tracing that development is crucial to understanding both the individual passage as well as the entire book. The structure of the passage and of the book reveals the author's thought as much as the words themselves. That structure can be identified by carefully noticing the *microstructure* and the *macrostructure* of the text. This is the end product of diagramming the passage as we discussed earlier in the chapter.

By forcing ourselves to see the development and hierarchical structure of an author's thought, we begin to understand what in the passage is truly the main thought and how that thought leads to other conclusions, qualities, or ramifications.

The microstructure is the most immediate level of structure and is revealed by the grammar and syntax of individual sentences. Taking note of an author's choice of a main (finite) verb as opposed to the participles or infinitives he hangs on it may reveal layers of meaning.

We can illustrate this level of meaning by using simple English sentences as illustrations. Consider the sentence, "Going to the store, I cried

when I saw a big, black dog bite an old man who was walking on the side-
walk." This sentence has several verbal forms, but it has only one main subject and verb. The subject is "I," and the main verb is "cried." Everything
else in this sentence hangs on one of them in some way. We might diagram
the sentence, then, like this:

```
I                         cried
    going to the store       when I saw
 L                        L
                                 a dog bite a man
                              L     big        old
                                 L black    L who
                                 L             L was walking
                                            L       on a sidewalk.
                                                 L
```

Admittedly, we don't diagram passages for the sheer joy of diagramming, but in order to see the author's development of thought. What is his
real point? Nothing reveals it like a diagram. On the level of microstructure,
it visually demonstrates what is the real action or thought of the sentence.
Diagramming imposes a discipline that forces us beyond our initial
response to what we read. In the example above, for instance, the image of
a big, black dog biting an old man might be so vivid in our minds that we
mistakenly see that as the main action of the sentence. But a closer look in
the diagram forces us to see that the subject and verb "I cried" serve as the
real core of the sentence, the real point that is being made. The speaker's
emphasis is on his tears, not the old man's plight.

To see how this works in a biblical passage, the Great Commission of
Jesus serves as an excellent example. Literally the verse reads in Greek, "So
having journeyed, disciple all the nations, baptizing them in the name of the
Father, and of the Son, and of the Holy Spirit, teaching them to keep all
things which I have commanded you." A diagram of the sentence would
look like this:

```
      ┌ having journeyed
(you) disciple all the nations
      └ baptizing them
          └ in the name of the Father
                  and of the Son
                  and of the Holy Spirit
       └ teaching them
              └ to keep all things
                      └ which I have commanded you
```

The main verb of the sentence on which everything else hangs is "disciple." Everything else is a participle that is grammatically subservient to the action of the main verb. Several shades of meaning emerge from this syntactical structure. First, their journeying is assumed, and *as they go,* they are to make disciples. The discipleship they administer is defined by two basic actions: baptizing them and teaching them. Based on the verbs, therefore, one can see a hierarchical structure in the sentence. Jesus' basic command is clear and simple: *make disciples.* Everything else in the sentence qualifies that basic command.

Notice that when we tie a word, phrase, or clause to something else, we are saying that this line answers a question or provides information about what it modifies. *When do they make disciples?* As they are going. *How do they make disciples?* By (1) baptizing them and (2) teaching them. *How are they to baptize them?* In the name of the Father, and of the Son, and of the Holy Spirit. *What are they to teach them?* To keep all things. *What things are they to keep?* Whatever Jesus has commanded the disciples.

The diagram, therefore, reveals that the Great Commission is not four separate commands—go, disciple, baptize, and teach—but one command that is qualified in three ways. (1) We are to make disciples *as we* go. (2) We are to make disciples *by baptizing* them. (3) We are to make disciples *by teaching* them to observe all of Jesus' commands.

Understanding the grammar and syntax is very important to understanding the Bible. If the author chose to say it a certain way, he did so for a reason, and that reason is normally revealed through the structure and syntax he used. Although we can still discover the general meaning without diagramming, we might easily fail to see the relationships and development of the author's thought.

We understand that not every preacher will take the time to diagram every passage that he preaches, so we offer a few words of advice on the subject. First, while we are convinced of the value of diagramming a text, we do believe that the basic meaning of the Scriptures are clear and comprehensible, even without diagramming. Physically laying out the passage on a desk pad helps understand the author's style, purpose, and meaning in a tremendous way, but we are definitely not saying that you cannot truly understand the Scriptures without it. Millions have done quite well without ever seeing a diagram, thank you.

What we are saying is that the discipline of writing it out burns the meaning and development of the text into your heart and mind like few other things you can do. Standing in the pulpit after you have worked through the text so thoroughly generates a passion and a confidence that are unmistakable and would alone be worth the effort. You *know* this text. You have worked through it and become intimate with it. You *can't wait* to share with your people the things God has shown you through such passionate attention to the author's intent.

Second, while those who have learned the Greek and Hebrew languages should do the diagram in the original language—that is, after all, why you spent so much time learning it—we also do not believe that a person cannot understand the Bible if he can only read it in English or in translation. We rejoice that the Word is so powerful and so plain that it can be understood in almost any translation, even in bad ones! The Word of God is so potent and the Holy Spirit so involved with the Word that some people have been born again even while using horrible translations. Many times Christians have witnessed to Jehovah's Witnesses, for example, from their very own Watchtower "translation" and, on occasion, some have been saved. How much more can one understand the Scriptures from legitimate translations? The point we are making is that we can understand the Word of God *more* clearly and *more* intimately when we take the time and discipline to diagram it, studying the structure as well as the words.

Third, while it is possible to diagram the text in an English translation, not every English translation can accurately reveal the structure of the text. Modern English simply does not have the same patterns of syntax and structure that _koine_ Greek used. Ephesians 1:3–14, for instance, is a single sentence in the Greek language.[9] The Revised Standard Version has six sentences instead of one, as does the New American Standard. In the New International Version, the translators divide it into eight sentences. The New Living Translation actually chops it up into fifteen sentences. These translators know that modern English speakers don't speak in long sentences and often have short attention spans. While their decisions to break it down for the receptor language may be legitimate translation choices, they simply don't lend themselves to accurate diagrams that reveal the hierarchy of thought and development of an argument.

For this reason we recommend the King James Version as the translation of choice for diagramming. While it may not be the best choice for preaching in a given context, its weakness for modern readers is its strength for preachers who diagram in English. The translators of the King James Version retained the Greek structure and syntax as much as possible. In Ephesians 1:3–14, for example, the KJV follows the same syntax as the Greek text.[10] One can diagram the passage in English with almost the same results as in Greek.

Finally, while not all biblical passages need to be diagrammed, all syntax needs to be understood. Certain narrative texts, for instance, are cut and dried. Mark's Gospel is often just a catalog of things that Jesus did, one right after another. The Book of Proverbs is normally just a collection of sayings, some in couplets, but rarely complex enough that they bear diagramming. Even so, we can _never_ afford to ignore the syntax. At the very least we locate subject, verb, and object or complement. We almost always diagram anything from the epistles, prophets, discourses, and more complex narratives. Understanding the sentence is basic and essential to understanding anything beyond that level.

Macrostructure is, as you might guess, the level of structure that occurs as we put sentences, paragraphs, and divisions together. Remember that the basic unit of thought is not the word or the sentence, but the paragraph. We need to discover not only the relationships between words within a sentence, but also the relationships between sentences within a paragraph, and the way paragraphs combine to form the divisions which compose the book.

While sentences are not grammatically related to each other in a paragraph, they are associated nonetheless through topic, thought, and logic. Following Walt Kaiser's methodology, we show that relationship in a diagram through indenting. A sentence that begins a section and serves as its heading would go all the way over to the left margin. Subsequent sentences that are still part of the same topic but are used epexegetically of that first sentence, we would indent to show that it is subservient to the prior sentence.

As we stated earlier, we want to observe and respect the natural divisions in the text. We can discover these inherent partitions and boundaries in several ways. The easiest (though sometimes misleading) way to notice the divisions is to notice them in the Bible translation we use or the paragraph divisions editors have given to the Greek or Hebrew text. One of the great benefits of modern translations is that they are often printed in a paragraph format rather than merely by chapter and verse divisions. The editors of Greek and Hebrew texts, like the translators of modern versions, usually get it right. One can normally see the reason for their divisions. Just bear in mind that the paragraph divisions, like chapter and verse divisions, are not original and can be wrong. Astute Bible students will always consider whether or not a division actually begins where a translator or text editor may place it.

The original texts of the New Testament were written in all capital letters with no punctuation (like commas, semicolons, or periods), no spaces between words or sentences, and certainly no numbered verses or chapters. Imagine reading a newspaper that looked like this:

INRELATEDDEVELOPMENTSTODAYTHEWHITE
HOUSEDENIEDREPORTSTHATTHEADMINISTRATIONHAS
INFORMATIONREGARDINGTHEARRESTOFCLANDESTI
NEENEMIESOFTHEGOVERNMENTONFOREIGNSOILTHE
FRENCHGOVERNMENTHOWEVERCLAIMSTHATITMADET
HEARRESTSATTHEBEHESTOFTHEIRAMERICANCOUNTER
PARTSANDREFUSESTOSHOULDERTHERESPONSBIL
ITYALONETURNINGNOWTOSPORTSTHEUNIVERSITY
OFKENTUCKYONCEAGAINWONTHENCAANATION
ALCHAMPIONSHIPINMENSBASKETBALL.

In the Old Testament, the Hebrew language originally had no vowels, either, so it might look something like this:

NRLTDDVLPMNTSTDYTHWHTHSDNDRPRTSTHT-
THDMNSTRTNHSNFRMTNRGRDNGTHRRSTFCLNDSTNN-
MSFTHGVRNMNTNFRGNSLTHFRNCHGVRNMNTHWVR-
CLMSTHTTMDTHRRSTSTTHBHSTFTHRMRCNCNTRPRTSN
DRFSSTSHLDRTHRSPNSBLTYLNTRNNGNWTSPRTSTHN-
VRSTFKNTCKNCGNWNTHNCNTNLCHMPNSHPNMNSBSKT-
BLL.

Textual editors and scholars, therefore, have to carefully read the texts, deciding where they think a sentence ends and another begins. Sometimes good scholars disagree. In Ephesians 1:4 and 5 we have a great example of an editing decision on which good scholars disagree. The question is whether the phrase "in love" should go with verse 4, thus reading, "According as he hath chosen us in him before the foundation of the world, that we should be holy and without blame before him in love" (KJV); or should it read "For he chose us in him before the creation of the world to be holy and blameless in his sight. In love he predestined us to be adopted as his sons through Jesus Christ" (NIV and most modern translations). Since there are no punctuation marks in the Greek text, scholars have to use their best judgment based on the author's typical way of writing, similar phrases found elsewhere in a corpus, or syntactical clues that emerge.

So while most divisions of sentence or paragraph or division are obvious and have virtually unanimous agreement, some passages present more of a challenge. Use all clues available to you to help you determine where a passage begins and ends. You will notice a clear overlap between structural analysis and thematic analysis (which we are soon to discuss), but together they help you determine the boundaries of an author's discussion of a given topic. You will often discover independent ideas that mark the logical units of a division or paragraph.

As you go through this stage carefully, do not be surprised to find that you have to go back and revise your planned preaching schedule. When you initially divided the book into preaching units, you relied on repeated reading of the text to give you a sense of the divisions. As you delve deeper into the structure as revealed through the diagrams, you may realize that you need more or less time for a passage or that you simply got the division wrong. Don't let that throw you. Just revise your preaching schedule by adding or subtracting the necessary folders in your files for the book and adjust the dates accordingly. Remember that the plan is your slave and not your master. Don't fear changing it or making it fit into the life of your church as necessary. You will find it far more desirable to change your schedule than to know you did not deal with the text in a worthy manner.

Thematic analysis. By adding this as a separate category we do not mean to suggest that you can actually separate structural and thematic views of the text. Naturally they go hand in hand. Just as we might write a letter to a friend in which we discuss three things and write it in three main parts, so the biblical authors usually intertwined form and function. The letters of the apostle John are thought by some to be a notable exception, but most biblical authors take up one theme or topic at a time and clue us in to these shifts in topics by structural conventions.

First, we look for *conventions of composition*. These are words or phrases that we use to signal a change in topic or a progression from a prior thought to one that results from it. If a man is talking to his wife and he wants to bring up something from the day before, he might say something like, "Now about that vacation you were asking me about . . ." and then proceed to take that up as his topic. Similarly, we spin off discussions by saying things like, "Speaking of bad music, have you ever listened to rap?" Biblical authors use compositional conventions and discourse markers all the time. Words and phrases like, "Now," "Therefore," "Wherefore," "I exhort you therefore," "The word of the Lord came to me saying," "Thus says the Lord," and many others serve in this way. They mark off a particular discussion, bracketing what follows as a distinct unit.

The Book of Hebrews serves as an excellent example. Chapter 1 functions as one distinct unit because its clear theme is all about the superiority of the Son. He is a better revelation of God and better than the angels. Chapter 2 begins with the statement, "We must pay more careful attention, *therefore*, to what we have heard, so that we do not drift away."

Do you see the change in tone and the discourse marker that accompanied it? First, the author changes from a discussion in verse 1 that is in the third person—all about Jesus being better. Suddenly he changes to an exhortation, the hortatory subjunctive, "Let us . . ." (chapter 4). He will repeat this device many times in the Book of Hebrews so that it becomes a primary way that he marks off the response of duty to the teaching of doctrine. To show this connection but also this progression, he uses the word *therefore*. He proceeds on through the argument of chapter 2, concluding that Jesus is a better High Priest because he was tempted so he can better help his people in their temptation. Then, to begin the new section in chapter 3, the author places another hinge between what has just been stated and where he now wants to go. "*Therefore*, holy brothers, who share in the heavenly calling, fix your thoughts on Jesus, the apostle and high priest whom we confess."

In other words, because Jesus is the faithful High Priest who can help us in our temptation and suffering, we must respond by focusing on him in that role. Then the author proceeds through the discussion of how Jesus is superior to Moses, too. When he moves to another part of the discussion in chapter 4, he uses the same device, writing "*Therefore,* since the promise of entering his rest still stands, let us be careful that none of you be found to have fallen short of it." For the writer of the Epistle to the Hebrews, using "therefore" in proximity with a hortatory subjunctive is clearly a compositional convention that serves as a discourse marker.

Another compositional convention that leads us to understand the theme of the text is repetition and variation. Whenever an author repeats a theme or a statement, he is obviously drawing the readers' attention to that topic or subject. Even more pronounced, however, is when the biblical author repeats himself several times and then varies the theme in some way. That is what some scholars have called a "zone of turbulence." By this they mean that the flow of the passage is interrupted in such a way that our attention is drawn to the cause.

Luke chapter 15 is one great example of repetition and variation. In response to the Pharisees' accusations and recriminations that he hangs out with and eats with sinners, Jesus told three parables. The first is the story of the lost sheep, the second is the story of the lost coin, and the third is commonly called the parable of the prodigal son. The first two parables are nearly identical in structure and theme; the only significant difference is the item that was lost. In the first example Jesus told of something that was lost, then it was found, and then they had a party. Likewise when the coin was lost, then it was found, and then they had a party.

But the third parable in the trilogy is different in several ways. First it is longer and far more emotional. This time the thing that was lost is neither an animal nor a piece of money, but a *son*. Still, at the core of the story Jesus repeated the three basic elements: something—in this case, some*one*—was lost, then it was found, and then they had a party. But now Jesus added a fourth element: someone got mad. By varying the pattern, the Master Teacher forces our attention on the very thing that was his object all along.

As beautiful as the heart of the father is, as tender as the repentant heart of the prodigal may strike us, Jesus' real objective was a rebuke to the Pharisees that they could not rejoice that sinners were coming to him.

Though heaven rejoiced, they sulked and whispered like pouting children. Luke's pattern of "same, same, same, *different*" is the device that drives us to the force of Jesus' words. One wonders how many sermons on the prodigal son have missed the point that Jesus was making! We cannot afford to miss the compositional conventions that an author exploits and think we will find his true intent.

Similarly, an author uses *literary conventions,* our second category of thematic clues that help in our pursuit of analyzing themes. Literary conventions are closely related to those of composition, but they typically involve more stylistic patterns. We find one obvious example in Hebrews chapter 11. There the author repeats the phrase "by faith" over and over. It would be hard for us to ignore it or fail to comprehend its prominence. The repeated use of "by faith" marks the parameters of the pericope as well as the subdivisions within it. When the author first uses it he announces his subject, and drives it deeper into our consciousness with each repetition.

Ancient writers had many such rhetorical devices and conventions available to them. While these devices may seem overwhelming to a modern Bible student, we must remind ourselves that this was simply the way the ancients communicated in written documents and even in oral speeches and presentations, especially in the Greco-Roman world. Aristotle's work on rhetoric, like that of Isocrates, had been around for centuries by the time the New Testament was written. Even during the time the New Testament was being written, rhetoricians like Quintilian were teaching the art of presenting an argument by following certain conventions. The culture had adopted these devices as easily as we have adopted starting a letter with "Dear." Even though it may seem complicated to us, expressing oneself in these ways simply became the norm. Complex as it seems to modern readers, such literary conventions make finding both the structure and the meaning of the text far easier than it would be in their absence.

But Old Testament writers, too, had their literary conventions that revealed their thoughts and hearts. The Book of Lamentations, written during the siege and overthrow of Jerusalem, is a protracted acrostic poem. Chapters 1, 2, 4, and 5 each have 22 verses, and each verse of each chapter begins with a consecutive letter of the Hebrew alphabet. Chapter 3, the center and focus of the book, contains 66 verses with every 3 verses beginning with a consecutive letter of the Hebrew alphabet.

Ancient writers were fond of a rhetorical device called *inclusio,* found often in the Bible, which was a technique of "bracketing" a subject by repeating at the end of a section a word or phrase that was used at the beginning. An inclusio, therefore, indicates the limits of a section and serves to emphasize the theme.

A good example of an *inclusio* is found in Hebrews 1:5: "For to which of the angels did God ever say, 'You are *my Son;* today I have become your Father'? Or again, 'I will be his Father, and he will be *my Son'*?" Notice how the word order deliberately places "son" at the beginning of the quote and then again at the end.[11] This word order is hardly accidental since the writer places the next six quotations from the Old Testament together as three pairs, each of which emphasizes a title for Jesus. The author is clearly emphasizing the sonship of Jesus in order to highlight the superiority of Jesus to the angels.

Related to inclusio, but usually more complicated in its structure is a *chiasm.*[12] The structure of a chiasm usually has at least four components, two pairs that relate to each other inversely, though often the structures are more sophisticated. Mark 2:27, for instance, is a simple chiasm: (A) The *Sabbath* was made (B) for *man,* (B) not *man* (A) for the *Sabbath.* This convention gets its name from the Greek letter *chi,* which looks like our X, because the structure can be portrayed like this:

Chiasms may be more complex, however. Sometimes authors will add other pairs of terms and will even put a central element at the core of the structure. First Thessalonians chapter 1, for example, is an extended chiasm. There Paul's structure follows a chiastic pattern with a central teaching.

A: (v. 3) Remembering your   (A1) work of faith

                                                (A2) labor of love

                                                (A3) patience of hope

  B: (v. 5) our gospel came to you

    C: (v. 6) you became followers of us

      D: (v. 6b) having received the Word

    C: (v. 7) so that you were examples

  B: (v. 8) from you sounded out the word

A: (vv. 9–10) how you   (A1) turned to God from idols

                                                (A2) to serve the living and true God

                                                (A3) to wait for his Son from heaven

The first part of the chiasm focuses on a motion *toward* the Thessalonians, and the second half emphasizes the movement of the gospel *out from* them. The triplet in verses 9 and 10 relate to and further explains the triplet of verse 3. Just as the gospel came to them (v. 5), so the Word sounded out from them (v. 8). The followers of verse 6 have become the examples of verse 7. And all of this revolves around the central truth and ground of all this activity: they received the Word.

This book on preaching is not intended as a technical explanation of ancient rhetorical devices, but we must make the point that the literary conventions an author used are important to discerning the boundaries of a unit and even of the meaning itself. To treat the author's theme adequately, we must find at least the smallest unit that completes the theme. Discovering the rhetorical devices and conventions that the author used insures that we do not miss the context or the full treatment of his theme.

In addition to compositional and literary conventions, the third type of thematic analysis at our disposal is to look for any *theological conventions*. Every passage of the Bible has something to say about God, his attributes, his character, his will, or his acts in history. To find the theological pattern we simply ask the question: what does this passage say about God?

Sometimes the theological pattern will not be what we notice first in a given passage, even though it may truly be the author's main point. The Book of Jonah, for instance, is often interpreted simply as the story of a reluctant prophet. After all, it would be hard to escape the attraction of a story about a rebellious preacher and a big fish. But on closer inspection, we come to see that the story is more about the heart of God than the action of a man—or even a fish. When we ask what the text says about God, certain theological patterns and truths emerge. God cared about the Ninevites, even though they were the enemies of his own people. He would not be disobeyed by Jonah, but orchestrated the circumstances of the prophet's life to make him willing to obey. God was forgiving of them, even though he sent his prophet to tell them of their impending destruction. In the end of the book, God revealed his heart to Jonah in an incredible lesson about his love for people. The passages of the book, therefore, are defined by the different truths about God that are presented: his anger at sin, his judgment, his demand for obedience, his control of his creation, his forgiveness, and finally his heart for the lost.

Sometimes the theological truths are overt, sometimes they are more subtle. The Book of Romans, for example, is clearly theological in most of its content. The Book of Esther, on the other hand, does not even mention the name of God, yet it reveals God's hand even when his face is hidden. In either case, we must go to the text looking for the theological patterns and themes in order to understand the author's meaning. By scouring the text for compositional, literary, and thematic conventions and patters, we hone in on the content which is not only revealed in the text, but which also guides the sermon we preach.

Lexical analysis. While not all passages under our study will contain formal flourishes of rhetoric and style such as those we have just mentioned, they all contain words. Understanding the meaning of those words is essential to understanding both context and content. Lexical analysis—knowing what the words mean—is the most basic and usual form of analysis in which we engage to find an author's intent.

For a preacher working in English translation, many helps are available. A good concordance such as Strong's or Young's is invaluable, as are many other more recent works that make an English reader aware of word meanings, synonyms, and word usage.

The preacher who has enough knowledge of Greek to use Greek reference works, however, will find many good books—even in electronic format for instantaneous use on computers—that make lexical analysis much easier. *A Greek-English Lexicon of the New Testament and Other Early Christian Literature (Third Edition)* by William Arndt, Walter Bauer, and Frederick W. Danker is the standard lexicon of the New Testament. Its advantage is its encyclopedic treatment of virtually every occurrence of every word in the New Testament. The *Greek-English Lexicon of the New Testament: Based on Semantic Domains* by Johannes P. Louw and Eugene Albert Nida is especially helpful because it takes context into account. The editors define words specifically with regard to the range of words with which they are used, also known as "semantic domain."

In addition to traditional books, computer programs are now readily available that include these and many other reference works that can pop up instantly at the click of a mouse. Cleon L. Rogers, Jr., and Cleon L. Rogers III have written *The New Linguistic and Exegetical Key to the Greek New Testament,* a helpful companion to the Greek text that not only provides definitions and morphological help, but also refers the reader to articles and other publications about the specific passage.

In the Old Testament, *The Brown-Driver-Briggs Hebrew and English Lexicon* (Peabody, Mass.: Hendrickson Publishers, 1996) is the most widely used lexicon. *The Englishman's Hebrew Concordance of the Old Testament* by George V. Wigram (Peabody, Mass.: Hendrickson Publishers, 1996) is a helpful reference for those who are not educated in Hebrew but want to do serious lexical study. *The Theological Wordbook of the Old Testament* by R. L. Harris, Gleason Archer, and Bruce Waltke (Chicago: Moody Press, 1980) is also a great resource that examines the theological content of most words in the Old Testament.

Though knowing the meaning of the words is essential, we caution against the so-called "word studies" that find meaning in the word that the author never intended. D. A. Carson's excellent *Exegetical Fallacies* has instructed us in the many ways that preachers have traditionally read meaning into the text that the author did not place there. We encourage every preacher to read Carson's book and disavow any practice that falls into that category.

By analyzing the text structurally, thematically, and lexically, we can be *confident* that we understand the author's meaning. The Bible was intended to be understood, and these procedures insure that we take all of the author's cues into consideration. The normal sense of the words, the strength of context, the logical development of a thought, and the Holy Spirit combine to reveal the content.

Nothing is more important for preaching than properly discerning the meaning of the text. Everything else in preaching hinges on this. No matter how great a communicator one may be, if the content of the sermon is not congruent with the Word of God, it cannot and will not achieve anything of eternal value. God blesses his Word—which is what makes all this careful effort worthwhile.

Discern the Concern

When we speak of the "concern" of the passage, we mean to determine how the passage applies. Nothing in the Bible is purely academic—knowledge for the sake of knowledge with no practical value. *Everything* in the Bible has a practical value that we must discern and apply to our lives. Our sermons, therefore, need to be saturated not only with the content of the text, but also with a practical application for our hearers.

Though later chapters will discuss in great detail how to build the sermon, two points need to be made right now. First, just as the *author's intent* guides our exegesis of the text, so the author's intent should guide our application. When the author wrote, he included stories, details, arguments, or whatever content he chose to address a specific situation. Perhaps an Old Testament author wrote to remind Israel of God's faithfulness and their own need to stay close to him. He may have written to call them to repentance. Paul often addressed his epistles to doctrinal problems or situations that required correction. As much as possible, we need to address our sermons to the same kind of situation addressed in the text. Sometimes the cultural difference will warrant an abstraction from the principles rather than from the specific situation of the text, but we want to stay as close as possible to the author's application.

Picture the authorial intent of the passage like a flowing river. It proceeds from the source, the author, and flows to his ultimate goal—the behavior and belief of his readers. When we preach the text and address our sermon to the *same kind of problem* that the author intended, we find ourselves in the main channel of the river, carried along by the strongest flow possible. We experience the maximum force of the passage and feel the blessing of the Holy Spirit as his Word is used as he intended. When we preach the text with an intent foreign to the original author, we fail to enjoy the maximum flow, even though everything we say may indeed be true. We may preach with a solid theological background and conviction that keeps us from saying things that are overtly false, but we stop short of reaching the torrential force that the passage offers. We might be standing in the edge of the river, our feet thoroughly wet, but we should not content ourselves with this. We want to be caught up in the power of the flow.

Understanding this makes us ask some important questions of the text. What situation was the author addressing? Why did he want them to know this? What encouragement was he offering? What correction was he administering? What sin was he confronting? If his listeners really believed what he wrote, what changes would they be compelled to make? What impact would this have on their lives?

Once we have a firm understanding of the author's intended application, we then proceed to the second area of concern: *contemporary meaning.* We move from the author's own application to one that fits our audience. Usually they are the same, but sometimes we have to build a bridge between cultures.

In the first century and in the ancient Near Eastern world, Paul wrote to the Thessalonians, "Avoid sexual immorality" (1 Thess. 4:3). He could write the same thing to the members of any church in any part of the twenty-first-century world. Regardless of culture or region, we face the same temptation and struggle today that Paul's audience did. So if we are to preach this passage, we must make direct application just as Paul did.

On the other hand, Paul wrote extensively to the Romans about whether they could eat meat sacrificed to idols (Rom. 14:1–23). While Christians in some parts of the world today may still face that same issue, hardly anyone in the Western world struggles with this particular custom. This does not mean, however, that Romans 14 has nothing to say to us today. To the contrary, the principles that Paul established there remain relevant and reliable guides for Christian conscience and behavior. But we must lead our listeners to identify with them and apply them to the same kind of issues that we face today.

Haddon Robinson has suggested a helpful mechanism that he calls "the ladder of abstraction" that serves as a guide to finding the proper application for contemporary listeners when the author's application is culturally distant.[13]

> I picture a "ladder of abstraction" that comes up from the biblical world and crosses over and down to the modern setting. I have to be conscious how I cross this "abstraction ladder." I want to make sure the biblical situation and the current situation are analogous at the points I am making them connect. I must be sure the center of the analogy connects, not the extremes.
>
> Sometimes, as I work with a text, I have to climb the abstraction ladder until I reach the text's intent.
>
> Leviticus says, "Don't boil a kid in its mother's milk." First, you have to ask, "What is this all about?" At face value, you might say, "If I have a young goat, and I want to cook it in its mother's milk for dinner tonight, I should think twice."

But we now know that the pagans did that when they worshipped their idolatrous gods. Therefore, what you have here is not a prohibition against boiling a kid in its mother's milk, but against being involved in the idolatry that surrounded God's people or bringing its practices into their religion.

If that's the case, it does no good for the preacher to bring this text straight over. You must climb the ladder of abstraction a couple of levels until you reach the principle: You should not associate yourself with idolatrous worship, even in ways that do not seem to have direct association with physically going to the idol.

One thing I always do with a passage [that can't come straight across] is abstract up to God. Every passage has a vision of God, such as God as Creator or Sustainer. Second I ask, "What is the depravity factor? What in humanity rebels against that vision of God?" These two questions are a helpful clue in application because God remains the same. Our depravity may look different, but it is the same pride, obstinacy, disobedience.

Take 1 Corinthians 8, in which Paul addresses the subject of eating meat offered to idols. The vision of God: He is our redeemer. Therefore, Paul argues, I will not eat meat, because if I wound my brother's weak conscience, I sin against Christ who redeemed him.[14]

Using Robinson's ladder as a means to move from culturally specific command to contemporary principles, we are able to make application that is relevant and specific.

Now with these three critical notions in place—context, content, and concern—we are ready to move ahead to building a sermon that connects these elements *and* connects with our listeners.

Abstraction Ladder

Climb by asking:
1) What does this teach about God?
2) What does this teach about human nature?

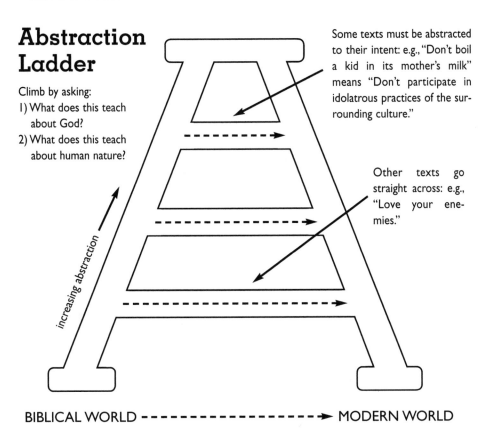

increasing abstraction

Some texts must be abstracted to their intent: e.g., "Don't boil a kid in its mother's milk" means "Don't participate in idolatrous practices of the surrounding culture."

Other texts go straight across: e.g., "Love your enemies."

BIBLICAL WORLD ➤ MODERN WORLD

CHAPTER 5
Moving Toward the Sermon

Fortunately, God does not anoint our preaching because of our education, our eloquence, our experience. While he certainly uses those things, he does not use *only* those who have the right credentials. We believe in the power of the Word of God so strongly, we affirm without apology that anyone who knows the Lord Jesus and is committed to his Word can be used by God to proclaim the gospel. That is why we determined to include instructions for those who are not trained in a Bible college or seminary and cannot study the Bible in the original languages as well as for those who can. The basic message of the Scriptures is not hidden or secret, and you don't need a Ph.D. in Greek to understand it—or even to preach it!

So if you are uncomfortable around all this talk about diagrams, thematic outlines, and homiletical outlines, you might want to move on to chapter 6. There you can learn a simpler, but very effective method, the Decker Method, of discerning the meaning and the application of a passage, as well as how to build a sermon that engages the audience. You may want to read over this chapter, too—we won't charge you extra—since much here works whether you work in the original languages or not. Just keep in mind that our purpose and mandate is always to understand the meaning and application of the passage.

Once you have discovered the meaning of a passage, especially if you have diagrammed it, you can see the author's main points and even the structure he uses to emphasize them. Now you are ready to begin the process of moving from text to sermon.

The first step is to build a *thematic outline* by reducing the text to an outline form. If the passage you are planning to preach is one that you needed to diagram, then the easiest way to do it is to write it out on the same sheet as the diagram itself. By visually connecting the diagram and the theme of the outline, you will find that you begin to think beyond merely restating the text to preaching it. If the passage does not require a diagram because it is a very simple structure, then look for the discourse markers and logical connectors within the text itself.

Keep in mind that you do not need to be creative at this stage. In fact, a thematic outline makes no pretense to creativity or application. *All* you want to do is get the meaning of the text. Making the outline artistic or applicational is a subsequent step. First, we just want to be sure of the meaning.

If you are preaching through a book of the Bible and are following the planning procedure that we suggested in chapter 4, we recommend that you diagram and write a thematic outline of the passage one to three weeks before you plan to preach it. This will allow your mind more time to ruminate on the text and to choose and edit illustrations, etc. before actually planning the sermon in detail. Put the completed diagram and thematic outline in the folder you have marked for the passage. Then on the Monday before you preach the text on the following Sunday, get out the appropriate folder. You will already have determined the structure, the theme, and the basic outline of the passage. You may also find that you put some possible illustrative material in the folder, as well. With all of that material already in place and a solid working knowledge of the text, your sermon planning will be much more effective and far less panicked.

AN EPISTOLARY PASSAGE

Let's look at 1 Corinthians chapter 5 (KJV) as an example.

1 CORINTHIANS 5:1-13

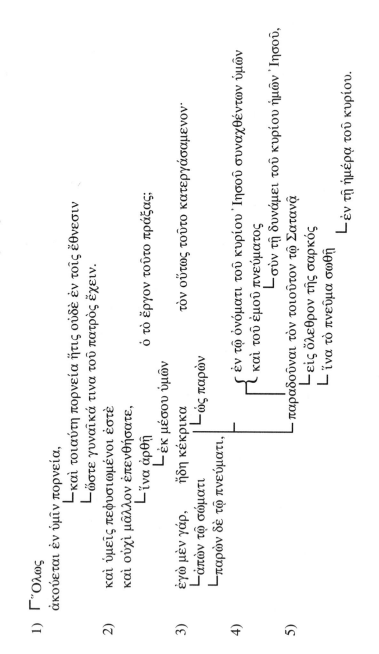

1 Corinthians 5:1-13

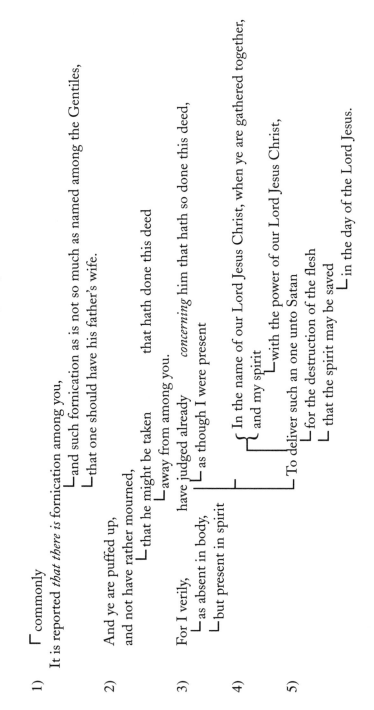

1) ┌ commonly
    It is reported *that there is* fornication among you,
          └ and such fornication as is not so much as named among the Gentiles,
          └ that one should have his father's wife.

2) And ye are puffed up,
    and not have rather mourned,
                              └ that he might be taken   that hath done this deed
                                └ away from among you.

3) For I verily,   have judged already   *concerning* him that hath so done this deed,
      └ as absent in body,   └ as though I were present
      └ but present in spirit

4)   ┌ In the name of our Lord Jesus Christ, when ye are gathered together,
       { └ and my spirit
          └ with the power of our Lord Jesus Christ,

5) └ To deliver such an one unto Satan
            └ for the destruction of the flesh
            └ that the spirit may be saved
                              └ in the day of the Lord Jesus.

6) Οὐ καλὸν τὸ καύχημα ὑμῶν.
   └ οὐκ οἴδατε ὅτι μικρὰ ζύμη ὅλον τὸ φύραμα ζυμοῖ;
7) └ ἐκκαθάρατε τὴν παλαιὰν ζύμην,
    └ ἵνα ἦτε νέον φύραμα,
      └ καθώς ἐστε ἄζυμοι·
    └ καὶ γὰρ τὸ πάσχα ἡμῶν ἐτύθη Χριστός.
8)   └ ὥστε ἑορτάζωμεν
      └ μὴ ἐν ζύμῃ παλαιᾷ
      └ μηδὲ ἐν ζύμῃ κακίας καὶ πονηρίας
      └ ἀλλ᾽ ἐν ἀζύμοις
        └ εἰλικρινείας
          καὶ
        └ ἀληθείας.

9) Ἔγραψα ὑμῖν ἐν τῇ ἐπιστολῇ μὴ συναναμίγνυσθαι πόρνοις,
10) └ οὐ πάντως τοῖς πόρνοις τοῦ κόσμου τούτου
     └ ἢ τοῖς πλεονέκταις
     └ καὶ ἅρπαξιν
     └ ἢ εἰδωλολάτραις,
     └ ἐπεὶ ὠφείλετε ἄρα ἐκ τοῦ κόσμου ἐξελθεῖν.

6) Your glorying is not good.
   └ Know ye not that a little leaven leaveneth the whole lump?

7) └ Purge out therefore the old leaven,
      └ that ye may be a new lump,
         └ as ye are unleavened.

8) └ For even Christ our passover is sacrificed for us:
      └ Therefore, let us keep the feast,
         └ not with old leaven,
         └ neither with the leaven of malice and wickedness;
         └ but with the unleavend *bread*
            └ of sincerity
               and
            └ truth.

9) I wrote unto you in an epistle not to company with fornicators:

10) └ Yet not altogether with the fornicators of this world,
       └ or with the covetous,
       └ or extortioners,
       └ or with idolaters;
       └ for then must ye needs go out of the world.

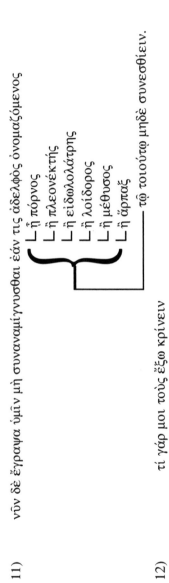

11) νῦν δὲ ἔγραψα ὑμῖν μὴ συναναμίγνυσθαι ἐάν τις ἀδελφὸς ὀνομαζόμενος

ἢ πόρνος
ἢ πλεονέκτης
ἢ εἰδωλολάτρης
ἢ λοίδορος
ἢ μέθυσος
ἢ ἅρπαξ

τῷ τοιούτῳ μηδὲ συνεσθίειν.

12) τί γάρ μοι τοὺς ἔξω κρίνειν
οὐχὶ τοὺς ἔσω ὑμεῖς κρίνετε

13) τοὺς δὲ ἔξω ὁ θεὸς κρινεῖ.
ἐξάρατε τὸν πονηρὸν ἐξ ὑμῶν αὐτῶν.

11) But now I have written unto you not to keep company, if any man that is called a brother be
    a fornicator
    or covetous,
    or an idolater,
    or a railer,
    or a drunkard,
    or an extortioner;
    with such an one no not to eat.

12) For what have I to do to judge them also that are without?
    do not ye judge them that are within?

13) But them that are without God judgeth.
    Therefore put away from among yourselves that wicked person.

Clearly, the passage breaks into three sections. In verses 1–5 Paul states the primary problem: there is sexual sin in the church, and not just your run-of-the-mill fornication, but sin so serious that even the pagans don't do it. He concludes the passage with a command to hand the offending member over to Satan for the destruction of his flesh that his spirit might be saved.

The second section begins in verse 6 and continues through verse 8. In these verses Paul points out the secondary problem that he alluded to in the first section. The church's response—or more accurately, their lack of a response—reveals a basic misunderstanding about the pervasive nature of sin. By using the Old Testament Passover feast as his model, Paul explains that those for whom Christ, the Passover Lamb, has been sacrificed cannot have leaven—sin—in their presence. The imperative of verse 7 echoes Paul's judgment in the first section: cast out the leaven.

The third section begins with verse 9 and continues through the remainder of the chapter. Its theme is the call to judge those within the church. Paul argues that the church has no responsibility to judge or to shun the world, but that they are commanded to judge those who call themselves a brother and to remove those who are in overt and public sin from their fellowship. He concludes with a third and final command to cast out the offending party.

So right beside the diagram we outline the passage like this:

I.   The Primary Problem: The Member's Sin (vv. 1–5)
   A. Its gravity (v. 1)
       1. Its impact on the Gentiles
       2. Description of the sin: incest
   B. Their response (v. 2)
       1. They are puffed up (they were proud of their "tolerance" perhaps)
       2. And have not mourned
           a. The mourning has a purpose
           b. That the guilty one should be taken away

    C. Paul's response (vv. 3–5)

        1. Based on action rather than on personality: "I have already judged"

        2. In the name of the Lord—that's how we gather

        3. In the power—that's how Paul is present

        4. **The command:** hand him over to Satan

            a. for his flesh's destruction

            b. for his spirit's salvation

II. The Secondary Problem: The Church's Attitude Toward Sin (vv. 6–8)

    A. They failed to appreciate the corporate impact of sin

        1. "A little leaven leavens the whole lump"

        2. So **purge out the leaven**

    B. They failed to appreciate the purpose of discipline

        1. Corporate purity

        2. Fellowship with Christ, our Passover

            a. Because Christ has been sacrificed we perpetually observe the Passover feast

            b. Not with the old way of life

            c. Not with malice and wickedness

            d. But with sincerity and truth

III. The Proper Response (vv. 9–13)

    A. Separation from sinners

        1. Not the sinners of the world

        2. But from those considered brothers

    B. Catalog of sins that separate

        1. Fornicator

        2. Covetous

        3. Idolater

        4. Railer

        5. Drunkard

     6. Extortioner

  C. Judgment is for those within the church

     1. It is the mark of family

     2. Let God judge those outside the church

  D. Conclusion: *Remove the wicked one* (v. 13)

While some preachers would be happy to stand up in their pulpits with a descriptive outline like this, we argue that this is not really preaching. This is dry commentary. Merely explaining the meaning of the text is certainly better than giving a great speech that goes nowhere near the Scriptures, but those are not our only options. We can explain the meaning of the text *and* apply it, all the while illustrating it, engaging our congregations, and sharing our passion for truth. We *must* get the meaning of the text before all else, but if that were all preaching required, we would probably be better off buying commentaries for our church members.

The thematic outline is simply our way of being certain that we understand the meaning of the text. Sometimes we wrestle with certain parts or verses. Writing out the outline of the passage forces us to see how it fits. In our example here, for instance, we might struggle a bit with verses 7 and 8. What is this business about the Passover Lamb? How does that fit in with a call to church discipline? At this point we simply cross reference the whole theme of Passover, and we discover that yeast was forbidden during Passover, not only in the bread but *in the entire house* (Exod. 12:15). Yeast is often a metaphor for sin in the Bible, just as the Passover lamb was a metaphor for Christ. We understand, then, that the basis of Paul's command is that, for the Christian, we live in a perpetual feast of the Passover, celebrating that Christ has been sacrificed for us and that death has passed over us. Yeast—sin—has no place in our house, therefore, because Christ has been sacrificed. Reducing the text to an outline form forces us through that thought process and, if we have not already figured it out, makes us see exactly how it fits in the overall structure.

As we write out the thematic outline, our minds start clicking. We start thinking of ways that we can preach it, of applications we must make to the lives and situations of our congregation, and even of illustrations that we can use. If that happens, use a different color pen or pencil and jot it down on the outline, too. Don't stifle the spontaneous ideas that begin to emerge, but distinguish them from the description of the text. More ideas will come later in the process, but don't lose the ones that surface at this point.

A Narrative Text

Read 2 Samuel 11:1–27 before reading further.

Unlike the epistles, narrative texts don't normally have sentences that last for several verses or much of a hierarchical structure at all. As in this example, the structure is usually on the order of, "He did this. And then he did that. And then he said this." The development of the passage is found in the development of the story. Our thematic outline of a narrative text, therefore, should reflect the simple storyline and themes that surface. Narrative texts typically show us something to either emulate or to avoid. Which one the author advocates in this pericope does not require a lot of thinking. Because of the simplicity of the text and of the message, we don't need to diagram this to discern the following simple outline:

1. David's first mistake: He didn't do what he should have done (v. 1)
2. David's second mistake: He did what he should not have done (v. 2)
3. David's third mistake: He acted on his impulses (vv. 3–4)
4. David's fourth mistake: He attempted a cover-up (vv. 5–13)
5. David's fifth mistake: He committed murder to cover his own sin (vv. 14–24)
6. David's sixth mistake: He continued with life as though God did not notice (vv. 25–27)

You may find other helpful and equally accurate ways to outline the text, but you shouldn't spend time looking for a hierarchical structure in the passage. The passage seems to unfold in steps, so we have suggested the simplest outline possible. Yet even as we write out this simple progression of sin in David's life, we are drawn into the story and start thinking of ways we can relate this to a contemporary audience. In the first two verses we notice the contrast between sins of omission and sins of commission, how omitting to do the things we ought to do leads us to commit the things we ought not.

Even though we are only outlining the passage, application is not far away. Our mind easily begins to list ways people in our culture act on impulse like David did. The word *cover-up* in our fourth point makes us think of famous political peccadilloes and the ensuing denials, but also times we have witnessed that in our own lives. As we see the awful progression of sin and the ensuing descent into disobedience and death in David's life, we may think of specific times we have seen it in others or even in our own lives. Our minds flood with illustrations and applications, especially as we write that final point: *He continued with life as though God did not notice.*

A Prophetic Text

Texts from the Major Prophets or the Minor Prophets, like those from the Gospels, are a mixed bag. In them we may find narrative, discourse, apocalyptic, poetic, or prophetic forms, or even mixtures of forms. Sometimes the individual pericopes are simple enough that we do not need to diagram them, but sometimes they are a bit more complex, and diagramming them proves fruitful.

The new covenant passage from Jeremiah 31:31–37 is a beautiful example of a prophecy that is full of promise and meaning for God's people.

31) ⌐Behold,
   The days come, saith the Lord,
   └that I will make a new covenant
       └with the house of Israel
          and
       └with the house of Judah:

32) └Not according to the covenant
       └that I made
          └with their fathers
          └in the day *that* I took them
             └by the hand
             └to bring them out
                └of the land of Egypt;
     └which covenant that brake,
       └although I was an husband to them, saith the Lord:

33) └But this shall be the covenant that I will make
       └with the house of Israel;
     ⌐After those days, saith the Lord,
     I will put my law
       └in their inward parts,
     and write it in their hearts;
     and will be their God,

34)
and they shall be my people.
And they shall teach no more every man his neighbor, and every man his brother,
    └saying, Know the Lord:
for they shall all know me,
    └from the least of them
    └unto the greatest of them, saith the Lord:
for I will forgive their iniquity,
and I will remember their sin no more.

35)
Thus saith the Lord,
    └which giveth
        └the sun for a light by day,
        └*and* the ordinances for a light by night,
            └of the moon
            └and of the stars
    └which divideth the sea
        └when the waves thereof roar;
    └The Lord of hosts is his name:

36) If those ordinances depart
  └from before me, saith the Lord,
    └*then* the seed of Israel also shall cease
      └from being a nation
        └before me
        └for ever.

37) Thus saith the Lord;
  If heaven above can be measurd,
  and the foundations of the earth searched out beneath,
  I will also cast off all the seed of Israel
    └for all that they have done, saith the Lord.

In this case we see that the prophecy that God gave to Jeremiah has an obvious structure. Verses 31–34 clearly go together. God announces the new covenant that he will make in verse 31. In the following three verses he states the negative—what it is *not* like—followed by the positive—what it *is*. The last three verses go together. Verses 35 and 36 are an extended promise of the new covenant's endurance, while verse 37 is a shorter form of a similar promise. Both of the subsections within the final section begin with the formula, "Thus saith the LORD," and contain a contrary-to-fact condition that guarantees that God will keep his covenant forever.

Our thematic outline, therefore, might look like this:

I.   The New Covenant (vv. 31–34)
  A. Who it is for (v. 31)
    1. The house of Israel
    2. The house of Judah
  B. What it is not (v. 32)
    1. Not like the covenant made with their fathers
    2. Not like the covenant that their fathers broke
  C. What it is (vv. 33–34)
    1. It is inward: "I will put it in their inward parts"
    2. It is relational: "I will be their God; they will be my people"
    3. Complete: "they will all know me"
    4. Merciful: "I will forgive their iniquity"

II. The Promise (vv. 35–37)
  A. Who God is (v. 35)
    1. The God of creation
    2. The Lord of hosts
  B. His first promise (v. 36)
      As long as his creation endures, so shall Israel
  C. His second promise (v. 37)
      If all creation can be measured, God will cast off Israel

As we diagram and build the thematic outline, the key words in the text begin to take hold in our minds. The contrast between the old, breakable covenant and the new covenant that God guarantees is striking. Knowing the dismal surroundings and the impending doom that Jeremiah faced only makes this piercing ray of hope that God gives him blaze more brightly. We are struck not only by the beautiful poetry of the text but also by the ominous context in which it is situated. The outward character of the old covenant and the inward character of the new leap off the page. Frankly, we often find that this stage of preparation leaves us with a quickened pulse and a passionate desire to find someone to whom we can immediately preach! Now we are ready to move a step closer to the sermon.

Part II
The Sermon

The sermon is the bridge we build between the text and the congregation. With Bible-based truth and listener-based delivery, the sermon carries God's Word to man's ears and on to his heart. So it is essential that we be committed both to biblical truth and also to culturally relevant styles of communication. Part II of this book is an accessible guide to sermon building.

Chapters 6 and 7 provide instruction in two different ways of building a sermon. Chapter 6 is less technical but explains how to discern the main points of a text and the best way to communicate those points to your audience, even without diagramming or an acquaintance with the original languages. The Decker Grid System™ is a proven system of speech building and communication that can easily be adapted to preaching. Preachers who need to wean themselves from reading a manuscript and those who frequently bore their audiences with superfluous detail will find it one of the most liberating techniques they could hope to find. Shedding those habits that weaken preaching and alienate congregations is crucial to preaching the Word in the way that it deserves, and the Decker Grid System™ will prove an invaluable aid to that end.

Chapter 7 is the more technical method of building a sermon. While some expository models emphasize explanation and other preaching methods emphasize application, we insist that good preaching accomplishes both. So Chapter 7 also explains how to make the sermon applicational rather than merely descriptive.

Chapters 8, 9, and 10 provide examples and instruction in how to illustrate the sermon clearly and how to plan effective introductions and conclusions. Although we present the content skills in this section and the delivery skills in

Part III, we emphasize that in a very real sense they are inseparable. Building the sermon, planning the outline, the illustrations, the introduction, and the conclusion all have to be done with the delivery in mind.

CHAPTER 6
Building a Sermon with The Decker Grid System™

There are three basic problems that we've seen repeatedly in the majority of preachers as well as those in other more informal settings. We find the same problem in meetings, at the other end of phone conversations, and even on voice mail.

Take a look at the following communication situations and see if you haven't heard preachers (or been a preacher) like this too many times:

Words, Words..............Point

BORING!

> *The Borer* may be well researched and even clear. He may share a lot of good information, facts, and data. He may appear logical, serious, earnest and sincere and may even have a point and yet . . . he is so boring as he drones on and on in a monotone. You have lost interest, or have fallen asleep, and at best there is certainly minimum impact.

Beware the LBOWs

Too often we see bluster and braggadocio in preaching, usually as preachers just air their own opinions. Little truth or communication wisdom is reflected in the sermons in which they use a lot of words that don't really say anything. We call these LBOWs or Lovely Bunch of Words. LBOWs occur when someone says something that sounds good, but means very little. Here's an example.

> *"A fool finds no pleasure in understanding but delights in airing his own opinions."*
> PROV. 18:2

> "I'm here to preach the Word to you today, and I want to talk on a subject that is familiar to all of us. It's an area that I've done a lot of research on, and is an area that we all need and should have an interest in, I think. So pray for me as I try to preach God's Word. I'm glad to be here. I've enjoyed my preliminary talks with many of you, and so I hope that you will be blessed by my sermon as I've enjoyed putting it together. The Lord laid this on my heart, and I think it will be valuable to us all. So in my sermon this evening . . ." Etc. etc. etc.

It is like "a resounding gong or a clanging cymbal." Signifying nothing. And that preacher who just airs his own opinions communicates loudly, but he is not the one who is respected by his parishioners, or the one who sees results in his preaching. The speaker who gets results is the one who first listens to God's wisdom. He is focused in his message, with a strong point of view, but he sends a listener-based message to create action. And he is clear in portraying and describing the benefits to his congregation.

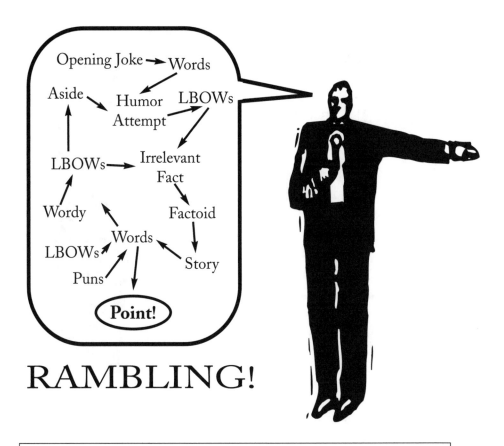

RAMBLING!

The Rambler may not talk in a monotone, and will get you laughing and even has a point–but he takes a long time in getting there. And by the time he does, you wonder whether the trip was worth it.

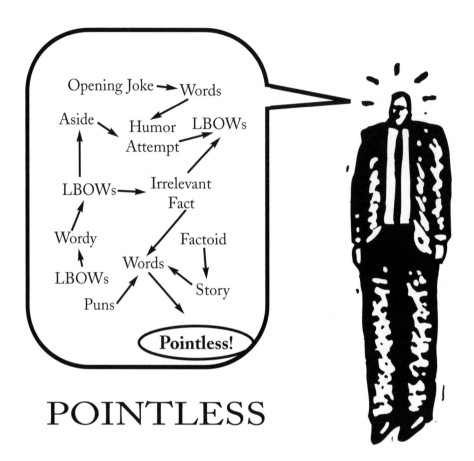

POINTLESS

The worst problem of all is the rambler who has no point at all. Although the trip might have been a diversion, it sure wasn't worth it!

It's Not Print

So that's our goal. To fully use the spoken communication channel to its maximum benefit, remember that it's not print. The difference between the written word and the spoken word is vast. When you want merely to get across information, do it in print. But when you want to create action, speak. That is why God has ordained "the foolishness of preaching" to proclaim his Word. Nothing reaches the heart and motivates action like passionate communication of the Word of God.

Combine your conviction and arresting content with energetic and authentic delivery. You want to use this powerful spoken communication channel in the right way. To move people. To teach. To motivate. To share how Jesus Christ has changed your life. To communicate to change lives.

So don't go back and write out a sermon! Don't get up and read a manuscript! There is a better way.

Summarize the Subject

Let's choose a passage of Scripture to serve as an example. For our purposes we will choose Philippians 2:1–11, but you can use some other example. If you would like to do this as an exercise, spaces are provided for you to fill in your own example. The adaptability of this system is one of its strengths, so don't be afraid to experiment a bit.

Reading through the passage, we first need to grasp the main theme or subject. The best place to locate the author's intent and emphasis is always the verbs, especially in an epistolary passage. And the most important verbs usually come early and seem to set the parameters for the others. When we look at the verbs of this translation, we immediately spot "make my joy complete" in verse 2, "Do nothing . . . but . . . consider" in verse 3, "look" in verse 4, and then "Your attitude should be" in verse 5. After that point, everything refers to Christ Jesus, whose attitude we should imitate.

Taking all of this into consideration, we can suggest several subjects. One subject in the text is certainly unity, because Paul is urging the Philippians to be united in their thinking. Another subject is joy, because Paul is asking them to make his joy complete. But the thrust of the passage, at least so far as the amount of ink is concerned, is being like Christ. In verses 1–4 it is implied, but in verses 5–11 it is explicit. So let's say that our subject is "Being Like Christ." So let's take that subject and just write it down on a piece of paper. Go ahead and do that now. Then think of that subject for a moment. Conjure up what you might say about it if you had someone sitting across from you and you had to give a little talk about the subject based on what you had just read in the text.

Being Like Christ

If you were to deliver a mini-sermon immediately, your ideas might look like this:

- Being like Christ makes Paul happy
- If Christians are like Christ, then we are like-minded
- Christlikeness produces humility
- Being like Jesus means caring for others and their things
- To be like Christ we first must understand his mind
- Jesus humbled himself, so we should, too
- . . . and a few more comments like that.

At this stage our ideas seem short, unfocused, and rambling. Let's see how we might fix it up:

What's the point of the text and, therefore, my point? What am I trying to accomplish with this sermon? How do I feel about Paul's exhortation to have the mind of Christ? Good, bad, or indifferent? Well, if I'm indifferent, I shouldn't be talking about it anyway!

But I feel passionate about the subject. I truly *want* to be like Christ! And so my point is that this command is good, and it should be taken seriously by every Christian. This will provide relief from the stress and complications of life. This is the secret to unity in the church. Only in this way will the world ever come to know Christ. This is the kind of life that God honors and exalts.

My point of view is clear and personal. Immediately, by focusing on my point of view I will begin to talk only about those things that will promote that point of view. My mind consistently attracts to it only those things that will help my cause. So long as I feel passionate about that cause, and if we believe the Word of God, how can we feel otherwise?

So in our talk on being like Christ, let's take the positive point of view and capture it with the following few words:

> # Being Like Christ
> ## is the secret of joy

Who am I talking to? When I'm preaching or teaching, I first want to be focused and sure of what I'm trying to accomplish, but then I want to know who I'm talking to—and where they are coming from. How much do they know about the subject? And are they for it or against it? And are they for or against me? What's their attitude? What does the group demographic look like? The truth may be the same for a child as for an adult, but I must communicate it differently. The point of the text may be the same for an American as for a Korean, but I probably will need different illustrations. I need to know my audience.

So for my sermon on being like Christ, let's imagine a specific audience that I might be talking to about this. Let's say I'm in a pretty dead, traditional church with people who live in a large city. They are:

- About half male and female/middle socioeconomic background
- Resistant to change
- A bit self-righteous, lukewarm
- Favorable attitude toward me

Think of the qualities of your specific audience and jot down a few comments here or on your own Post-it note:

```
┌─────────────────────────────────────────────────┐
│                                                 │
│                                                 │
│                                                 │
│                                                 │
│                                                 │
│                                                 │
│                                                 │
└─────────────────────────────────────────────────┘
```

What do I want them to *do?* Usually when I'm just talking I don't automatically think of an "action" step for my listener or listeners. But if I'm preaching rather than chatting and I feel passionate about the subject and have a point of view, shouldn't I want them to *do* something? You bet! Remember that our goal is never merely cognitive, but behavioral. We want nothing less than changed lives.

With Christlikeness as my subject, my general objective would be to get them to strive to have Christ's mind in the way that Paul describes. But we want our actions steps to be specific. *Whenever we find command forms in the text, we want to use those.* If the text is a narrative, then our action steps will usually be either to imitate or to avoid the actions of the characters in the story. In this text we find several commands that we can contextualize. Just as we see Paul using the considerable resource of his relationship with the Philippians to get them to do the right thing, we can do the same thing. So to make a more specific action step to move them to my point of view, I might advocate to:

> • Make your pastor happy by being unified,
> • Choose to surrender your rights and preferences about matters that threaten church unity, or
> • Be more concerned for others than for self

Go ahead and write your specific action step(s) for your audience:

What's the benefit for them? What's in it for them—the audience? Too often we are focused on the benefits for us, and to be effective we have to reverse that. If my listeners don't see the benefits for them, they will be very unlikely to take my action step, and my purpose will not be met.

"People don't care how much you know until they know how much you care."

So in our current example, the benefits to my audience of striving to be like Christ might be:

> • You will enjoy a unified church
> • You will make your leader happy
> • God will exalt you in due time

What would be three benefits for your audience if they were to buy into your point of view and take your action step? Write them here:

Benefits

Laying the Cornerstones

We have just built a foundation for a clear, focused sermon on our text. Now if we were to briefly summarize our talk as we did at the outset, we might start it like this:

Point of view:	Being like Christ is the secret of joy.
Action step:	Be more concerned for others than for yourself.
Benefits:	God will exalt you in due time.

If I had to give a little talk on the subject of being like Christ, my thoughts might go like this:

- Having the mind of Christ brings joy.
- The church reflects Christ through unity.
- The fellowship of the Spirit leads us to be like Christ.
- Having Christ's attitude is a choice we make.
- I am most like Christ when I care for others.
- If Jesus didn't demand his rights, neither should I.
- The unity of the church was the thing that made Paul happiest.
- Jesus' humility is one of downward progression: servant, human, obedience, death, cross.
- When we humble ourselves, God exalts us.
- There is no place for selfishness in the church.
- Each of us needs to choose a way to put others before ourselves.

Now take your subject and write down the key words from your point of view, action step, and benefits here:

Your point of view

Your action step(s)

Benefits to your audience

Now go ahead and imagine preaching a mini-sermon now to the same person on the same subject or text as you did several minutes ago. Wouldn't the focus and ability to present many more ideas in a cogent and confident manner have increased dramatically? Actually do it out loud if you can, and see what happens!

WHAT WE'VE JUST DONE

In this exercise we have just done the "Cornerstones" step, the first of four steps in The Decker Grid System™. We are just familiarizing ourselves with how to think through a text. In the next few pages we will take you through the Decker Grid in specific detail, so you will be able to prepare all of your messages and speeches with this useful tool. It will not only insure that you have listener-based, focused messages, but it can cut your preparation time in half while unleashing your creativity at the same time.

In seminars when we do this exercise and people have done the cornerstones like this, and then take that same subject they talked about the first time and talk about it again—the results are amazing. The mini-talks are more focused, energetic, confident, interesting, longer, and more arresting. The energy in the room doubles. All from a simple, ten-minute exercise. If people can do that with a quick look at a biblical text, think of what you can do after studying the passage for context, content, and concern!

The Decker Grid System™

Many messages, lessons, and sermons are often boring, rambling, or point-less, but The Decker Grid System™ almost guarantees you won't have those problems. It forces you to have a listener-based message, encouraging spontaneity and the human touch in your content. In addition, it allows you to create your messages in about half the time.

The System Itself

In the rest of this several chapter we will continue to take you through The Decker Grid System™ in an interactive way, so you will be able to actually use it in real life. We urge you to do the exercises and not just read through them. Then test the process in your own ministry. It can change your life and ministry because the way you present yourself and your sermon is important. Lives are touched and changed as a result, so we want to build sermons that have real impact.

"Give us the tools, and we will finish the job."
WINSTON CHURCHILL

Creating Messages That Motivate

The Decker Grid is a four-part process that will help you create messages that motivate. It is based on the way the mind actually works—quickly and spontaneously. It uses three basic concepts, or tools.

1. *Trigger words.* When you prepare a spoken message, don't write out sentences. Use trigger words instead. You are far more efficient when you create with building blocks, each one made up of the concepts and ideas you wish to communicate. These building blocks, or trigger words, prompt the wealth of working knowledge within your mind—representing ideas, facts, stories, etc. You can think of them as file names or key words within files.

A trigger word is the shortest word, group of words, or symbol about which you could talk for thirty seconds to five minutes.

2. *Grid message folders.* In the following pages you will need a message folder. You can use a regular manila folder that you adapt for this purpose or you can order specially designed folders from Bold Assurance. Be sure to use a separate folder for each sermon or lesson so it can be created, delivered and saved. Trigger words are used with the message folders in the four-step Decker Grid process.

3. *Post-it™ notes.* The trigger words are jotted on those familiar sticky notes. Your notes will move around, so Post-it notes work much better than the often-used 3x5 cards or note pads. You won't use all of your ideas. The ones that you use could end up in any order. Post-it notes allow you to shuffle ideas around quickly, sorting and discarding them as if they were playing cards, until you finally arrange them for maximum clarity and impact. The Decker Grid System™ prompts you through this activity so that you achieve order from chaos very rapidly.

When you use Post-its in The Decker Grid System™, place them "upside-down" with the sticky portion at the bottom. Post-its or similar notes are usually used with the sticky portion at the top, but this allows the bottoms of the notes to curl up away from you, and they are more difficult to read when you are using them as notes. When you start with them upside down, they will curl toward you as you lay the sheet of paper down on a lectern or pulpit for your notes. And remember to use the 1½ x 2-inch Post-its. Not only does this size fit the system, but they will encourage you to be sparing in jotting down your "trigger words" so you don't keep your nose down in your notes all the time.

THE FOUR-STEP PROCESS

The Decker Grid System™ is a four-step process which is simple in execution and profound in impact. It takes common-sense ideas and puts them together in a different way. Here are the basic four steps:

1. When you lay your *Cornerstones,* you create the context for your

The Four-Step Process

1. Cornerstones
2. Create
3. Cluster
4. Compose

message. The Cornerstones establish the purpose, or foundation. They stimulate your thinking and focus your attention on your listener's perspective, what you want your listener to do, and how he or she will benefit.

2. When you *Create,* you unleash your mind's potential to generate ideas to support your subject.

3. When you *Cluster,* you naturally group your ideas according to common themes.

4. When you *Compose,* you organize and edit your clusters. The end result is your best ideas, arranged and ready to be communicated.

Setting the Cornerstones

The purpose of The Decker Grid System™ is to help you organize and deliver your ideas in a rapid and memorable manner and to ensure that you are focused on what you want to say and clear of purpose.

Preparing sermons this way offers various benefits. You will be on target with any listener or audience, be able to organize your ideas quickly, and develop a new way of thinking.

Begin your work on the following pages. You can use the Cornerstones you did in the previous example if you like, but why not start a new grid on the new template! Here are the instructions:

i. The Cornerstones Step

Building the Cornerstones

1. Pick a biblical text to preach, and write its main theme in a word or two on a Post-it. Place it in the subject "cloud."

2. Think of your point of view—how do you feel about this subject? Define your passion with an active verb.

3. Think of and describe your audience, specific demographic, congregation, or class, and put that Post-it on the listener square.

4. Think of the general and specific action steps. What does this text demand of our lives? How should we respond to it? Place those two Post-its on the action step box.

5. Think of three benefits for the audience if they do your action steps—write and place them.

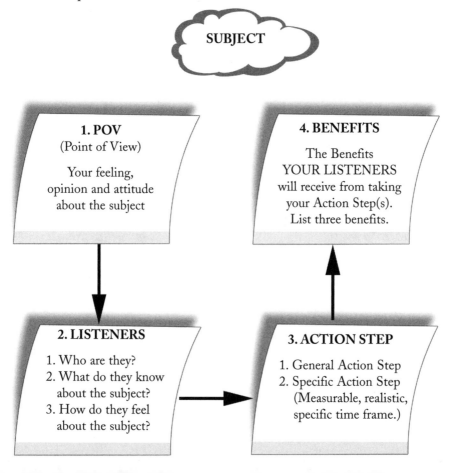

James 1:2–6 Example

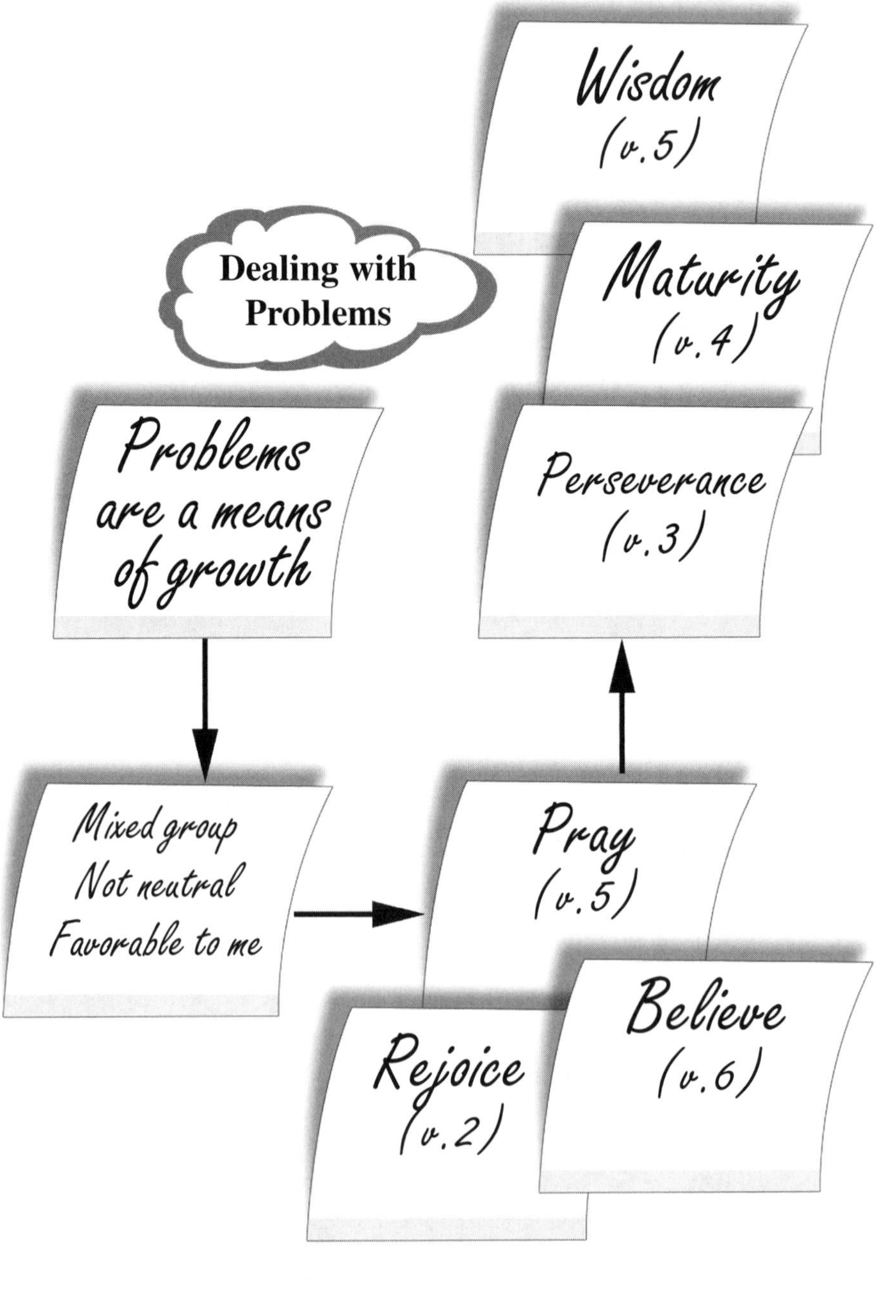

Wisdom
(v. 5)

Dealing with
Problems

Maturity
(v. 4)

Problems
are a means
of growth

Perseverance
(v. 3)

Mixed group
Not neutral
Favorable to me

Pray
(v. 5)

Believe
(v. 6)

Rejoice
(v. 2)

BUILD *Your* CORNERSTONES

Use this blank template to either place your cornerstones that you did in the previous pages, or better yet, do a new subject and new cornerstones to gain even more experience.

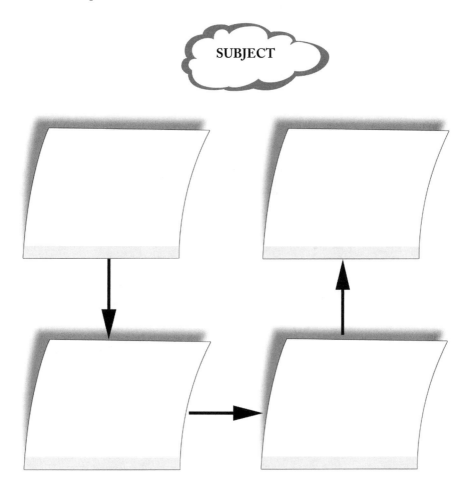

Delivering the Cornerstones

There will be times when you don't have time to go on to steps 2, 3 and 4 and Create, Cluster, and Compose. Then the Cornerstones become more than the beginning tool for structuring your mind—you can actually sequence them and deliver your message from just having the Cornerstones.

If you are delivering the Cornerstones, all you have to do is
 1. State your point of view
 2. State your action step
 3. State your benefit, or benefits

It's as simple as that. You will want to verbally add and embellish on your Cornerstones even as you are speaking, but in effect you have already "memorized" your message and can deliver it in about thirty seconds to five minutes or more if necessary.

Here is the delivery order:

Delivery

The Spiritual Cornerstones

There are many references in the Bible to communicating (well over four hundred), and many advocate having a clear and focused message. Here are four specific writings of Paul and James that relate to the four Cornerstones:

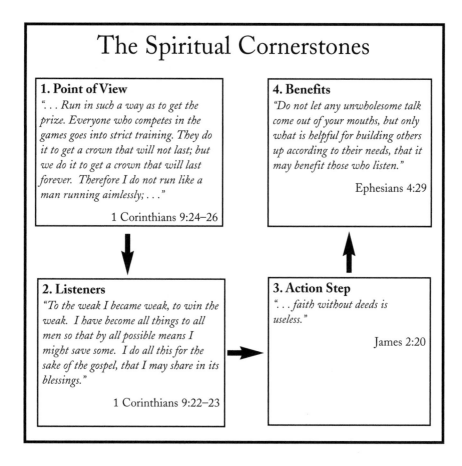

The Spiritual Cornerstones

1. Point of View

"... Run in such a way as to get the prize. Everyone who competes in the games goes into strict training. They do it to get a crown that will not last; but we do it to get a crown that will last forever. Therefore I do not run like a man running aimlessly; ..."

1 Corinthians 9:24–26

4. Benefits

"Do not let any unwholesome talk come out of your mouths, but only what is helpful for building others up according to their needs, that it may benefit those who listen."

Ephesians 4:29

2. Listeners

"To the weak I became weak, to win the weak. I have become all things to all men so that by all possible means I might save some. I do all this for the sake of the gospel, that I may share in its blessings."

1 Corinthians 9:22–23

3. Action Step

"... faith without deeds is useless."

James 2:20

Create, Cluster, and Compose

Remember that The Decker Grid System™ has four specific steps. The most important step is the Cornerstones step—because you have to do that first to determine where you are going. Although you can actually deliver a mini-sermon or lesson with just the Cornerstones, the next three steps of creating your ideas, grouping them, and then organizing and editing them is critical to the complete presentation. Here are the four steps again:

The Four-Step Process
1. Setting the Cornerstones
2. Create
3. Cluster
4. Compose

In this chapter we will take all three of the steps, give the description, then an example, then provide a working page for you to do your sample interactive exercise on your chosen text and subject.

STEP 2: THE CREATE STEP

The purpose of the Create step is to brainstorm for a few minutes to get as many ideas as possible out on the page, using only a trigger word or two for each Post-it. Do this only after you have thoroughly read and studied the text so that you understand its meaning. But once you know the passage well, you are ready to create. You do not edit or organize at this stage—you want the top-of-mind ideas that relate to your four Cornerstones—facts and figures, stories, data, examples, concepts, etc. As many as you can think of, you quickly put on the page, so that after about three minutes you should have about fifteen ideas on your Create page, which might look like this:

idea
idea
idea
idea
idea
idea
idea
idea
idea
idea
idea
idea
idea
idea
idea
idea
idea
idea

The James 1:2–6 Create Example

Sanctify

Respond correctly to problems

Pray (v. 5)

You will be more like Jesus

Rom. 8:28

Better or bitter

They purify (like gold)

Change your attitude

Varied (v. 2)

My seminary job

1Thess. 5:18

1 Peter 4:12

Make me like Jesus (mature)

Purify Gold story

Fruitful they produce (V. 3)

Inevitable (v. 2)

Guaranteed answer

Believe (v. 6)

Diamonds coal under pressure

Unpredictable (V. 2)

Are a test (v. 3)

God's great purpose

John 17:17

Knowledge Determines Atttitude

See from God's POV

God gives Wisdom

Traffic jams

Rejoice (V. 2)

Tempered Steel

Your Create Example

Now give yourself a time limit of three minutes. Time yourself and work to get at least fifteen trigger words written down on Post-its (upside down) that relate to your text and subject—ideas, facts, stories, quotes, numbers, etc. Remember the principles of brainstorming—no censoring or editing here (that comes later). Let one idea trigger another. Your goal is quantity, not quality.

Step 3: The Cluster Step

The purpose of the Cluster step is to begin the editing process by organizing your random ideas that you brainstormed in the Create step. It's a bottoms-up process where you simply group your ideas naturally—remembering that like attracts like. Begin by determining how many *logical points* the author makes in the text you are planning to preach. Make sure that you phrase the key point in an applicational way. Usually that means put it in a command format. Make it action-oriented, not merely descriptive. Write each of those key applicational points on a Post-it note, underline it to show that it is a thematic point, place it in a corner of the page, and then put other related ideas with it. Here is how it might look:

Tempered Steel

Rom. 8:28

See from God's POV

Sanctify

Purify Gold story

God's great purpose

Respond correctly to problems

Believe (v. 6)

Are a test (v. 3)

Unpredictable (v. 2)

Change your attitude

Varied (v. 2)

Inevitable (v. 2)

They purify (like gold)

Make me like Jesus (mature)

Better or bitter

Guaranteed answer

God's great purpose

Pray (v. 5)

God gives Wisdom

You will be more like Jesus

1 Thess. 5:18

Diamonds coal under pressure

John 17:17

1 Peter 4:12

My seminary job

Fruitful they produce (V 3)

Traffic jams

Rejoice (v. 2)

Knowledge determines attitude

Your Cluster Example

Now take about five minutes or so, and cluster the Post-its that you created in step 2: the Create step. You could transfer them to this page, although it is easier to just do the clustering on the Create page itself. Remember that the creating process never ends. When you think of a new idea, illustration, application, fact, or story, just write it on another Post-it and cluster it. When you are done, your cluster page will look something like this:

STEP 4: THE COMPOSE STEP

The purpose of the Compose step is to edit your ideas, keeping the best. Keep it simple, using the rule of three. While the number of key points depends on the biblical author, you should limit your subpoints to three per key point. Try to have one subpoint as explanation and one as illustration. That leaves one for discretionary use. Some passages need more illustration, others more explanation. Remember that the application should be in the key point itself. These are general suggestions, but they will tend to make the sermon meet our goal of changing behavior. Place your key points on the Compose page, putting them in the order of their occurrence in the text or their logical order. Then take your best subpoints for each key point and place them under their key points. Assuming you have three key points, you should end up with twelve Post-its on the page, looking like this:

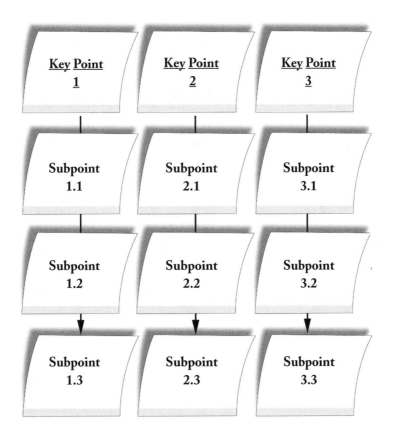

The James 2:2–6 Compose Example

Rejoice (v. 2)	Pray (v. 5)	Believe (v. 6)
Knowledge determines attitude (v. 3)	Better or bitter?	Rom. 8:28
Fruiful— they produce (v. 3)	God gives wisdom	Tempered Steel
Diamonds are coal under pressure	guaranteed answer	see from God's POV

Your Compose Example

Now take about ten minutes and arrange the key points from your cluster working page, and place them in order of occurrence or importance on the key points sample on this Compose page. Most of the time it is best to preach the key points in the same order as they occur in the Scripture passage. On rare occasions, however, you may need to rearrange them for the sake of clarity or some rhetorical device. After you arrange the key points, then take the three best subpoints of each key point and place them underneath. Notice that you will not be able to use all your ideas—that's OK. You want to use the KISS principle—"Keep It Simple, Sweetheart." Less is more. You can always speak any of your ideas when you are talking, but as notes, you just want to have your best ideas on the page to trigger your mind when you need to. You don't want a cluttered page.

After you have the key points and three subpoints for each, then look again at any of your ideas that you did not use. If any are better than those you have on your final grid, see if you can replace them. You will find that usually an idea left over can fit in and make sense under a different key point. The object is to end up with your best ideas on the page.

Delivery—with Opening and Closing

When you deliver your Decker Grid presentation, you will add a simple opening and closing. This one never fails. Start with a story or quote (SHARP principle; see chapter 8), and then state your point of view, action step, and second best benefit. (You'll save the best benefit for last.) Then tell your listeners key point 1, then subpoints 1, then key points 2 and subpoints 2, then key points 3 and subpoints 3. Then close by restating your point of view, action step, and best benefit. And to end with a flourish, add another SHARP principle. It would look like this:

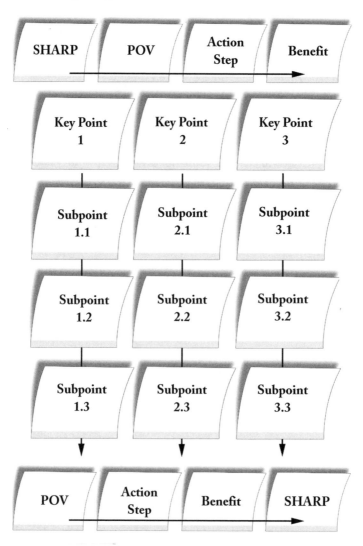

The James 1:2–6 Delivery Example

My seminary job	God's great purpose	Respond correctly to problems	Make me like Jesus

Rejoice (v. 2)	Pray (v. 8)	Believe (v. 6)
Knowledge determines attitude (v. 3)	Better or Bitter?	Romans 8:28
Fruitful— they produce (v. 3)	God gives wisdom	Tempered Steel
Diamonds = coal under pressure	guaranteed answer	see from God's POV

God's great purpose	change your attitude	You'll be more like Jesus	Purifying gold story

Your Delivery Example

Now you can either move your Decker Grid Post-its that you did in the Compose step a few pages back to this page and then use this template, or leave the Post-its there and do these final delivery steps on that page a few pages back.

Either way, take these final few minutes to complete your opening and closing. For the opening, place your point of view, action steps and second best benefit above your completed Compose step grid. Add a SHARP at the front end to complete your opening.

For the closing you will then repeat placing new Post-its, duplicating where necessary your point of view, action step and the best benefit at the bottom of your grid, as in the sample. Then choose a final SHARP quote or story to end with, and you will have completed your closing.

Then all that is left is to deliver it. Note the delivery order on the next page.

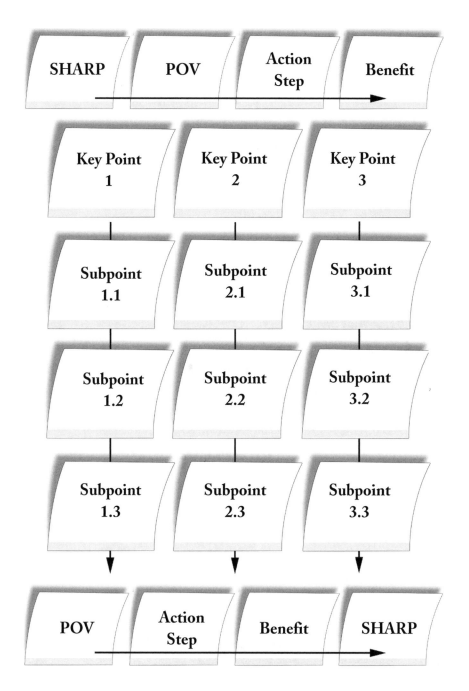

CHAPTER 7
Building Sermons to Change Lives

It's one thing to know what the text means, but it's quite another to be able to relate it to others. That is why the sermon is crucial. Like the preacher himself, the sermon is part of the delivery system for God's truth. Preaching involves three elements: the *text*, the *sermon*, and the *delivery*. Ideally, our goal is to convey the message that God gave in his Word and for our hearers to receive and comprehend that message.

THE COMMUNICATION MODEL

A basic understanding of communication is helpful in understanding the preaching task.

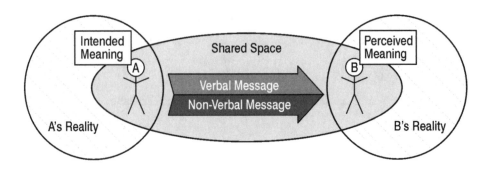

In the diagram, person A is the *source*. He *encodes* and sends a *signal*—whether verbal or nonverbal—that contains meaning to person B, the *receptor*, who must *decode* that signal in an attempt to perceive the meaning of the source. In other words, person A has an idea that he has to express in some way that is meaningful to person B. He might express his idea with words. If they share a common language and vocabulary, person B will be able to decode it. But words are not the only bearers of meaning. We don't call it body language for nothing! Person A might pump his fist menacingly, or wink playfully, or smile seductively. So long as person B receives and understands these signals, they communicate. If person A is unclear, or if person B infuses the words or actions with meaning that person A did not intend, then they failed to communicate properly. Communication is successful *only* when the receptor accurately decodes the signal and comprehends the meaning that the source intended.

Modern theories of art and literature have attempted to remove the source from the equation entirely. For centuries people read a book or looked at a painting and asked themselves what the author or artist was trying to convey. The big question was, "What does it mean?" But for the past century, things have shifted. Literary and art critics think that the source is irrelevant. Now the question has become, "What does it mean *to you?*" Some have gone beyond claiming the irrelevance of understanding the source's intent. They actually claim the *impossibility* of knowing the author's intent. Preachers who believe that are left to preach their own opinions and the felt needs of their listeners, hoping to strike a chord that resonates in their hearts and helps them cope with life.

But common experience tells us that we can know an author's intent. That is why we sign mortgage contracts and leave wills for our heirs and put instructions on a shampoo bottle! Words have agreed-upon meanings. Communication is possible. One human being really can know what another person means. All that is necessary is that they use mutually understood signals in their shared space.

If we apply this communication model to preaching, we identify three levels on which it occurs. On the first level, God is the ultimate source. He has revealed himself and his Word to humans.

Level 1: God ▶ (((signal))) ▶ Biblical authors

On the second level, the "holy men of old" who received God's Word then became the sources. Each of them sent a written signal in the various books of the Bible, which we readers decode in order to discover their intended meaning.

Level 2: Biblical authors ▶ (((signal))) ▶ Readers

On the third level, we preachers shift from being receptors who read and decode meaning to being sources who convey meaning to our receptors, the listeners who hear our sermons.

Level 3: Preacher ▶ (((signal))) ▶ Listener

Our goal, therefore, is to preach so that our listeners hear and perceive the same message that God originally gave. And to the degree that we faithfully preach the text, we speak God's words.

But we must understand the serious task to which we are called. Because we are called to preach *God's* Word, we have no right to substitute our own message. At the same time, we have the responsibility to use every aspect of the communication process to ensure that those who hear us understand correctly what God says. And that is why the sermon is so important.

When we construct a sermon, we want to keep an eye on our source—the biblical text—*and* on our receptors—the ones who will hear the sermon. We have to build the sermon for both. On the one hand, we must be faithful to the text. What the text says, we say. On the other hand, we want to say it in a way that *best* conveys the text to our listeners. We must say it in a way that relates the textual truth in a manner that they "get it."

On the textual side, we think *conceptually,* but on the listener side, we think *perceptually.*

By studying the text, diagramming it, and writing a thematic outline, we have thought carefully and thoroughly on the conceptual side. In transitioning to a homiletical outline—the outline we will actually preach—we must account for the perceptual element. We ask ourselves one simple question: *how can I say this so they really understand and act on it?* With that question in mind, we are ready to begin a step-by-step method of constructing the sermon.[15]

DISCOVER THE PROPOSITION

Every sermon should have one core proposition. More than a central theme or a big idea, a proposition is the main point stated in an applicational way. The proposition arises from the text—which is why we say it must be discovered, coming from the main theme and thrust of the passage. If the text is in an imperative format ("Consider it pure joy, my brothers, whenever you face trials of many kinds," James 1:2), then build the proposition from the commands found in the text. If the text is a doctrinal passage, look for clues about what behavior or error the writer was correcting or what action the doctrine requires. In a narrative text, look for the main thing the reader is being shown to emulate or to avoid. Regardless of the form of the passage, the proposition bridges the gap between the text and the sermon.

Sometimes discovering the proposition takes time, prayer, and a lot of investigation, but it is worth the effort. Just remember that no text is purely academic. Every passage in the Bible has a purpose. Find that purpose and preach it.

Be sure to word the proposition in a way that relates to and meets the needs of your congregation. If you are preaching a passage on covetousness, for instance, you would probably word it differently for a lower middle-class or lower economic congregation than if you were preaching to an upper-class church. Covetousness, though the same at its core, takes on different forms. The proposition should take such distinctions into account.

Most importantly, build application right into the proposition. Don't bury it in the conclusion or even in the exegesis, but lay it out from the very beginning. Let application drive the sermon. That is what you are preaching for. Don't be afraid to tell the people what they must do. Don't expect them to discover inductively how they should apply it personally. Tell them.

So what should a good proposition look like? Here are some examples:

Wrong: God expects his children to be holy.

Right: Every Christian should strive for personal holiness.

Wrong: David's sin with Bathsheba reaped dire consequences.

Right: To avoid the consequences of sin, don't indulge your flesh.

Wrong: Jesus died for our sins.

Right: Accept Jesus as your Savior.

Wrong: God chose us in Christ.

Right: Live a holy life in gratitude to God for choosing you.

Everything in the sermon must relate to that proposition. It is our compass. If an illustration does not help us get the proposition across, we need to eliminate it. If a point does not relate directly to the proposition, we need to restate it. The introduction should lead the listeners directly to the proposition, and the conclusion should drive it home.

DEVELOP THE MAIN CONTENT POINTS

Go back to your diagram and your thematic outline. If you did not need to diagram the text, you should still make a thematic outline in which you state briefly what is happening in the text. If you see discernible sections in the development of the story or of the argument, ask yourself: (1) what is the main truth being presented in that section and (2) what is the proper response to it? In other words, you are trying to locate not only the meaning, but the *implications* of that meaning. So if the meaning of 2 Samuel 11:1 is that David stayed in Jerusalem when he should have gone to battle, then we must discern the author's feeling about the act in the story.

Is the author suggesting that David did the right thing? Hardly, since nothing in the text indicates that. Is he suggesting that David did the wrong thing? Well, why else would he include this little detail to introduce the tawdry business that follows? Clearly the author is cluing us in to a behavior we should avoid. He did not have to incorporate the time of year into the narrative, but he did it for a purpose. He was pointing out that if David had been doing what he should have been doing, he could not have done what he should not do. And there is our point. To make it personal and applicational, we would state as the first point of the passage: *Defeat the t   ptation of neglect.*

Continuing through the text, we can develop other applicational points that we reveal as we move through the narrative. Each of them relates to our proposition, "To avoid the consequences of sin, don't indulge your flesh." So the sermon becomes, in essence, a how-to sermon. Our proposition is that we should not indulge our flesh and if we get five applicational points from the narrative, we then have a sermon on "Five Ways to Defeat Temptation."

Genre and the forms within them will usually determine whether application is obvious or more subtle. Some passages from the prophets, for example, are more challenging than others. Often the prophets were preaching directly for an action. *Repent. Stop taking advantage of the poor. Don't worship false gods.* But if we are preaching from a prophetic passage such as the new covenant passage in Jeremiah 31:31–37, we often find that the text has no clear imperative. In this case God simply informed Jeremiah that a new covenant was coming. He didn't tell him to *do* anything. That, in fact, is precisely the point of the new covenant, isn't it? So should we really impose an imperative on this text?

We answer with an unequivocal "Yes!" First of all, though we are stating the main points as imperatives, we are not "forcing" that on the text. We are simply saying that the text drives us toward application, so we are just putting it up front. We are stating what the implication of the text is. Why did God give Jeremiah the promise of the new covenant? Did God just want Jeremiah to know it? Did God merely want the prophet to have this bit of information for no particular reason other than to fill his head?

The answer is obviously "no." Of course, God had a purpose, some intended effect that knowledge of the new covenant would have. *That* is the application we seek. Maybe God wanted to give Jeremiah hope in the middle of his horrible ordeal. Perhaps he just wanted him to take heart. Certainly he wanted Jeremiah to respond in praise for his graciousness. All of these are possible applications for the passage, but that is not an imposition on the text.

Obviously, many preachers do not feel the need to make their points applicational. They opt for outlines that are little more than the descriptive outlines we have already talked about in chapter 5. They may dress them up a bit, alliterating them or rhyming them. But no matter how many times you say, "The Problem, The Process, The Promise" or "The Cause, The Condition, The Conclusion," all you do is point out the structure of the passage and perhaps its meaning in its original context. You still fail to build a bridge to your listeners. You are preaching a sermon that even the devil can agree with. He can be in complete agreement with your analysis of the text. The most backslidden member of your church can nod in sympathy with your description of the new covenant—or of any other biblical truth. Applicational points in which you show the mandate of the text and its claim on our lives awaken people to their own need for conformity to the image of Christ. When you preach applicational points, the devil can't agree and the backslidden (or lost) can't stay comfortable.

Some preachers outline the text in a descriptive way ("The Sent One, The Scorned One, The Saving One"), but put application within each point. Though we do not feel like this is the unpardonable sin, we still believe that the real "point" of the sermon is *always* application, so let's just be honest and reflect that in the points of the sermon. Don't hide it somewhere between explanation and illustration, but unfurl it and fly it high like a banner leading the troops into battle.

Another common mistake is to save all the application of the sermon for the end. This is a particularly serious mistake for several reasons. First, it makes application an afterthought rather than the real point of the passage. Second, it is hard to have a gripping conclusion when you are busy making sure the people understand the implications since this is the first they have heard of it in the entire sermon. Third, most preachers run out of time and rush their conclusions anyway. If you discover that you have preached longer than you planned and you must do some extemporaneous editing, your only choice is to cut the application. And exegesis divorced from application produces Christians with big heads and no heart.

By moving from descriptive points to applicational points, you make the outline itself have content *and* interpretive impact, not merely structural value. The purpose of the outline, after all, is to help get the message of the text across and not merely to provide a structure to your sermons.

Rely heavily on your diagram and thematic outline to determine the breakdown of the sections within the passage. Make it your goal to *let the structure of the passage determine the structure of your sermon.* If you see three sections or movements in the text, then show that in the number of main points. Admittedly, this is sometimes hard if not occasionally impossible, but we have to believe that the Holy Spirit was involved in composing the structure of the text as well as choosing the vocabulary.

DEVELOP THE TRANSITIONAL SENTENCE

Typically, it is best to state the proposition at the end of the conclusion, but do not shift abruptly into your first point. The proposition is the main theme of the sermon, but the first point in the body is just one part of that theme. You need a transition sentence, therefore, to take your textual development and show its relevance to the congregation. If the proposition is the bud, the transition sentence makes it blossom into the sermon.

If possible, the transition sentence should have a plural key word that reflects the proposition and anticipates the main points of the sermon. For instance, if the proposition is "To avoid the consequences of sin, don't indulge your flesh," the transition sentence could be, *"Through the example of David's sin with Bathsheba, we discover five* temptations *we must defeat in order to live godly lives and spare ourselves the pain of sinful consequences."* The transition sentence is tied to the proposition through the mention of the sinful consequences we want to avoid, but it looks ahead to the main points of the sermon by using the word *temptations.* Each point of the sermon would then be a *temptation* that David indulged that we must defeat.

In other words, the key word of our transition is repeated either actually or in principle in each of the main points of the sermon (that is, "Defeat the *Temptation* of Neglect, Defeat the *Temptation* of Lust," etc.).

FILL IN THE MAIN POINTS

Once you have the main points of the text in mind, you can plan exactly how you will flesh it out and explain the text. Traditionally, expositors have advocated explanation, illustration, and application (in that order) for each point. But if you compose applicational points and let application drive the sermon from the time you state the proposition, then you are creating an expectation in the congregation that has to be met with each point. You have read them the text, told them the proposition, and established the sermon as a how-to sermon. Each point reiterates that how-to aspect, but the people need to see clearly how you are deriving the instructions you are giving them from the text.

So in each point, therefore, you begin with application because your main point is in an imperative form, but then you have to take them through the text. You have to explain its meaning and demonstrate how the text you read leads to the point you are making. Do not underestimate the importance of this step. Beyond this one sermon you are also training your congregation in how to discern God's will for themselves from the Scriptures. Take the time to get them in the text. Build it into your outline.

The form of each point, therefore, is simple. You begin with application, because that is the form of your main point. You immediately move to explanation, showing them the textual basis for the command. You illustrate as necessary, and then conclude the division by restating the original point, which brings you back to the applicational foundation. The sermon, therefore, looks like this:

Introduction →	**Main Point 1** (Application) →	**Main Point 2** (Application)
Proposition	Explanation	Explanation
Transition	Illustration	Illustration
Sentence	Application (Restated)	Application (Restated)

Continue through the body of the sermon, filling in the explanations of the text required for each content point. Keep your listeners in the text, referring to it frequently. If you occasionally need them to turn elsewhere in the Bible for a cross reference, always get them back to you main text.

Choose the Main Point Illustrations

We make the case for illustrations and explain how to use them in the next chapter, chapter 8, but here we need to emphasize the basis on which you choose an illustration. Ideally, you should have at least one illustration per main point. Admittedly, sometimes time does not allow it and also the point is so obvious that it does not need it. Usually the audience finds it easier to listen, stay involved, and understand when each point is illustrated.

Determine what exactly needs illustrating in each point. For instance, if you are preaching from Galatians 2:20, you determine that you need to illustrate how closely we are identified with Christ, that what happens to him happens to us. That is not a normal or natural concept for most people to grasp, so that is the point you wish to illustrate. On the other hand, sometimes you determine that even though the text is clear, your audience just doesn't think about it much, so you really need to drive it home with an illustration.

We can think of illustrations best when we visualize what the lives of our listeners (and of ourselves) will look like if they obey the mandate of the text. Once you know that, then you can decide what kind of illustration will help them visualize the concept you are advocating. The illustration can be one of comparison or of contrast, but it needs to be as analogous as possible. Remember to *think on the perceptual level.* Ask not only if it truly illustrates the text, but how your congregation will hear it.

Develop Specific Applications

As we have argued previously, one of the secrets of powerful preaching is specific application. And even though we are crafting the main points in an applicational fashion, we want to be specific. We want to get in their lives, in their shoes, in their jobs and confront whatever is dissonant with our text and encourage conformity to Christ.

So to continue with our example of David's sin with Bathsheba, we must not content ourselves with an applicational point like "Defeat the Temptation of Neglect." David neglected to do what kings do, and it cost him. What are some ways that our people neglect to do the things they should do and it leads to sin? How many men have become addicted to Internet pornography because they neglected to do the things they *ought* to do and thus turned to wasting time on their computers? How many church splits have occurred because church members got distracted by secondary matters when they lost their burden for the lost? Might there be someone in your congregation who stands in danger of an affair because he or she wastes too much time at work talking to a coworker of the opposite sex?

Each main point provides opportunities for specific applications that fit within the main point. And as you do this personal application each week, your parishioners begin to apply the text instinctively to their lives in personal ways, too.

One word of warning is in order: make certain that your applications arise legitimately from the point of the text. Don't ride your own personal hobby horse or use this as an opportunity to shoot at all the ecclesiastical or personal idiosyncrasies that annoy you. Church members can tell the difference! If there is a particular church problem that everyone knows about (the same way they notice an elephant in the living room), you are better off ignoring it and sticking to the general application that the text makes plain. Never use application as an excuse for personal venting.

WRITE TRANSITIONS BETWEEN MAIN POINTS

The difference between a good sermon and a great sermon often lies in the lack of three or four sentences. Amazingly, preachers who spend hours in the study, doing all the exegetical work, praying over their text and seeking the proper application for their people, never take a few moments to plan intentionally the transitions between points. These transitional sentences smooth out the presentation of the sermon. Each transitional sentence acts like a hitch between the boxcars of a train. It not only connects one main point to another, but it helps the listener follow the development of the sermon.

Avoid cliché transitions like, "Our first point was, but the second point is." That is just too heavy handed and intrusive. It highlights the structure more than the meaning. The transition should recap the previous point, but it should propel us forward into the next point. It can be in the form of a question, a statement, or some other rhetorical device, so long as it smoothly meets those criteria.

DEVELOP THE CONCLUSION AND THE INTRODUCTION

The conclusion and introduction cannot be written well until the body of the sermon is complete. When all else is done, turn to the beginning and ending of the sermon. No part of the sermon is more crucial for getting your congregation to become involved in the text and to change their lives as a result. They are so important that we devoted chapters 9 and 10 to explain carefully how to introduce and conclude the sermon well.

While we are not so bold as to suggest that this is the only way to preach, we hold a settled confidence that the pastor who will follow this structure and methodology about 80 percent of the time will see spiritual results in his congregation. They will always go to the Word of God asking for direction and instruction. They will learn that obedience is the consequence of knowledge. Do not be afraid to try other methodologies of preaching, but let applicational preaching be your "bread and butter."

REDUCE THE SERMON TO OUTLINE FORM

We have purposely not advocated a particular form of writing the sermon. One could follow every instruction of this chapter and write a sermon in full manuscript form, and one could just as easily write it out in an outline. The precise manner in which you create is a personal choice and needs to fit your own style of thinking. If you need to write everything out in detail, go for it. If you can create through a more truncated outline (and still remember later what those notes meant), that is fine.

The creative process is a personal matter, but your delivery is very, very public. Which is why we have a word to say about using a manuscript in the pulpit.

Don't.

No.

Never.

Please.

We know exactly what some of you are thinking when you do it. You really want to get it right. You want to say exactly what you mean and you want to say it eloquently. So you work hard in your study to craft the sermon of a wordsmith. And the only way you can get it right is to read that manuscript.

That may seem like a lofty and noble goal, but that is actually self-centered preaching. That perspective considers self ("I don't want to embarrass myself") and it considers the sermon ("I want it to be just right"), but it does not consider the listener. Honestly, who ever brags that their preacher reads his sermons? When you want to have a heart-to-heart talk with your wife or children, do you write it out and read it? Then you probably won't get to the hearts of your congregation either.

While it may be wise to write out your sermon in a detailed outline or complete form for your files, the pulpit does not lend itself to extended looks at a meticulous manuscript. For your files you need an outline or manuscript of the sermon that is complete enough to recognize it five years later (or more), but for the pulpit all you need is a brief reminder of your points and illustrations. If you are prone to keep your eyes on your sermon notes, you need to reduce them to as brief a form as possible, even if it means you have a detailed copy of the sermon for posterity and a sketchy one for the pulpit. Just make sure that you do whatever you must to guarantee that the sermon notes are a blessing and not a curse.

A sermon outline that is detailed enough to include all the necessary details but brief enough to prevent ignoring the audience is optimal. We suggest that after you write a detailed outline or manuscript, then reduce its main points to Post-it notes and put them in a folder or even on the opposing leaf of your Bible. Those Post-it notes probably won't be complete enough for you to remember five years later what they meant, but they will be perfect for your delivery after all of your study in the passage. To illustrate this technique, we have included an example in the appendix at the back of the book. However you do it, when the time comes to preach, *don't read your sermon!*

CHAPTER 8
Illustrating the Sermon

Jesus was a master communicator because he not only spoke from his own heart, but he also directed his speech to the hearts of others. From his heart to theirs, Jesus changed minds by touching hearts. Jesus demonstrated that the way to really connect with people was to give them more than just information. While there are elements of Jesus' teaching and preaching that we cannot emulate because they are the prerogatives of divinity, in this case we can confidently affirm that we must follow his example. The key is to *give them one's self.*

That is why illustrations in sermons are so powerful. Whether we like it or not, people remember our illustrations far better than they remember the main points of the sermon. No matter how much time we might spend coming up with an outline that accurately and artistically portrays the text, they will not be nearly so taken by the logic of our outline as by the emotion of our stories. The trick for the preacher is to strike the balance between content and emotion, between head and heart. Illustrations of all kinds help us do exactly that. By illustrating the sermon, we are able to shed light on the text and make its meaning plain, establish an emotional connection with our hearers, and provide a hook by which they can remember and apply the exhortations of the sermon.

THE JESUS METHOD

Jesus certainly taught a lot of information. He spoke of money, heaven, hell, the end times, legalism, Judaism, taxes, ethics, biblical interpretation, salvation, and a host of other things that were important to him and those he loved. The entire Bible hinges on his life and teaching. The Old Testament would make no sense without it. Paul would have nothing to write were it not for Jesus. We still study what Jesus said so we may know God's will. But isn't it ironic that Jesus' teaching was so simple, usually directed at common, uneducated people? He used stories and parables. He did not just impart information. He never gave a lecture on evangelism, for instance, but he told the parables of the lost sheep, the lost coin, and the prodigal son (Luke 15). When questioned about the extent of the law and defining who our neighbor is, he responded not with an academic discussion of the definition of "neighbor," but with the heart-tugging story of the good Samaritan.

Jesus never trivialized his answers with mere sentimentality, but he never confused or alienated his audience with mere doctrine, data, and details either. Jesus demonstrated perfectly that no one has to make a choice between information and emotion. He exemplified the ideal balance and interplay between the two.

Even today his stories and parables still have emotional impact. Only the most hardened reader could peruse the story of the rich man and Lazarus and not feel the terror of a man in hell, crying and begging for someone to warn his living brothers of the judgment to come. At the conclusion of the Sermon on the Mount, the greatest sermon ever preached, Jesus summed it all up with a story: the tale of the wise man and the foolish man and the way they built their houses. After laying the highest ethical standards the world had ever heard, Jesus closed with a stark, emotional word picture of the calm and stalwart assurance of the person who obeys him and the complete calamity of the one who hears but disregards his teaching.

Over and over again, Jesus tugged at the hearts of his audience. Sometimes his words startled and shocked, but they nevertheless connected on an *emotional* level, not primarily a cerebral level. Imagine being with him when a Gentile woman came and asked for a miracle. Contrary to anything we might expect, Jesus answered, "It is not right to take the children's bread and toss it to their dogs" (Mark 7:27). Yet Jesus knew exactly what he was doing. In being so raw and apparently abrasive, he was demonstrating the faith of the woman and her correct comprehension that she was not worthy of God's grace. She had to cross the greatest barrier to the gospel message: pride. Then he used the incident to teach a lesson about faith. This emotional exchange was one of the first times that Jesus revealed his mission to the Gentiles. Had he merely granted her request, the scene and the lesson would not have been nearly as memorable, or even as theologically rich.

CONNECTION, NOT EMOTIONALISM

Jesus never resorted to *emotionalism*—making mere emotion the goal—but on the other hand he certainly wasn't afraid of using the emotions as a vehicle for his truth. Some communicators are content to tell a heart-rending story that really has nothing to do with the point they are trying to make. They mistakenly think that if they can just get an audience to cry or laugh or sympathize then they have done their job: "Get 'em crying and you can get 'em down the aisle." Jesus unquestionably touched emotions, but it was always appropriate and fitting to his subject matter and to his listeners. Emotions were genuine, not manipulative or manufactured.

Some preachers fall short on the opposite extreme. The ones who fail to communicate on an emotional level have the best of intentions. They usually believe that all they need is to communicate the information, deliver the data, and that the Holy Spirit will energize and apply the truth of the Word, no matter how poorly they deliver it. Some even excuse their own laziness and lack of preparation in this way, feeling that if they don't give the Holy Spirit some obstacles to overcome he just might be robbed of his glory and they might be tempted to take the credit.

No one would argue that the Holy Spirit can and sometimes does use the Word of God even when it is poorly preached. We could all cite stories and individuals whose testimonies bear witness to this. But the issue is not what the Holy Spirit *can* do, but what he *usually* does and what pleases him. Frankly, we are presumptuous to give him less than our best. We fail miserably when we communicate the most exciting and liberating message in the world with anything less than passion and excellence—and even emotion.

History bears witness to God's use of those who are willing to surrender all of their time and energy to his cause. God did not use Chrysostom, Augustine, Luther, Calvin, Whitefield, Wesley, Spurgeon, Moody, or Graham *because of* their eloquence or passion, but they *used* whatever passion and eloquence they had about their convictions and their message—and God blessed them.

Jesus spoke to hearts and changed minds, and that is still the most effective way of communicating God's truth today. Our message should be filled with images, with emotional impact, with stories and parables that highlight and drive home the content of our message.

THE PLACEMENT OF ILLUSTRATIONS

Since form follows function, the structure of the sermon should dictate the place of our illustrations, but illustrations usually fit at certain places in the sermon. The most important places for illustrations are *in the introduction and the conclusion.* Nothing arouses audience interest or drives home the message of the sermon like a well-placed illustration to begin or to conclude the sermon. Nothing can open people up emotionally to receive difficult truth like a good illustration or story.

Paul wrote 1 Corinthians chapter 5 to instruct the Corinthians in their need to practice discipline and to remove a man from membership because of gross and publicly known immorality. Frankly, church discipline is a difficult truth for modern Christians to accept. Like the Corinthians, we seem to take pride in our tolerance rather than taking the initiative to confront and correct members who are in sin. When I preached through 1 Corinthians and came to that passage, I was aware that I had to get across that cultural predisposition against confrontation and discipline. So in the introduction, I used illustrations to open them up to the loving nature of discipline and the truth that discipline *leads to fellowship and successful living*; it does not destroy it.

I began by telling about my high school wrestling coach and the awful things he put me through, all with the promise that it would make me a better wrestler. Then I talked about how I disciplined my sons, even spanking them when they were small, and yet how that discipline has led to incredible fellowship between father and sons. I even read a card that my youngest son sent me for no special reason, just to tell me that he thinks I am a great dad and role model. Choked with emotion, I explained how the loving discipline that I had given him was the basis of the love and respect we now shared.

Those very personal illustrations predisposed the audience to see discipline in a different way than they had perhaps ever thought. Now my task of working through the meaning of the text and urging them to adopt a proactive and positive practice of church discipline was much easier. I could then easily argue that the exercise of discipline was an act of love, but leaving someone in their sin was the greatest act of cruelty.

To use another example, I once preached on Numbers 20:1–13, in which God tells Moses that he will not enter the Promised Land because he violated God's expressed instructions and struck the rock rather than speaking to it. I was preaching to a large gathering of preachers and wanted to emphasize that our calling demands total obedience, that the price of leadership is a stricter standard of judgment. I know that most of us read that text and, on an emotional level, we sometimes sit in judgment on God, wondering why he was so tough on Moses. We feel like the punishment was too harsh for what seems, in the broad scheme of his life, a minor infraction for so large a soul as Moses.

The opening illustration had to be both riveting and relevant, so I told at some length the story of Sir George Mallory, arguably the greatest mountain climber of his day. Here is the image I gave them right after reading the text:

At 38 years of age, Mallory had already achieved worldwide acclaim for his mountaineering skill. He wanted to conquer the "one great challenge that yet remained," Everest. So on June 8, 1924, Mallory and his young, inexperienced, but strong and agile companion, Sandy Irvine, took off from their high camp to climb through the "death zone" for the summit. At 12:50 P.M., as the mist and clouds parted for a fleeting moment, one of the other members of their group, Noel Odell, thought he saw two figures ascending one of the steps high on the ridge. It seemed that they were behind schedule, but that they might yet make the summit. But just as quickly as they had given way, the thick clouds veiled the mountain in a dark mist and Odell could not see them any more.

It was the last time they were ever seen. In 1933 Irvine's ice ax was found. In 1975 a member of a Chinese expedition reported that he saw an "English dead" on the mountain, but he died the day after telling a few details. In the following years many expeditions were launched in an attempt to find Mallory and Irvine. The conventional wisdom was that the inexperienced Irvine must have fallen and Mallory died trying to save him.

In April 1999, almost 75 years later exactly, one more expedition was launched in search of the solution to mountain climbing's greatest mystery. Conrad Anker came across the bleached remains of a body some thousand feet below the summit ridge. It was not so unusual to find bodies on Everest. In fact, it is now all too common. When someone dies on Everest, they are there until the resurrection. It is impossible to move them, bury them, or even for their bodies to decay. Several climbers die on the mountain every year, and their bodies litter the trails. But the body that lay before Conrad Anker was not near any trail. He found its face hidden in the gravel of the mountain, its hands clutching at the earth. He noticed that the man had a broken leg, that his shirt had blown open, exposing a muscular back. The old hobnail boots on the cadaver's feet and the kind of clothes he wore told the searcher that this must be one of the two they were searching for, and the position a thousand feet below the ridge told him that this must be Irvine.

As his companions answered his call and came, standing around in disbelief, one of them bent down and turned back the collar on the man's neck. It had the initials G.L.M. marked inside. They looked at each other more puzzled than ever and one of them actually said, "Why was he wearing Mallory's shirt?" It was inconceivable to them that Mallory, the greatest mountaineer of all time, was capable of falling, but the body before them bore witness that even the greatest climbers are vulnerable in the inhospitable and unforgiving environs of the world's tallest mountain.[16]

It is not unlike the way we feel when we think about Moses, the great prophet of God. It seems all but impossible that he should do such great wonders, that he should have such a zeal and devotion to God, that he should come through the plagues of Egypt, the waters of the Red Sea, the temptations of Sinai and the deprivations of the wilderness only to die on a hillside on the wrong side of the River Jordan.

In fact, *we want to excuse Moses.* Here at Kadesh he had a terribly difficult time. Here Moses faced *defeat and dispute* of the will of God when the Israelites refused to enter the Promised Land. Here his life had been touched by *death* as he said an earthly goodbye to the sister who had reared him. Here was a place of *deprivation* of water, one of the necessities of life, and it resulted in *dissent* of the people.

God had given Moses specific instructions: (1) take the rod, (2) assemble the people, (3) speak to the rock before their eyes, (4) give them water. And what pastor can't understand Moses' anger. Couldn't they come up with a more original or clever way to voice their discontent? Couldn't they do anything for themselves? Had he ever let them down before? I can hear Moses saying, "Cut me some slack, God! Just this once let me have my say." And for one sin—one that we might even think small— Moses paid a great price. He did not get to enter the Promised Land, but he died there.

Do you think sin a light thing? When it comes to preaching his word and picturing him before the people, God takes it *extremely* seriously. And if you want to finish well, if you want to enter the rest God has prepared, then there are three errors you have to avoid.

The illustration not only gained interest but also it set up a paradigm by which the pastors in the audience could relate to God's action with Moses. If we want to climb the high mountains of leadership, we can expect no margin for moral error or disobedience. That is the price we pay; that is what we signed on for.

In the same way, placing a great illustration at the conclusion of the sermon sums up the main theme of the sermon and points them to application. In the Numbers 20 sermon, for instance, I returned to an Everest illustration to conclude the sermon. During the body of the sermon I had told story after story of great men of God who had failed in spite of their advantages. David sinned with Bathsheba. Elijah ran and hid in the desert. Every month we hear disturbing stories of preachers and pastors all around us who have fallen morally. So I concluded by relating the story of the book *Into Thin Air* by Jon Krakauer.

These days it seems comparatively easy to climb Mt. Everest. For $70,000 you can join an expedition. With crampons on boots, ladders across crevices, fixed ropes up the slopes, oxygen tanks, and modern thermal clothing, making the summit is much easier for climbers today than it was for Mallory or Sir Edmund Hillary.

Yet the unforgiving and hostile nature of the mountain cannot be controlled. For all of their technological advances, climbers still face the dangers of the mountain with very little margin for error. Everest made this point unmistakably clear in 1996 when some of the climbers on two expeditions faced tragedy. Rob Hall and Scott Fisher, two of the greatest mountain climbers in the world, were taking clients up to the summit. They set a turn-around time of 2 P.M. whether they had summitted or not, but they missed it. They failed to take warning from the bodies along the way. They failed to turn around before it was too late, and eight climbers—including Scott Fisher—paid the ultimate price of their lives.[17]

We, too, need to heed the bodies along the trail. Every time we hear of a pastor who has fallen into sin, we need to examine ourselves. Each time we find ourselves excusing sin in others, we had best repent and hate sin in our lives. We dare not minister in the power and strength of the flesh, but rather in complete reliance on the Holy Spirit and with an unrelenting submission to the commands and will of God. If Mallory can fall, if David can sin, if Moses can miss out on the Promised Land, you dare not trust your flesh either.

Not only does this concluding illustration have the vivid and emotional impact of the bodies along the trail on Mt. Everest, serving as silent warnings that this is serious business, but it also serves as an *inclusio,* the bracketing effect that comes when we reintroduce an earlier subject. Just as we began the sermon on the unforgiving slopes of the world's highest mountain peak, we ended it there, driving home the point that ministry may seem easier these days, but the consequences of failure are just as serious.

The SHARP Principles

While it is usually best to utilize the strongest illustrations in the introduction and conclusion, illustrations are also needed in the body of the sermon. Within the various points of the message they further explain the point, give the audience time to digest the truth that is being presented, and connect emotionally with them so they begin to adopt a positive attitude toward the teaching of the text. Remember that our goal is always to move from the "what" of textual meaning to the "so what" of contemporary application. Illustrations can promote that development by portraying what obedience to the text looks like. That is precisely the way Jesus used illustrations like the good Samaritan and the prodigal son.

No matter where you use illustrations, you can exercise the same principles that Jesus used to get to a person's heart. There are five methods you can use to help you make the emotional connection that Jesus demonstrated. Together the five techniques form the acronym SHARP. They hone your message to pierce the armor of resistance and boredom that listeners often wear. By punctuating your message with these five methods, you make your audience want to hear you and to pay attention to your content. You give them a handle for understanding and remembering your content. SHARP stands for Story, Humor, Analogies, References, and Pictures.

The Story

The first technique is to tell a *story*. Including a story that is interesting, engaging, entertaining, relevant to their lives, and related to the point you are making is one of the most effective ways to generate and hold interest in what you are saying. It is one thing to tell a person that Jesus can save him, but it is much more effective to tell him how he saved *you*. Anyone can tell a person whose marriage is in trouble that God *can* deliver him, but he will be much more encouraged if you can tell him a story of when and how he restored a couple's marriage when they were in trouble, too. The story helps people identify with the truth and also to remember it in a context.

Jesus' teaching is full of stories. He loved to tell stories that the simplest people could understand. Jesus' technique was obviously successful because his stories were preserved in an early oral tradition until they were written down by the Gospel writers as they were inspired by the Holy Spirit.

When Jesus told stories, he used images and parables that evoked familiar settings. He told the kind of tales that made his listeners have the "aha" of recognition and identification. Be sure that your stories are related to the lives of your hearers. You can use the occasional stories about ancient conquerors and personalities, but mix them in with more contemporary and relevant anecdotes.

Humor

Nothing predisposes people to like you and to listen to you, like a good sense of humor. Having the ability to take a light-hearted look at oneself or surrounding events is one of the secrets of great communicators. Humor creates a special bond between you and your listeners. It's virtually impossible to dislike someone who makes us laugh, who helps us enjoy ourselves. A sense of humor—whether sharp and explosive or dry and witty—makes you appear more genial, warmer, more likeable. The strong, pleasurable emotions people associate with good fun and high spirits make your message enjoyable to listen to—and *memorable.*

The feeling part of our brain uses strong emotions—including the emotions that trigger smiles and laughter—to saturate our consciousness with vivid impressions that result in greater retention of the message. Humor is different, though, from telling jokes. Our advice is: *don't tell jokes.* Leave the jokes to comedians. Too often preachers try to be funny by telling jokes, and they flop for numerous reasons. The slightest variation in timing can ruin a joke. A single misplaced word can destroy a punch line. Telling a joke that everyone knows or that another preacher told recently just makes you look silly. Jokes are not the best way to be humorous, but the ability to laugh at oneself, at the world around you, or at the human condition can really open your audience to like you. Remember that comedy is not your goal, but *connection* is. You just want to put your listeners at ease so they get the message of the text. Find your natural sense of humor and put it to use.

Analogies

A powerful way to make your sermon memorable and picturesque is to use analogies like Jesus did. Jesus used earthly analogies to describe heavenly truths. What is the kingdom of heaven like? It is like a man sowing, a pearl of great price, a mustard seed. A rich man getting into heaven is like a camel going through the eye of a needle. Jesus is the shepherd, the door, the bread, the water.

Whenever Jesus used an analogy, he fixed an image in the minds of his audience that would not soon go away. Analogies are like hinges on which the doors of our minds swing. (There is an example of one right there!)

Analogies provide a simple eloquence that can help speakers of limited vocabulary express themselves powerfully and at the same time can help listeners comprehend and grasp meaning. An analogy is a one-line illustration, a porthole of light illuminating your message and pegging it to your listener's memory.

References

If you want to lead your listeners to really hear and to accept your message, learn to use references effectively. References can either appeal to commonly accepted knowledge, reminding an audience of generally accepted facts, or they can lend support to your point of view by appealing to the authority or wisdom of others.

Jesus frequently referred to the Old Testament because it is God's inspired Word, recognized as such by the Jews, and the revelation of God's will. His ministry was saturated with Old Testament references used as an appeal to authority. Jesus often exposed the erroneous thinking of his contemporaries by citing the Old Testament. This lent support and authority to his message. When the Sadducees criticized his preaching of the resurrection, Jesus quoted the familiar Old Testament declaration that the Lord is the God of Abraham, Isaac, and Jacob, and that as such he is the God of the living, not of the dead.

Jesus also used references to establish commonly accepted views that needed correction, too. In the Sermon on the Mount, for instance, Jesus followed the formula, "You have heard it said . . . but I say unto you." In this way Jesus was reminding them of some beliefs that needed correction.

Your purpose in using references is not to impress, but to impact. Don't weigh down your presentation, but a sparing use of appropriate quotations, poems, and references to common cultural or current events can help turn on the lights for an audience.

Pictures

In addition to making your own presence as interesting as possible, give your listeners something visual to look at whenever it is appropriate. Make your sermon memorable with the use of bold, striking graphic aids, props, overheads, computer presentations, or other sensory enhancements.

Pastors, professors, and teachers are increasingly finding the benefit of using PowerPoint presentations as they speak. Coupled with a fill-in-the-blank outline, sermon and lesson outlines flashed on a screen behind an active speaker are a powerful combination.

For added impact, mix assorted kinds of media (for example, use projected outlines *and* video clips of appropriate testimonies) in order to keep the visual dimension varied and interesting. Rehearse the visual part of your presentation so transitions will be fluid rather than fumbling. Involve your listeners with your visuals; for example, ask questions of your audience and briefly tabulate their answers on an overhead transparency.

If you are teaching your church how to share their faith, for instance, write a script and rehearse a scenario with some willing church members. Anything you do to help your audience visually picture the truth you are teaching is a great help. When Jesus told his followers that they had to become like a child to enter heaven, he first took a little child in his lap. As they saw the simple adoration and obedience of that child, Jesus' words had a stronger impact on them because they were visual.

One word of warning is in order: *do it with excellence!* If you try to use any kind of visual aid or graphic presentation that fails—the person advancing the slides gets behind or ahead, the projector doesn't work—it will absolutely *destroy* your sermon. The rewards are great when it works, but the price of failure is huge. Don't use a technology until everyone involved with it has mastered it.

The content of our message is crucial, but we must follow Jesus' pattern to make sure that our content gets first to the heart. By using the SHARP principles to gain and maintain our listeners' interest, we can have greater impact and lasting effect—just like Jesus.

HINTS FOR GREAT ILLUSTRATIONS

Illustrations should only be used when they *truly* help you reach the goal of your sermon. Whether it is to aid in explanation of a difficult concept, to provide a hook that will stay with them and help them apply the truth of the text, or to show them the urgency of accepting the truth of the text, your illustrations should have a purpose other than light filler between substantive points. If you want your supporting material to help you hit your target, we offer some guidelines that will help you create, find, and use the right kind of illustrations.

Use only illustrations that relate to your text. Preachers sometimes settle for a good story instead of a relevant story. If you just heard a great sermon on tape or at a conference, resist the temptation to put that great illustration into your next sermon just because it is a good story. And let's be honest: it is easy to come up with some convoluted logic that appears to tie it in, even when you know it just doesn't fit. *Don't do it!* File and save that illustration for a time when it will be appropriate to the text. If you don't, the chances are good that you will confuse your audience.

Use illustrations relevant to your culture. My wife Tanya is a great communicator and speaker, frequently traveling to share in women's conferences and retreats. She used to have a presentation on the stages of a woman's life as illustrated by her purse and its contents. She used this creative and entertaining speech to help women enjoy the stages of life and rejoice in what God was doing right then in their lives. She would begin with a little girl's purse, stuffed with hair berets, doll paraphernalia, and crackers. Continuing to speak, she would unveil the purse of a teenager, a newlywed, a young mother, a career woman, and a grandmother. She would delight audiences as she pulled items out of the purse that characterized the different seasons of a woman's life.

Once she was invited by a missionary friend to come to eastern Kentucky, the most rural part of the state, and speak to a group of women. She took her boxes of purses and made the drive from our city to the mountains to address these ladies and, she hoped, to bless them. When she got back late that night, I was waiting up for her and asked how things went.

"Terrible," she replied with a dejected look. "They never laughed, cracked a smile, or even nodded with the slightest hint of enjoyment. It was just awful."

"What happened? That talk *always* works!" I responded.

"They don't carry purses!" she explained.

That is what happens when we use an illustration in a culture that has nothing in common with the premise of the illustration. When I go to the Amazon region of Brazil, I may preach the same sermon, but I do not use the same illustrations or tell the same stories. A lady living on a floating house in the Amazon does not have the same kinds of issues or experiences as a woman living in a Manhattan apartment. Though they may have the same core needs, the point of entry to those needs may be miles apart. Illustrations have to take culture into account.

You may be thinking that this is obvious, but the illustrations about Napoleon, Alexander the Great, and Fanny Crosby that are so common indicate otherwise. Rick Warren calls these "dead Englishman illustrations," and you just can't use many of them. You run the risk of speaking about purses to people who don't carry purses. You might get away with using one on occasion—*if* it is well told—but most people today just don't see that Napoleon's exile on Elba is like our alienation from God. The best illustrations are the ones that get a nod of recognition.

Comedians know this, so they base their humor on things that cause a flash of recognition in their audience. They joke about the way people feel territorial about their shopping carts even though they haven't actually bought anything yet, or the hairnet on the lunch lady in every elementary school in America, or men who still wear 32-inch jeans even though their bellies are twice that size. Every time you hear something like *that,* you feel connected. You've been there. You can *relate.* And isn't that the point?

By the way, this is why most books of illustrations are worthless. They are filled with weathered and well-worn clichés that everyone has heard and no one cares about. Some books or illustration services are refreshing exceptions, but not many. Wherever you find them or create them, be sure they are relevant to the culture.

Make them vivid. One of the keys of power in preaching is focus. The more specific, the more intensely focused the details of a story, the more you pull the audience in, creating "involuntary listening" and drawing them into the story and ultimately the application and meaning.

Refer back to the earlier illustration about George Mallory. Notice all of the detail. Frankly, the oral presentation of that story in an actual sermon is even more vivid than the one we have included here. We actually trimmed it for the sake of space. But contrast it with this version of the same illustration: "In 1924 Sir George Mallory, arguably the greatest mountain climber of his day, mysteriously disappeared on Mt. Everest. For years climbers and students of high-altitude climbing wondered what had happened. They assumed that he fell because his inexperienced partner fell and Mallory tried to save him. Finally, just a few years ago, some men found his body and were shocked to discover that he had fallen to his death, even though he was such a great climber."

What that illustration gains in time, it more than loses in effectiveness. Vivid language is a secret to powerful stories, illustrations, and even preaching. Word pictures, vibrant description, and strong action verbs are the life blood of engaging preaching. The great preachers and sermons of the past, from Jonathan Edwards' "Sinners in the Hands of an Angry God" to R. G. Lee's "Payday Someday" to W. A. Criswell's "If We Live or Die" (and just about anything Spurgeon preached) relied heavily on vivid images and language.

To get into the habit of using picturesque speech, read a great sermon or two every day. Listen to great preaching on tape, CD, or in streaming audio from the internet. Enroll in some type of personal program to enrich and increase your vocabulary. Learn a new word or two every week and force yourself to use them. Finally, read a lot. And when you read, keep a running list of new words that you encounter. Look up their definitions and make them your own. Remember that learning *big* words is not the goal. You are not out to impress others with your knowledge. Learning *useful* words that vividly describe what you want your listeners to picture is the goal.

Make them personal. Probably nothing else we say about illustrations will be as debatable as this piece of advice, but we are great believers in using tasteful, appropriate personal illustrations. Other kinds of stories and anecdotes may work fine, but you will be amazed to discover that the people who give you their time every Sunday morning are most interested in your personal stories. They enjoy hearing about your struggles, your victories, and even your thoughts. They don't have to be stories of earth-shattering drama or personal crisis, just little insights that shed some light on the subject of the text.

Once while preaching through the Book of Colossians, I came to that wonderful passage that includes the end of chapter 2 and the beginning of chapter 3—the great text in which Paul explains that you cannot be holy by keeping the law, but that holiness comes through focusing on Christ and heavenly things. He goes on to explain that the "old man," that person who existed before we trusted Christ, is actually dead, but that we must go on to put off the things that are related to the old man—his deeds and desires—and that we must clothe ourselves in the things that belong to the "new man." I wanted to illustrate that God has clothed us in the righteousness of Christ and that our deeds must match it like a pair of shoes should match a suit or a dress.

I related that Tanya had forced me to get rid of an old, worn-out, dilapidated pair of topsiders that made my feet feel wonderful—but they looked disgusting! The soles were separating from the shoe so that they seemed to talk with every step! Months after I thought she had thrown them away, I was getting ready to preach one Sunday morning and was rummaging in my closet looking for something when I was delighted to find my favorite pair of shoes. I was elated! It was like running into an old friend. I already had on my suit pants and shirt, but I had to run out to the car for something, so I just stepped into those old ugly shoes. I felt as though I was stepping into warm water when I put those shoes on.

Later that morning as I was preaching, just as I was making a dramatic point, my eyes fell to my feet and, to my horror, I realized that I was still wearing those shoes. Right in the pulpit, in front of hundreds of people and a television audience, and with a nice suit, I was wearing ugly, frayed, and frazzled topsiders because I had forgotten that I was wearing them. To say the least, I was terribly embarrassed.

So when preaching the passage about putting off the things that belong to the old man, I told that story and then I made my point: "Have you ever rummaged through the forgotten store of memories long hiding in the corner of your mind, when suddenly you discovered the memory of a sin long past, long ago forsaken. But instead of repulsion, it brings delight to your mind. You remember it fondly rather than in shame. You think of it as pleasurable, and before you know it, you have fallen into it again. You are still a child of God, still clothed in the righteousness of God, but you have slipped into the comfort of past sin, and it doesn't go with what you are wearing now. It belongs to the old man."

For such a simple illustration, drawn from my everyday life, it had a profound impact. For years following that sermon, struggling church members would come into my office, hang their heads, and softly say, "Pastor, I slipped into an old pair of shoes this week." Immediately I knew what they meant. The power of a simple image had helped them recognize and deal with sin in their lives in a way that mere information probably would not have done.

A few words of warning about personal illustrations are worth mentioning. First, your illustrations can be personal, but they cannot be *too* personal. In other words, no one wants to know about your sexual practices or sins (no matter how long ago they occurred), your struggles with money, or your dislike of your in-laws. You can't talk about any sin or weakness in your life that is still unresolved or even too fresh. In the same way, you might get away with telling in a humorous fashion about an argument you once had with your wife years ago, but don't tell them about the fuss you had yesterday! They aren't necessarily sure your marriage will survive it!

And when it comes to illustrations about family, ask permission from any family member you will mention before you dare use it. Their answer will depend on their personality and their confidence in you, but if they say no, respect it and accept that answer. Do not let your family feel like they have no privacy or control of how their private lives are presented to the congregation. Let sanctified common sense guide your use of personal illustrations and you will find them worthwhile.

Look for illustrations everywhere. If a pastor averages preaching just two sermons a week, fifty weeks per year, he will preach one hundred sermons. And if he uses one illustration for every introduction, conclusion, and three main points per sermon, then he requires five illustrations per sermon and five hundred illustrations per year! If he stays in one church for long, he will discover how difficult coming up with fresh illustrations can be. Many pastors have actually discovered that they can repeat whole sermon series in the same church years later—so long as they change the illustrations. But if a pastor repeats an illustration, no matter how good it may be, his congregation may think of his preaching as tired, worn-out, and stale—even if the sermon is new and only the illustration is repeated.

Obviously, the constant pressure to find new, relevant, and appealing illustrations is a consuming fire. Deal with it. You can get better at diagramming, outlining, and communicating, but finding fresh illustrations seems to get harder the longer one is in the ministry. Buying illustration books is seldom the answer. Craig Brian Larson's books and those in *Leadership* magazine are rare exceptions, but most collections have more useless material than anything. High-priced illustration subscription services are not any better, unfortunately. You will find that you often have to read one hundred such illustrations for a single serviceable story.

The solution is to become a human vacuum cleaner, sucking up interesting stories and tidbits as you go through life. Look for them in the vehicle registration line. Observe human behavior and interaction. Look for the quirks and challenges of life. Listen to the songs your teenagers are playing. Watch TV. Keep up with what is happening in the culture. Read the books on the *New York Times* bestseller list. Peruse the movie reviews in your local newspaper. Find web sites that provide daily or weekly headlines. Subscribe to news magazines. All of these things put you in touch with the culture around us which is an abundant source of material for illustrating sermons.

We also recommend quirkier sources. Learn to look for illustrations where no one else is looking. We particularly like books about strange and unusual oddities and peculiarities of history or culture. Odd and quirky dead Englishmen seem to be the exception to the rule. They still hold the interest of an audience, even though they are from distant centuries or cultures. *Condemned to Repeat It: The Philosopher Who Flunked Life and Other Great Lessons from History* by Wick Allison, Jeremy Adams, and Gavin Hambly (New York: Viking, 1998) is a great example. Filled with lessons drawn from strange or little-known history events, the book is a treasure of great illustrations and lessons. Charles Panati wrote *Extraordinary Origins of Everyday Things* (New York: Harper & Row, 1987) and *Panati's Extraordinary Endings of Practically Everything and Everybody* (New York: Harper & Row, 1987). These books provide endless sources of ideas, humor, and ways to make biblical ideas come to life.

Typhoid Mary's spread of death can be compared to the Judaizers of Galatians. Earl Tupper's innovative way of turning his fledgling company into an economic power through empowering individuals to host "Tupperware parties" can illustrate the power of personal evangelism or home Bible studies. The most famous and humorous "last words" recorded in history make a great introduction to just about any of Paul's epistolary conclusions. We have already noted nonfiction books like *Into Thin Air* and *Ghosts of Everest,* which are endless supplies of material. Kent Hughes's

Preaching the Word series is an excellent source of supporting material, complete with references so you can look it up for yourself.

Using contemporary movies or television for illustrations demands sensitivity to the conscience of others. As a general rule, don't refer to movies or television shows that you cannot recommend. Stay away from references to R-rated movies or other forms of offensive entertainment, even if you did not personally see them. By the time you explain to everyone that you did not see the movie and that you don't go see objectionable movies but that you happen to know about this one because you read the reviews, you have so weakened the power of the illustration as to make it ineffective.

You can also find illustrations in poems or songs, but follow this one rule: *don't read them.* If you use a poem, memorize it and deliver it well. If you can't memorize it, just eliminate it. If you refer to a song, quote it without reading it. Better yet, sing it—but only if you have a voice that will help and not hurt your sermon. You really don't want to make the audience uncomfortable on your behalf because you cannot sing, but try it anyway.

While you may find some great material in statistics, our advice is to avoid them unless you can present them visually. Most people just can't digest statistics, especially in rapid succession. If you feel like you simply must cite some stats, use them sparingly and make sure that you can actually document them.

Once again, the best place to look for illustrations is in the thousands of apparently ordinary things that happen to you. The trick is to record them, and then to relate them to the subjects you find in your homiletical crosshairs.

I was invited to speak at a deacons' banquet at a large church in the deep South, a job I relished because I love deacons and also I had tremendous love and respect for the pastor. At the close of the banquet the chairman of deacons began to thank the people who had worked hard to make the dinner happen, and he presented each one with a small gift. I was more than a little surprised when he called my name and asked me to return to the lectern to accept a token of their appreciation. I thanked him, took the gift back to my seat, but thought no more about it for the time being.

A staff member was driving me back to my hotel when I began to wonder what was in the neatly wrapped white package. Shaking it and weighing it, I guessed that they had given me a nice paperweight or desk plaque. Sensing my curiosity, he suggested that I open it. "Let's see what you got!"

"Why not?" I wondered aloud, and began to rip through the perfectly folded wrapping.

Soon I found myself gazing at a beautiful red box, but I opened it without particularly noticing the name inscribed on the outside. "It's a pen!" I said, but the staff member driving the car was already way ahead of me.

"Oh my goodness!" he exclaimed. "They gave you a *Dupont!*"

"What's a Dupont?" I wondered aloud, thinking to myself that I have always been a Bic kind of guy.

"That's a $500 pen!" he informed me, and proceeded to tell me all about my pen. "That's the Orpheo fountain pen. It takes cartridges or it comes with an adapter pump for an ink well. That is a gold nib, gold trim, and Chinese black lacquer. S. T. Dupont is a French company known for making luxury items, and you, my friend, just got one of their best pens."

Wow! I couldn't believe it. I had never even heard of S. T. Dupont before that night, but as soon as I got back to the hotel room, I got on the Internet and read all about the company, my pen, Chinese lacquer, and the fine cobalt blue ink that I had to order. I was hooked. I loved my pen. I treated it like we had given birth to another child! No more cheap Bics for me. I had arrived.

A few weeks later, I was sitting on the front pew on a Sunday morning, just moments away from preaching. Thinking through the sermon and my impending delivery, suddenly a thought came to me, a point that I wanted to add. Maybe I was just looking for an excuse to use my pen, but I effortlessly reached a hand into my coat pocket and unholstered my elegant writing instrument. Uncapping it, I began to record on my sermon outline my last-minute flash of brilliance when, to my abject horror, my $500 pen would not write. I scribbled, shook it, tapped it, and tried again, but with the same fruitless results. All that was left on the paper was the indentation of my increasingly frustrated pressure on the gold nib. Finally, I dismantled the beast to see what foreign matter might be impeding the flow of the cobalt blue blood through its noble artery. No ink. Not a drop. It was at that moment that an obscene thought pierced through my mind and hit me right between the eyes. An S. T. Dupont Chinese black lacquer Orpheo fountain pen that has run out of ink is no more helpful than a broken Bic.

A couple of Sundays later I was preaching from a passage in 2 Timothy in which Paul commends his friend Onesiphorus for the way he refreshed him with his presence after tenaciously seeking him until he found him, even in the great metropolis of Rome. I was struck by the way Onesiphorus hardly appears in Scripture. If Paul did not mention him in 2 Timothy, he would be completely unknown and unsung to us today. But simply because of his friendship, the way he refreshed Paul like a cool breeze on a hot summer afternoon, he is immortalized in the pages of Scripture. I was looking for a way to get that point across, urging my listeners that they, too, had to leave a legacy of friendships and rich, refreshing relationships if their lives were to be remembered and treasured after their passing.

So I asked, "How can I really picture the importance of friendship? What image can I present to them that captures how empty their lives will be without real relationships?" So I began to think about the words *empty* and *useless* in the context of friendships, but it took me to the "empty, useless" Dupont. All my studies in 2 Timothy 1:16–18 made me confident that I had a handle on the *conceptual* aspects of the text, but now I needed to move to the *perceptual*. I had to explain the text in a way that gripped them and pinned their minds to the meaning of the text. I knew that in the story of the pen, I had an image that could make my congregation visualize a life without meaningful relationships.

So after working through the text, explaining its context, its content, the applicational concern that it required in us, I closed the sermon with one final exhortation to be an Onesiphorus for someone, to refresh someone as he had refreshed Paul. Then I told the story of my Dupont. I told it much like I wrote it above, but with all the added visual cues that oral communication affords. At the end of the story they were laughing and smiling at my affection for this pen that would not write because, for all of its fine craftsmanship, it was out of ink. I let the laughter subside, a pause hang in the air, and then I said, barely above a whisper, "Friendships are the ink of life, the indelible substance with which we write our legacies. You can drive a fine car, live in a palatial estate, and enjoy every material possession imaginable, but if you are never a true friend to others, if your entrance into a room never lightens the load or alleviates the pain of others, you will die without a legacy, as meaningless as a pen without ink."

While that story is not dramatic, it *is* effective because it sneaks up on listeners. They aren't really sure where the story is going until I draw the parallel at the end, but when I do, it makes sense. The experience is common enough and simple enough that listeners can relate. While not many people have a Dupont pen, everyone has tried to write with a pen that has run out of ink. Connecting that with the legacy that we leave, the legacy that Onesiphorus left, simply works. The response to that sermon, especially to that illustration, was overwhelming. It made that emotional connection—reaching the heart first—that is prerequisite to reaching the mind.

CHAPTER 9
Introducing the Sermon

Pilots have long joked that flying is really hours of boredom punctuated by moments of sheer terror. Their humor belies the fact that once a plane is airborne, keeping it flying is the easiest part of the job. As we have seen with tragic results, even terrorists with minimum training can direct a plane that is already in the air. The tough parts are at the beginning and the end of the flight: the takeoff and the landing. Those actions require more skill, more concentration, and more attention than any other part of piloting an airplane.

Preaching is similar. Once we diagram and exegete our text, the structure and meaning of the passage can propel us forward of its own force after we get started. Once we have read the text and are into the flow of the passage, the current carries us along. The danger is that we may lose them by that time.

Within the first few moments of seeing and hearing us, listeners will subconsciously decide whether or not they find us credible, whether they will allow our information in. If we botch those first moments, if we do not seize their attention and draw them into our own passion, we stand in danger of losing them. If we were salespeople, losing their attention would be unfortunate, but as preachers of the gospel, failing to earn and hold their interest is *tragic*. Our message, our audience, and our Lord deserve our best efforts and planning.

Devising the introduction and conclusion is the final step of building the sermon. Only after we have done our exegetical work, determined the appropriate application, built the outline, and found our illustrations are we ready to plan the best way to verbally grab our listeners by the lapel and convince them that they need to know the message we are bringing to them.

Keep in mind the concept we have already mentioned several times: we have to think and plan on the *perceptual level* and not just the conceptual level. In order to do that from the very beginning of the sermon, we need to understand the *six main goals of a sermon introduction*.

Establish a Rapport

If you doubt the necessity of establishing a rapport immediately with your congregation, carefully read part III and then return to this page. The manner in which we relate to our audience in the first moments of a sermon will either close the shutters in our listener's minds, or it will throw them wide open and make them receptive to all that follows.

Admittedly, this step is not as crucial for pastors who already have a relationship with their congregations, but we must not forget that each Sunday brings the possibility and opportunity of having first-time guests. While church members who know you and love you may easily forgive your stumbles and stutters, first-timers may relegate you to a category you really don't want to be placed in. Whether we want to admit it or not, so much of that person's experience of our churches rests squarely on the shoulders of the pastor who proclaims the Word. People seldom join a church in which they just don't like the pastor. To the contrary, liking the pastor is *essential* and usually one of the most important factors in the decision to return a second time and to join eventually. But for the preacher facing an unfamiliar audience, *everyone* is a first-time listener.

So those first moments are crucial. Our demeanor, our countenance, the tone of voice, and the construction and content of those first remarks often determine whether or not they allow our information in and really hear it. No matter how good the content of our sermons, if we put them to sleep or turn them off needlessly, they will not get the benefit of the message we have to give them.

We evaluate credibility—whether we will _trust_ someone or not—on much more than just words. On a subconscious level, we are constantly processing all kinds of visual and verbal clues whenever we communicate with someone.

Our behavior is the conduit that conveys the content of our speech. In other words, you might have the most thrilling, exciting news in the world as the content of your sermon, but if your behavior conveys anything less than that—if you send a mixed signal—you will not only confuse your audience; _you will lose them._

Just put yourself in the pew for a moment. Imagine a preacher smiling as he preaches on the horrors of eternal punishment. Wouldn't that make you feel strange and uncomfortable? The mixed signal makes you question his credibility, his theology, his judgment, and his qualifications.

Conversely, imagine that as you stand to share the gospel—the most exciting, life-changing story in history—you seem unmoved, monotone, with no smile or hint of excitement on your face. You even look at your watch repeatedly while you speak. Do you really expect your congregation to stay interested and be excited about what you are saying?

Although only God can apply his truth to someone's life, _you_ are responsible to get your message to that person's ear. No one will give an honest and thoughtful hearing to a message that is incongruent with everything else he sees in your expression, posture, and body language.

We do not mean to imply that you will always get the results you want or that your magnetism and charm can sway everyone. Learning effective communication does not mean that people will always do whatever you want them to do or even that they will always be interested in everything you say. It means that you must send a _clear message_ in words and actions that they can receive and appreciate without being distracted by any behavior that makes them question the reliability of that message.

And nowhere is that message more critically important than when you introduce your sermon. If you do not establish a relationship and rapport with the people immediately, you will probably dig a hole that will be hard to climb out of for the duration of the sermon.

A common mistake we see that destroys healthy rapport is including apologies and "homiletical travelogue" in the introduction. Apologies hurt rapport and undermine the preacher's authority. If you have a sore throat, don't tell them about it. If you didn't have much time for preparation because you were at the hospital with a member, don't whine (or brag); it just looks like you want sympathy. Remember that an audience only gets what you give them. If you have a cold, some will figure it out without you announcing it. Others won't necessarily notice, so why call attention to it? If your preparation time was cut short by a church crisis, apologizing up front just sounds like, "This sermon is going to be lousy, so don't expect much." It might feel natural to ask their indulgence up front, but it actually demeans the Word of God.

The homiletical travelogue occurs when the preacher relates the details of how he chose his text or why he was planning on preaching another but changed his mind at the last minute. "When I first thought about preaching this morning, I planned to preach from the book of Zechariah, but at the last minute God told me to preach from John 3:16." The congregation did not come to hear about the rigors of study, the hermeneutical obstacles, or your thought processes. They came in need of a word from God. Preach the Word, not how you got to the Word.

INTRODUCE THE SUBJECT

The main purpose of a good introduction, of course, is to set up the subject and to let the audience know a little about where you are taking them. The apostle Paul used this technique in the first verses of his first epistle to the Corinthians:

> Paul, called to be an apostle of Christ Jesus by the will of God,
> and our brother Sosthenes, To the church of God in Corinth, to
> those sanctified in Christ Jesus and called to be holy, together

with all those everywhere who call on the name of our Lord Jesus Christ—their Lord and ours: Grace and peace to you from God our Father and the Lord Jesus Christ. I always thank God for you because of his grace given you in Christ Jesus. For in him you have been enriched in every way—in all your speaking and in all your knowledge—because our testimony about Christ was confirmed in you. Therefore you do not lack any spiritual gift as you eagerly wait for our Lord Jesus Christ to be revealed. He will keep you strong to the end, so that you will be blameless on the day of our Lord Jesus Christ. (1 Cor. 1:1–8)

Not only does Paul write words of kindness and tenderness to them, but he lays out the threads of discussion that he will later pick up. He builds rapport by conveying his desire for them to enjoy grace and peace, his gratitude to God for the grace they have received, and for their enrichment with abundant spiritual gifts. He even notes that they don't lack *any* spiritual gifts. But while he is ingratiating himself to them through his prayer and commendation, he is also introducing the subjects that will frame the rest of his letter. Sanctification, unity, spiritual gifts of speaking and knowledge, and their security in Christ on the coming day of the Lord are important themes in the book.

In the same way, our introductions should not only establish and strengthen the bond between preacher and congregation, but they should also establish the theme of the sermon. Only rarely can a very well-designed sermon create an air of mystery and allow people to ask safely, "Where is he going with this?" Normally, if they are asking themselves that question, we have not done what we needed to do. That introduction should tip them off to the subject matter.

Thankfully, we can use many methods to accomplish this task. By applying the SHARP principles that we learned in the previous chapter, we can introduce our subject in an engaging manner that also fulfills the third goal of an introduction.

CREATE INTEREST

Don't be fooled by the light filtering through the stained glass, the exuberant worship, or even the faithful attendance of the people who fill the pews every Sunday. They may not voice it, but if you listen closely, you can hear it. Just as you rise to the pulpit and open your Bible, in the rustling pages and shuffling of coats, they are all saying the same thing: "Why do I need to know this? What good is this going to do me?"

And it's a fair question. They are entrusting you with the better part of an hour of their discretionary time. They are placing the largest portion of their worship time right into your hands. So you had best not waste it.

Not only should you use the SHARP principles to get their attention, but you need to grab them by the lapels, shake them awake, get in their face, and put them on alert that what you have to say is something they desperately need that will change their lives! You cannot literally do that, of course, but you can do something *better*. You can draw them into your sermon through *involuntary listening*.

Involuntary listening is what takes place when a member of the audience who is not necessarily disposed to pay attention cannot help himself and finds himself engrossed in what the speaker is saying. That is quite a skill, wouldn't you say? And the good news is that *you can do that!*

You have the ability to create involuntary listening by using nine techniques that draw people into your sermon, even when they were not necessarily intending to listen. If you think of your own experience, you will recall times that you were trying to do something, but you suddenly heard a whisper, and were inexorably drawn into someone else's conversation. Can you remember a time when you were sitting through someone else's sermon, hardly paying attention, probably thinking how much better you could do, when suddenly the preacher began to choke with emotion and your head lifted up to hear him? Have you found yourself drifting through a class lecture when the rest of the class laughed, and then you tuned in to see what you missed?

These are all examples of involuntary attention,[18] those moments when we cannot help ourselves, when we *have to tune in* and listen. That is the response we are going for, *especially* in an introduction. If you really want to create interest in your introduction, or even in the rest of your sermon, include some of these elements:

- *Novelty.* our attention is always drawn to something new and different, out of the ordinary. Don't make every introduction follow the same pattern or rhythm.
- *Movement.* When everything else is still, movement draws our focus and attention.
- *Proximity.* Those things that are perceived as near to us (whether physically, emotionally, or experientially) draw our attention.
- *Concreteness.* Vivid and concrete details stand out in contrast to things that are abstract and general.
- *Familiarity.* Awakening a sense of common experience and knowledge gains greater interest.
- *Suspense.* We are naturally drawn in when a few pieces of the puzzle remain missing.
- *Intensity.* People don't pay attention to lethargy, but to passionate energy and intense emotion.
- *Humor.* A funny look at life and self is irresistible. Self-deprecation is the safest form of humor.
- *Life relatedness.* Things which people can readily identify with or which are directly connected to their lives creates great interest.

Ideally, you can find a story or an illustration of some kind that involves your listeners in one or more of these ways. Clearly, finding an element of the introduction that does everything you want it to do—establishing rapport, introducing the subject, and creating interest—takes a lot of thought, searching, and creativity. We told you that you had to have a commitment to clear, hard thinking! But do not despair. You will find ways to do it. Just don't be lazy and hurriedly settle for something less than you know you can and should do.

SET UP AND READ THE TEXT

The timing of reading your text may vary from sermon to sermon or may even be a function of the liturgical approach of your church. Some churches use a layperson to read the text during the worship time and then the pastor preaches the sermon by referring to the earlier reading without going through it a second time. Other pastors read the text when they first get to the pulpit and then introduce the sermon in reflection on the text. Still other preachers may go through at least a portion of the introduction and use that to transition into the actual reading of the passage.

No matter which way you do it, we strongly urge you to ensure that someone indeed reads the text at some point during the service. Paul wrote to Timothy, "Until I come, devote yourself to the public reading of Scripture, to preaching and to teaching" (1 Tim. 4:13). Most evangelical church services would indicate our belief in preaching and teaching, but the ranks of those who believe in the public reading of Scripture have grown perilously thin. We cannot expect our people to treasure a book whose words we hardly read. You always reproduce whatever you honor, and if you honor the reading of the Word, then you will reproduce an attention to reading it in the lives of your people.

We suggest that the placement of the text, whether it be before, during, or after the introduction, should be a function of your development of the sermon itself. Just don't do it the same way every time. Sometimes you may deem it best to read the passage, pause a moment, and then begin your introduction. You may begin with some introductory material, setting up a question or a problem which you know the text addresses, and then say something like, "The Corinthian church was facing precisely that kind of a dilemma, too. They may have been surprised when they received a letter from their beloved apostle which read . . ." Just make certain that you give the congregation sufficient cues that they can follow along and that they see the text as the heart of the sermon.

Not only must the text be set up rhetorically, but you also need to locate the passage biblically. How does it fit into its larger context? What factors outside the immediate text inform one's understanding of the passage? Be selective. Your congregation probably doesn't need to know all about the proximity of Ephesus to the Meander River in Asia Minor just because you are preaching from the Book of Ephesians. Learn to leave some of your knowledge and discoveries on the cutting-room floor. Make the scriptural background as brief as you can make it and yet be sufficient for understanding the text you are preaching.

STATE THE PROPOSITION

Remember the proposition we talked about earlier in chapter 6? The proposition is the core truth, the central idea that we want our listeners to leave with, putting it into practice in their lives. The proposition is the demand that the text makes on us if we understand it properly and wish to be more like Christ as a result.

The best place for the proposition to emerge is at the end of the introduction, just as we move into the body of the sermon. The introduction sets it up while the body of the sermon proves it. While some sermons may be built with a sense of mystery and an eventual revelation of the proposition, most of the time we ought to just state it convincingly at the end of the introduction. It serves as the homiletical compass, the sermon's true north by which everything else is measured. We don't normally want our listeners to wonder where we are going. Tell them up front and then develop it, showing them step by step how the text leads us to this proposition.

TRANSITION INTO THE BODY OF THE SERMON

The parts of the sermon are not like building blocks, stacked but not actually connected. They are more like the cars of a train. The cars are distinct but they are hinged together and they move the same direction, one right after another. Good transitions are the difference between a good sermon and a great one. No transitional statement is more important than those that lead the listeners into and out of the body of the sermon. Usually the propositional statement itself can double as a transition into the body of the sermon, but sometimes a little more explanation is required.

If you follow our advice and make the points of the sermon applicational and imperative, the format of transition into the text might work like this:

Proposition: Every believer ought to strive for holiness by striving for Christlikeness rather than by keeping the works of the law.

Transitional statement: Paul wrote to the Colossians—and to us—to tell us three ways we can be like Jesus and live holy lives.

First point: To live a holy life, set your affection on things above.

With the right introduction, the audience is engaged, interested, and receptive to the message that is to follow. They are thinking about action! By spending a little extra time and thought planning a good entrance to the body of the sermon, you can help hearts and minds open to hear the message you preach. When you finish the introduction, people should be feeling that they are interested in the subject, perhaps because they realize that they struggle in that area or that they have been wondering about it themselves.

CHAPTER 10
Concluding the Sermon

People remember last words. When my sons were young and were going to spend the night at a friend's house, we would save the most important words for the last. Just as we dropped them off at their friend's house, we would say, "Remember to use your manners. Say 'yes ma'am' and 'no ma'am' to Billy's mother. Don't eat too fast. Don't eat too much candy. Take a shower. Flush the toilet when you use it. And one other thing—I love you lots."

We hear a lot about famous last words, the final utterances before death. Buddha said, "Never forget it. Decay is inherent in all things."[19] Oscar Wilde, clever right to the end, looked around the room and said, "This wallpaper is killing me. One of us has got to go."[20] John Paul Jones's famous words are still quoted in almost every school in the United States: "I have not yet begun to fight!"[21]

In the same way, people remember the final words of a sermon more easily than anything else in the whole message—with the possible exception of the introduction. Preachers, therefore, should restate the most important themes at the conclusion and do so in a way that is especially memorable. What is the thing you most want them to remember?

Unfortunately, many great sermons have been all but ruined by the lack of a satisfying conclusion. Some preachers work hard on the proper exegesis and explanation of the scriptural passage but pay little attention to how they want to drive it home at the very end. We will go so far as to say that the *greatest error* most otherwise good preachers make is in their conclusion—or lack thereof. When the Word is preached and the Holy Spirit uses that Word, people feel a need to respond. A sermon that does not tell them how to apply the truth and respond to it will only frustrate them. When congregants leave the church saying, "I really felt like God wanted me to respond in some way, but I just wasn't sure *how,*" then the preacher has not done a good job.

Like introductions, conclusions should be planned only after the body of the sermon is finished. Ideally, conclusions will accomplish four basic tasks.

Summarize the Main Subject

Saying that the conclusion should summarize the theme of the sermon may seem obvious, but the hundreds of sermons we hear each year from students and pastors testify otherwise. While we definitely propose in subsequent paragraphs that the conclusion should definitely make an emotional connection with the listeners, we also must issue a warning. If that is *all* the preacher does, then he is guilty of *emotionalism,* not emotional connection. Too often, the preacher who is willing to abuse the principles of communication will opt for a moving story at the end of sermon, even though it has no relation to the theme of the sermon. If he can get the audience crying by reminding them of the death of Old Yeller or singing "Tie a Yellow Ribbon 'Round the Old Oak Tree," he will do it with glee (even through his feigned tears). At best, he has missed a great opportunity. At worst—and probably more accurately—he has manipulated his audience. While there is nothing wrong with genuine emotion, it should serve only as a means to get listeners to keep and apply the meaning of the text.

Whatever else the conclusion accomplishes, it *must* summarize the proposition and the main points of the sermon. *The conclusion is the sermon in microcosm.* In the conclusion the preacher finally weaves all the various threads of the sermon together. The conclusion is the funnel into which all the other elements of the sermon are poured and emerge in a single, unified stream.

The safest way to do this is simply to restate the proposition and the main points, but you can find more artistic ways to do it. Let's take another look at a sermon we used earlier as an example. In 2 Timothy 1:16–18, the *theme* was "How to Be a Refreshing Friend," and the *proposition* was "Because of Christ in our lives, Christians should be refreshing friends to others, just as Onesiphorus was to Paul." The *main points* of the sermon were: (1) Practice a Refreshing Religion (v. 16a), (2) Be a Faithful Friend (v. 16b), (3) Be Tenacious in the Task (v. 17), and (4) Expect Mercy for Your Ministry (v. 18). In chapter 7 we used our conclusion as an example of illustration, but now let's flesh it out as the conclusion. Here we will repeat the previous illustration, but we add the elements that tie the sermon together at the end, noting them by editorial comments in brackets.

> I was invited to speak at a deacons' banquet at a large church in the deep South, a job I relished because I love deacons and I also had tremendous love and respect for the pastor. At the close of the banquet the chairman of deacons began to thank the people who had worked hard to make the dinner happen, and he presented each one with a small gift. I was more than a little surprised when he called my name and asked me to return to the lectern to accept a token of their appreciation. I thanked him, took the gift back to my seat, but thought no more about it for the time being.
>
> A staff member was driving me back to my hotel when I began to wonder what was in the neatly wrapped white package. Shaking it and weighing it, I guessed that they had given me a nice paperweight or desk plaque. Sensing my curiosity, he suggested that I open it. "Let's see what you got!"
>
> "Why not?" I wondered aloud, and began to rip through the perfectly folded wrapping.
>
> Soon I found myself gazing at a beautiful red box, but I opened it without particularly noticing the name inscribed on the outside. "It's a pen!" I said, but the staff member driving the car was already way ahead of me.

"Oh my goodness!" he exclaimed. "They gave you a Dupont!"

"What's a Dupont?" I wondered aloud, thinking to myself that I have always been a Bic kind of guy.

"That's a $500 pen!" he informed me, and proceeded to tell me all about my pen. "That's the Orpheo fountain pen. It takes cartridges or it comes with an adapter pump for an ink well. That is a gold nib, gold trim, and Chinese black lacquer. S. T. Dupont is a French company known for making luxury items, and you, my friend, just got one of their best pens."

Wow! I couldn't believe it. I had never even heard of S. T. Dupont before that night, but as soon as I got back to the hotel room, I got on the internet and read all about the company, my pen, Chinese lacquer, and the fine cobalt blue ink that I had to order. I was hooked. I loved my pen. I treated it like we had given birth to another child! No more cheap Bics for me. I had arrived.

A few weeks later, I was sitting on the front pew on a Sunday morning, just moments away from preaching. Thinking through the sermon and my impending delivery, suddenly a thought came to me, a point that I wanted to add. Maybe I was just looking for an excuse to use my pen, but I effortlessly reached a hand into my coat pocket and unholstered my elegant writing instrument. Uncapping it, I began to record on my sermon outline my last-minute flash of brilliance when, to my abject horror, my $500 pen would not write. I scribbled, shook it, tapped it, and tried again, but with the same fruitless results. All that was left on the paper was the indentation of my increasingly frustrated pressure on the gold nib. Finally, I dismantled the beast to see what foreign matter might be impeding the flow of the cobalt blue blood through its noble artery. No ink. Not a drop.

It was at that moment that an obscene thought pierced through my mind and hit me right between the eyes. An S. T. Dupont Chinese black lacquer Orpheo fountain pen that has run out of ink is no more helpful than a broken Bic. The value of the pen is not nearly as important as the presence of ink.

Friendships are the ink of life, the indelible essence with which we write our legacies. *[restate point 2]* You can drive a fine car, live in a palatial estate, and enjoy every material possession imaginable, but if you are never a faithful friend to others, the material wealth you gained won't matter. *[restate point 1]* If your entrance into a room never refreshes them like a cool breeze on a hot August afternoon, if your presence never lightens the load or alleviates the pain of others, your life simply won't leave a lasting legacy. *[restate point 3]* If you aren't the kind of person who doggedly stuck by the side of a friend in his moment of fear or shame, you will probably die without a heritage, as meaningless as a pen without ink. *[restate point 4]* And the great tragedy is that when you need a friend, when you need mercy, no one will be there for you—perhaps not even on that day when we stand before God, *[restate the proposition]* because the great proof that you have been befriended by Christ is that you befriend others.

Notice that we did not restate the points verbatim or even in order, but wove them together. Neither did we announce crudely to our listeners, "Remember our first point was . . ." and so forth, but used a bit more subtlety than that. The final paragraph was both the interpretation of the illustration and also the summary of the theme of the sermon. Its intent is to encapsulate the whole sermon so they can both comprehend it and keep it.

Focus on Long-Range Application

At the risk of beating this point to death, once again we insist that the goal of our preaching is always a change in the behavior and character of those who hear the Word. We don't just want them to *know* the truth; we want them to *do* the truth. Our conclusion, therefore, should reflect that commitment. We mustn't merely summarize principles that are cognitive, therefore, but we must urge on them the changes in their behavior that the text demands.

This emphasis on application has two elements. One is long-term and is the primary focus of the sermon, and the other is the immediate response of making a commitment. The long-term application tells people how their lives must change; the short-term and immediate application tells them how they can respond right now through the invitation or in prayer.

Long-term application needs to be expressed throughout the sermon, but *especially* in the conclusion. Be specific. Think carefully through the implications of the text as well as the life situations of your listeners and bring the two together. For instance, if you are preaching on Ephesians 6:4, "Fathers, do not exasperate your children; instead, bring them up in the training and instruction of the Lord," you have to know and explain exactly what that means for their lives. If you just leave it open, every father present will convince himself that he does not exasperate his children. Half of them may not even know what that word means! But if you get very specific in application, not only will you make them see the application that *you* make, but you will set the wheels of their minds in motion so they start making their own applications, too.

Part of the conclusion of a sermon on that passage might sound something like this:

> As God is speaking to the hearts of you fathers through this text, you may realize that some major adjustments are required in your life. You may not actively provoke your children, but today you may understand that you exasperate your children by your absence. For some of you that means you must make a major lifestyle change. You need to turn down a raise or a promotion because it would mean more time away from your family. Others need to spend less time on your hobbies and pleasures and more time mentoring and nurturing your children. Some realize that the greatest source of exasperation and anger in your child's life is the poor relationship that he or she witnesses between you and

your wife, and today God is telling you that you need to ask forgiveness and chart a new course for your marriage. Still others
need to change the way you talk to your children. Confess that
you have demeaned them and hurt them, and ask their forgiveness, promising that by the grace of God you are going to change
the way you speak to them.

This part of the conclusion is clearly focused on more than walking an
aisle or lifting a hand. You are portraying vividly what their lives must look
like if they get serious about obeying the text. Some well-respected authors
and preachers have suggested that such specific application is not effective
because it leaves too many people out. Our experience is actually the opposite. When a preacher starts getting specific with application, so long as he
does not claim that this is the *only* application, people catch on and per-
sonalize and contextualize it for themselves. Specificity and detail are
always more powerful than broad generalities.

Ask for Immediate Response

The way we offer immediate application depends on our individual contexts, especially on whether or not we invite people to respond publicly after
the sermon. Some denominations and churches offer a public invitation at
the conclusion of the message, while others do not. Scores of books and
articles have been written about the merits of the invitation system. We
cannot possibly say anything that has not been said better elsewhere. But we
feel it necessary to comment, especially for those who believe in the public
invitation system because it is implicitly bound with our preaching.

For that reason, we make the following points. First, many of the objections to offering a public invitation are based on perceived abuses of the
invitation. As anyone who wishes to think logically knows, one cannot
argue against a thing because someone somewhere at some time abuses it.
In that case we must argue against the abuse, but not the thing. Some husbands abuse their wives, but we are not against marriage. Some parents

abuse their children, but we are not against discipline, even corporal discipline. Some people stab their victims, but we are not against knives. In the
same way, we have certainly seen all kinds of emotional manipulation take
place in public invitations. We have literally witnessed scenes in which
evangelists asked everyone who loved his or her mother to come forward
just so they could claim that they had X number of "decisions." But that is
hardly a legitimate reason to refuse to call on men and women to put their
trust in Christ publicly and to make it known by coming forward in a
church service.

Second, the public invitation should be just one of many ways a church
urges people to respond to the gospel and to the sermon. You can have min-
isters or counselors available after the service. You can have cards available
for people to indicate that they require a visit or an appointment. You can
have a day of the week set aside on which the pastor meets with inquirers.
Now you can even have web site and e-mail responses. Do it all, so long as
you do it with integrity and sensitivity. But by all means, keep in mind that
when people hear the word preached, they often feel the need to seal their
inward response with an outward action. The invitation system allows for
that.

Third, never equate walking an aisle with trusting Christ or doing the
will of God. Make it plain that this action is merely the way they are seal-
ing their decision publicly or else coming for further prayer or instruction.
The best thing a pastor can do is to train church members to counsel those
who respond. Equip them to discern the needs of people, share the gospel
when appropriate, pray when needed, and refer them to pastoral staff when
necessary.

So for a sermon on Ephesians 6:4, *after* the long-range application is
portrayed, the preacher might then ask all those who will commit to those
kinds of changes in his life and home to come forward for a time of prayer.
The appeal might go something like this:

> While you may feel the Holy Spirit speaking to your heart and
> leading you to make some changes, we have to admit that it is

easy to be stirred by a sermon and to make a secret commitment, only to forget it by two o'clock this afternoon. But if you are really serious about making some changes, why not seal that decision by coming here to this altar with the other men who feel led as you do, and letting me pray with you? There is nothing magic about walking this aisle or letting me pray for you, but when we step out openly, when we let our wives and our children see us on our faces before God, we make ourselves accountable for our commitments.

So if you really mean business with God, if you truly desire to make the changes in your life that you feel God directing you to make, when we begin to sing a hymn of commitment in just a moment, step out and come here to the altar and join all the other men who are making the same commitment that you are making. When you get here, just silently pray, or kneel, or allow someone to put his arm around you and pray for you until I can lead us all in a prayer of commitment to the Lord. By your coming you are saying that you want to honor God and follow him as a godly husband and father.

It is appropriate to give an invitation that is directly related to the sermon you just preached. In this case the text was about fathers, and so our invitation was directed to the dads. But we must also recognize that the Holy Spirit works in other ways, sometimes even unrelated to our sermon. Even though you just preached to dads, you may find someone in the audience who trusted Christ on an evangelistic visit during the week. That person may want to come for baptism. You may find families who have been visiting and checking out the church for months, and they came that day prepared to join the church. Still others may be under conviction of sin and ready to trust Christ because they have heard the gospel in the past.

Even though your sermon is specifically about fatherhood, you also need to enable listeners to respond in other ways that are fitting, yet unrelated to the message. The best way to do that is to pause after the first appeal is completed and then mention the other ways that listeners may feel led to respond and instruct them that they are free to do so now. Remember that if you preach in the power of the Holy Spirit and apply the text accurately, many people will *want* to respond. If you do not give them the opportunity to do so, you will only frustrate and confuse them.

SET A HOOK

Make the conclusion memorable! If you *must* make a choice between using a great illustration in the body of the sermon or in the conclusion, use it at the end. This is the place where you need to get their hearts open to reach their minds.

One goal of the conclusion is to help listeners visualize themselves acting on the truth presented and changing their lives to reflect that understanding. A gripping illustration that portrays that behavior or demonstrates that new understanding will help them know what that behavior looks like and will help them see the implications for their own lives.

Giving a conclusion takes a good amount of time. Too often, preachers fail in their conclusions because they realize that time has slipped away and their conclusion is a rushed, "If you feel God leading you to respond, come forward as we sing." No wonder we don't see greater results! When we fail to draw the net and challenge listeners to commit to obedience, we fail in our calling. As surely as we make time for our exegesis, we must reserve adequate time for our conclusion, including that required to draw the net through illustration, summarization, and appeal.

A good conclusion will require at least five minutes, so plan for it. Determine at what time the sermon should end, and begin the conclusion at least five minutes before that. Allow yourself time for the emotional connection and direct appeal that the text deserves. Far better to shorten the amount of text you cover in the body of the sermon, leaving ample room for a solid conclusion, than to just dump data and end the message abruptly.

Admittedly, this is a lot to accomplish in a brief conclusion, but that only highlights the need for forethought and planning. Repeatedly thinking through these elements of the conclusion and incorporating them into your sermons will make you more adept at it, however, and you will soon develop an instinct for strong conclusions.

Part III
Delivery

Up to this point we have talked about the substance of your sermon. But what is the most important thing in communicating? Is it substance or style? Is it content or delivery? Simply put—it's *both*. You cannot effectively have one without the other. If you divorce them from each other you will fail to be the preacher and teacher God wants you to be.

As noted in chapter 4, we typically find three kinds of preachers. The first is the "great" preacher who really doesn't say much. He is all flash and no substance. He engages his audience, using humor and making an emotional connection. Time passes swiftly as he tells stories, puts his audience at ease, and makes them feel right at home with his personal style. But when he is finished, you aren't really sure what his point was. Like eating cotton candy, you leave feeling like you enjoyed him, but on reflection you realize that you took nothing of substance away with you.

The second kind of preacher is the person who has great content, but you really didn't get it because he put you to sleep. He was very educated about his theology. In fact, he told you more about it than you ever wanted to know, but you got lost in the original Greek and the monotony of it all. You didn't doubt that his information was important, but you just didn't get it all because your attention waned. Like eating broccoli, you know you need it—it's good for you—but you really don't look forward to it.

Then there is the kind of preacher that we aspire to be. He has something important to say, and he says it *well*. We strive to know what to say and how to connect with a person or an audience so they get it and embrace it. When we have life-changing information, our countenance, posture, expression, and energy clue our listeners in that what we have to say is worthwhile, that it has changed our lives, too. We strive for nutrition *and* taste.

According to the New Testament, people stood for hours listening to Jesus, even going hungry while his impassioned words enthralled and challenged them. Did they do it only because they had not yet had their attention spans shortened by television? Or was it because everything about Jesus communicated that he could be trusted and that his message was what they desperately needed?

Just in case someone might think that this approach is modern or takes away from the work of the Holy Spirit, we can produce ample evidence that godly and great preachers through the centuries have advocated a passionate form of delivery. Solomon Stoddard was the maternal grandfather of Jonathan Edwards, and one of the greatest influences on Edwards's preaching. In 1723, Stoddard preached a sermon entitled "The Defects of Preachers Reproved" in which he rebuked his Puritan contemporaries for reading their sermons:

> When sermons are delivered without notes, the looks and gestures of the minister is a great means to command attention and to stir up affection. Men are apt to be drowsy in hearing the word, and the liveliness of the preacher is a means to stir up the attention of the hearers and beget suitable affection in them. Sermons that are read are not delivered with authority, they savour of the sermons of the scribes. Experience shows that sermons read are not so profitable as others. It may be argued that it is harder to remember rhetorical sermons than mere rational discourses, but it may be answered that it is far more profitable to preach in the demonstration of the Spirit than with the enticing words of man's wisdom.[22]

Some advocates of preaching from a manuscript have cited Jonathan Edwards as an example of a minister who could preach powerfully even though he read his sermon. Nothing could be further from the truth. To the contrary, during the Great Awakening Jonathan Edwards found himself accused by his preaching colleagues of being far too emotional and of appealing to the "affections" (as emotions were then called). Edwards responded by admitting that he preached to move people's hearts, and he was therefore unapologetically guilty of their accusation: "I am bold to assert that there never was any considerable change wrought in the mind or conversation of any one person, by anything of a religious nature, that ever he read, heard or saw, that had not his affections moved."[23]

Edwards's understanding of the "mind," that it contains both an intellect and a heart, prompted him to craft his sermons so they appealed to both equally.[24] Edwards scholars report that as Edwards grew older and continued preaching, his notes grew sketchier. He relied on key words and phrases and spoke passionately from notes that were largely indecipherable to others.

No less an authority than the great John A. Broadus argued for the same emphasis on both message and manner. His classic work *On the Preparation and Delivery of Sermons* contains notable chapters on both. He included chapters on style, energy, elegance, and imagination. Preachers who assert that Broadus advocated simply commenting on the Scripture have obviously never read Broadus. He wrote: "When a man who is apt in teaching, whose soul is on fire with the truth which he trusts has saved him and will save others, speaks to his fellow-men, face to face, eye to eye, and electric sympathies flash to and fro between him and his hearers, till they lift each other up, higher and higher, into the most intense thought, and the most impassioned emotion—higher and yet higher, till they are borne as on chariots of fire above the world, there is a power to move men, to influence character, life, destiny, such as no printed page can ever possess."[25]

The balance between content and delivery, between style and substance, is probably not what you have been taught or what you might think. And knowing that balance can transform your preaching. What you will learn in this section is that *building trust in your listener* is critical and is based on some surprising fundamentals. By learning how to build credibility and gain the trust of your congregation, you are giving the life-changing message of truth, the weight and significance that it deserves. Just as you have spent years of study and preparation in learning how to handle the text, so must you learn how to handle the tools of delivering the message so that the message reaches your intended listeners.

CHAPTER 11
Building Trust in the Messenger

What is it that makes us hear a sermon? Why does the advice some people offer make us appreciate them, while the same advice given by others makes us mad? What is the magic ingredient that makes a person's message compelling? Why do we intuitively receive and believe some people while we mistrust others?

TRUST IS THE KEY

Everyone wants to be believed, but unfortunately we share the planet with a lot of dishonest and unscrupulous characters. It is natural and healthy to take much of what we hear with a grain of salt, to have a healthy degree of skepticism. Though we all listen that way, we hate to be heard that way. We don't want to think that anyone questions our sincerity, our intention, or even our information. We want to be *trusted*.

And make no mistake about it: *trust is the most critical element in communication*. You've got to be believed to be heard. People won't care what your message is if they don't trust you. In fact, your audience, whether it be of one or one thousand, rarely hears your message if something in your behavior makes them think, even on a subconscious level, that you are not trustworthy.

If we want our sermons to be heard and accepted, then we must do everything possible to gain trust. If we are doing anything that unwittingly undermines our message, we must ruthlessly eliminate that behavior. Everything about our expression, demeanor, posture, tone, and attitude must demonstrate that we are sincere, that we are passionate about our message.

So how do we do that?

The Importance of Behavior

There are nine basic behavioral skills that have such an impact on our communications that they will determine the impact of our sermons. Though some of them seem like common sense, most people don't understand how they work as the primary conduits of credibility. We will explore each of them in depth in the next few chapters:

- Eye Communication
- Gestures and Facial Expression
- Posture and Movement
- Dress and Appearance
- Voice and Vocal Variety
- Words and Fillers
- Humor
- Listener Involvement
- The Natural Self

If our behavior lacks those communication skills, we invite our listeners to doubt our word. In essence, we send a mixed signal. Our words say, "Believe me," but our behavior triggers doubt and creates distrust.

No matter how skillful our words, how profound our truth, how artistic our presentation, we must never forget that we *are* the message. People won't hear us if our behavior gets in the way. Conversely, if we distract with behavior that is obtrusive, they see us, but not our message.

Sending a Mixed Message

When we carry a positive message but we have a negative behavior, our listeners are confused. When a husband tells his wife that he loves her but he leers at other women, he sends a mixed message. When a pastor is listening to a parishioner's hurts but he glances at his watch, he is really saying that he has something else that is more important. When a Christian looks grim as he shares the gospel, he is not making that lost person feel like Christianity is something that he wants.

When we send a mixed message—saying one thing with our words but another with our actions—which one do you think has the greatest impact?

A spoken message is made up of only three components: the *verbal,* the *vocal,* and the *visual.* Several years ago, Professor Albert Mehrabian of UCLA conducted a landmark study on the relationships between these "Three V's" of spoken communication. He measured the effect that each of these three components has on the *believability* of our message.

The verbal element is the message itself—the words you say. Most of us tend to concentrate only on the verbal element, mistakenly assuming this to be the message, when in fact it is only *part* of the message. The second part of the message is the vocal element—the intonation, projection, and resonance of your voice as it carries the words. And the third part is the visual element—what people see—the motion and expression of your body and face as you speak.

Let's do an experiment. Think for a moment about how these three elements of your spoken message—verbal, vocal, and visual—work together to reach and persuade your listener. Write these three words on a piece of paper, and then beside each of them write your estimate of the percentage of impact each element has on the believability of your message. If you think the verbal part of the message accounts for 50 percent of a person's determination of believability, then write that. Or maybe 25/25/50 percent. Or if you think they are all equal, write 33 1/3 percent for each. Make sure that your percentages add up to 100 percent.

Write them down, and when you are finished, you can compare your answers to what Mehrabian's studies determined—on page 203. We think you will be quite surprised at what you thought, and what the research has shown. The truth of the relationships between these three communication

What Counts: _Believability_

Verbal _____

Vocal _____

Visual _____

Total **100%**

components is not the way we are taught communications in school—or in seminaries, the business world, or life for that matter.

(Make sure you have written your answers before you turn the page to get the full impact of this important finding.)

In his research, Albert Mehrabian found that when we send out an inconsistent message, our verbal content is virtually smothered by the vocal and visual components. Just look at his results:

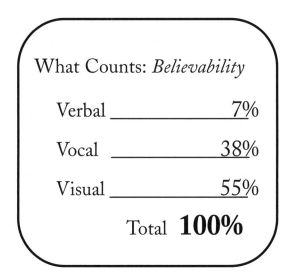

How did Mehrabian's actual results compare with your estimate on the previous page? Surprised? Yet it's absolutely true! When the vocal and visual components of our message are inconsistent with the verbal content of our message, we will simply not be believed.

Don't misunderstand these statistics. This does not mean that a person only gets 7 percent of a speaker's verbal content or that 93 percent of their judgment of a speaker is based on "body language." What Professor Mehrabian found is that these percentages are valid *when there is an inconsistent message.* In other words, if your demeanor matches the content of what you say, your audience is free to more carefully listen to actual content and to judge rationally. But when their eye sees and their ear hears a discrepancy between what you say and how you are saying it, the manner of your speech and behavior carries the overwhelmingly major impact.

When we learn how to coordinate all three of these components to form one totally consistent message, we are not only believable; *we have impact.* The excitement and enthusiasm of your voice work with the energy and animation of your face and body to reflect the conviction of your message. When your words, your voice, and your delivery are all working in harmony, your message dynamically and persuasively reaches your listener, having the fully intended impact.

On the other hand, when you appear nervous, awkward, or under pressure, your verbal content is blocked by your inconsistent vocal and visual message. For example, when someone says, "I'm happy to be here," but looks at the floor, talking in a halting, tremulous voice, clasping his hands together in front of his body in an edgy, inhibited "fig-leaf" position—he is sending out an inconsistent message. Those words will not be trusted, because it is the visual channel that dominates what is believed.

What does the visual channel tell the listener about us when we send out an inconsistent message? Perhaps it says we are insincere or lacking in confidence, or that we have something to hide. Perhaps it just conveys to the listener a feeling of anxiety or out-and-out boredom.

WYSIWYG is a computer term that stands for "What You See Is What You Get." It applies to personal impact as well. The message you *see* is the message you *get*. Clearly, the primary path to believability is through the visual channel.

Making It Work

Now that you know this powerful reality, you must put it to work for you and, most importantly, for those you want to impact. Do you want your children to *really* know that you love them? Maybe you might look them in the eye when you say it, get down on a knee to talk to a three-year-old, pause, and pay attention. Do you want your Bible study class to really get the life-changing power of the Bible? Then your energy and excitement when you teach must convey the excitement and power that you have discovered. Do you want to lead your coworker to Christ, even though you know he has a low opinion of Christianity and of most Christians? Then you must learn to convey nonjudgmental love and concern in the way you speak to him, especially when you share the gospel.

Do you want your audience to believe your message? Then first you must get them to believe *you*.

CHAPTER 12

The Victory of the Visual

Many preachers find these concepts of communication difficult to accept. For years they have spent so much time getting the facts, preparing a sermon or organizing a talk, and planning *what* to say, that they have hardly thought at all about *how* to say it. They recoil at the thought that they could have invested so much for so little return.

But that is precisely what we do. Like it or not, God has made us visual creatures. Pastors don't mail printed texts of their sermons to parishioners; they deliver them in person. Philips Brooks, the great preacher of the nineteenth century knew this when, in his Yale Lectures on Preaching he defined preaching as "truth through personality." And more than anything else, personality, that part of us that really convinces our audience of our own commitment, is revealed *visually*. In other words, they consciously and subconsciously are looking for clues on whether they can trust our message or not.

We've used the term WYSIWYG, which stands for What You See Is What You Get. Good communicators understand that the audience gets what they see. If they see nervousness, even if the speaker is giving a talk on "Ten Reasons Why Worry Is a Sin," then they will get a very different message than the one the speaker intended.

Why is the visual element so important in communication? Why must we come to the inescapable conclusion that we must give attention to the way we behave as we speak? Put simply, because that is the way God made us.

God's Glorious Design

The visual is very powerful. The nerve pathways of the eye to the brain are twenty-five times larger than the nerve pathways from the ear to the brain. The eye is the only sensory organ that contains brain cells. Memory improvement experts emphasize techniques that link the information you want to remember to a *visual* image. Over the past few years a huge body of research has been amassed, demonstrating that of all the sensory input the brain registers, it is the visual input that makes the greatest impact. Clearly, the *visual* sense dominates *all* of the senses.

God made us very sensitive creatures. During those periods of human history when survival was threatened almost daily, we had to pick up on subtle nuances. Our very lives could depend on our ability to differentiate between a threat and a haven.

Be Careful Little Eyes What You See

Why does the visual sense so dominate? According to scientific estimates, the nerve endings of our eyes are struck by 700,000 stimuli every instant. We cannot escape the massive impact of this bombardment on our brain. Psychologists have said that viewing something three times has the power of one actual experience. This fact alone has enormous consequence in our movie and TV habits and in how we use our powers of visualization. This has no doubt contributed to recent rashes of school violence.

Consider the impact of viewing *The Texas Chain Saw Massacre* or a pornographic movie three times. The psychological, emotional, and destructive impact of seeing those scenes portrayed three times would be similar to seeing the actual event just once. The power of vision can be used for good or ill. But there is no question that it is a strong power.

The advent of television has exaggerated this natural phenomenon of visual dominance in this age. Most of today's adults were raised on television, so they are much more visually sophisticated than their parents. Television is used as a convenient babysitter so that today's children will probably be even more visually oriented. The subtleties of a glance or a coy smile are significant—and they communicate. Such nuances weren't as critical in previous times.

Once you understand the significance of the visual and how it is even exaggerated today, you soon begin to appreciate both the power and the responsibility of communication. The visual element of communication often determines whether or not people hear the content of our message.

GETTING PAST THE GATEKEEPER

It should be obvious by now that effective communication is a lot more than simply transferring information. Every time you hear someone speak or teach, there is a gateway to your mind through which communication must pass. Standing guard before the house of your rational mind is a gatekeeper. This gatekeeper makes a quick assessment of the messenger to determine whether he will let the information pass into the intellect. We call this gatekeeper the *first brain*. Will the gatekeeper open or close the gate of communication? Will our message get through, or will it be blocked?

Whenever we communicate, our listener's gatekeeper is right there on guard, figuratively asking, "Friend or foe?" The gatekeeper has power to grant or deny access to our listener's higher analytical and decision-making processes. The best communicator is the person who knows how to befriend the gatekeeper, who knows how to become "first brain-friendly," so that his or her message can get through effectively and persuasively.

When it comes to communicating the Word of God, we know that no human can get the message from the ear to a person's heart. Only God can do that. But it is our job to get the message to their ear, and *they won't really hear us* unless we learn to get past the gatekeeper.

FIRST BRAINS FIRST

We literally have a brain within a brain. We tend to think of our cerebral cortex, the analytical thinking brain, as our entire brain—but there's more to it. Housed inside all that surface brain area that is the cerebral cortex is what we call the "first brain," which is composed of the brain stem and the limbic system. The cerebral cortex, of which God gave the majority share to his human beings, is our rational side. And the first brain contains the limbic system which is our emotional brain and the brain stem which is our unconscious "immediate response system." This more primitive brain he gave in more generous portion to the animals. But we have it as well, and we use it continuously since it is the seat of human emotion.

Without going into scientific details, suffice it to say that all of our sensory input—particularly the stimulus of seeing and hearing—go into the first brain areas before they are later analyzed by the thinking brain. So when we say first brain, we mean the nonrational gatekeeper that subconsciously takes in all visual and auditory cues and clues and decides whether to accept the information first, and then how to accept it.

To communicate effectively you *must* be aware of the language of the first brain—and you must *use* it. The language of the first brain is mostly a *visual* language.

Cutaway views of the thinking brain (cerebral cortex) and the first brain (limbic system and brain stem)

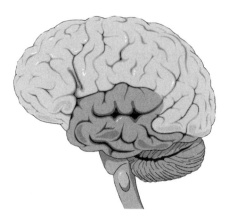

Thinking Brain

First Brain

The Thinking Brain and the First Brain Work Together

Thinking Brain

- Intellectual and Advanced
- Rational
- Conscious
- Source of thought, memory language, creativity, planning, and decision making
- Uniquely human

First Brain

- Instinctual and primitive
- Emotional
- Preconscious/Unconscious
- Source of instinctive survival responses: hunger, thirst, danger, sex, and parental care
- Common to many animals

THE MOST COMMON MISTAKE

When most people speak, they think only of the rational part of the brain as their target. Bible study teachers think that if they just lay the facts out there, the class members will "get it" and their lives will be changed. Preachers assume that if they organize a sermon and choose their words carefully, their parishioners will be moved to conviction and commitment.

Don't think for a moment that the rational part of the brain—that cognitive part that digests facts, evaluates data, and makes decisions—is unimportant or uninvolved. To the contrary, that part of the brain is one of God's most marvelous gifts to mankind. But to reach that rational part of the brain, our message must first pass through the first brain, the emotional part of the brain.

THE ISSUES OF LIFE

The wise author of Proverbs wrote, "Guard your heart, for it is the well-spring of life" (Prov. 4:23). He recognized that the emotional part of a person is the key to his or her core existence. So the most important language in effective communication is the language of trust. In order to communicate effectively, we must make *emotional contact* with listeners. They must see that we are absolutely persuaded of what we are saying. And when they see our passion and belief, they are more apt to *really hear* what we are saying.

Quite frankly, most people hate to admit that they are less than perfectly rational and deliberative people. We delude ourselves that we are never swayed by emotions, certainly not in the most important decisions of life. But that is not the way most people work, because that is not the way our minds work.

Salesmen have long known that *people buy on emotion and justify with fact.* No matter how much we resist that principle, it remains true—and we can prove it. Think back to the major decisions you have made—your profession, your purchases of a house or car, or even choosing your spouse. These are major life-affecting decisions, and we all like to think we make such decisions in a rational way.

But when you were making any of those big decisions, did you take out a yellow legal pad, write "Pro" and "Con" at the top, and make a list of all the reasons for deciding yes or no? When you chose your wife, did you make a list of her physical qualities, her prospects for income or childbearing? Did you estimate her future maintenance costs based on the life span of her parents?

Even if we consider a decision like buying a house, you probably didn't make it purely on those practical reasons. Did you visit twenty houses and make a profile of every house you visited and compare and contrast the pros and cons? And if you actually did that, did you then make your choice purely on the basis of the weight of those answers? And what then were the primary, scale-tipping reasons for your decision? Even if you took those practical considerations into mind, your decision probably had more to do with how you felt in that house than any other factor. If the house was attractively presented and clean and colorful, and then you saw a breakfast nook that appealed to you, or a play room ideal for the children, or a back-yard with a little garden grove. These are the types of things that probably swayed you. Then, *after* you made a decision of the heart, you got your head involved and made sure the facts supported the way you felt.

We aren't saying you didn't do research or give the decision a lot of thought. We are saying that most of our major decisions are overwhelmingly influenced at the emotional level, the preconscious level. We decide (or "buy") at that level and then use our intellect to justify our decisions. Those emotions serve as the conduit to the intellect.

If you want to reach a person's intellect, you must go through his heart, his emotions, his first brain *first*. Do you want that Bible study class to get excited about the principles you are teaching them from the Sermon on the Mount? Then you must appear credible, excited, and make that emotional connection! If we are energetic, enthusiastic, and believable, our words will actually be given more impact and energy by the listener's first brain before they are switched to the rational part of the brain. But if we appear boring, anxious, or insincere, our words will not even reach their destination. Instead, our message will be discolored or even tuned out at the switching station by our lack of believability. If we lack believability, we risk failure that has eternal consequences.

Use or Abuse?

Can these principles be abused? Certainly! Charlatans, manipulators, crooks, and politicians abuse them all the time! There are also unsavory characters who abuse food, sex, money, and talent. But food, sex, money, and talent are not evil, nor do they cause the problem. The unregenerate and selfish heart of man that wants to glorify self is the problem. Those things can either be used to glorify God within their proper use and enjoyment, or they can be used for selfish and destructive ends.

And that is no less true with those who understand these powerful principles of communication. These principles are neither good nor bad. They just are! They are descriptive and cognizant of the way God has made us. As with all knowledge, a great responsibility rests on the shoulders of those who understand. James knew that when he reminded us that teachers will be held to a high standard of judgment (James 3:1), and then he explained the awesome power of the tongue.

Yet at the conclusion of that chapter, after warning us of the destructive ability of the tongue, he continues, "But the wisdom that is from above is first *pure, then peaceable, gentle, and easy to be intreated, full of mercy and good fruits, without partiality, and* without hypocrisy" (James 3:17 KJV, emphasis added). What a description of the correct use of the tongue and communication principles!

Do We Sell the Gospel?

Please understand that the gospel is far more than something that we sell. No matter how persuasive or sincere we are, it still takes the work of the Holy Spirit and the grace of God to save a person. We are not at all suggesting that people accept the gospel based on the sophistication of our presentation. What we are suggesting is that they will not even *hear* the gospel if they do not find us credible. They must have an emotional response to *the evangelist* before they can ever hear *the evangel*. Although God can and does use many means to reach a person's heart, this is his primary means.

Have you ever heard of someone being led to Christ by a person he thought was a liar or a cheat? Of course not! The one thing we have to contribute to the gospel is simply our belief—and *that* is what we want them to see.

Just think of the person whom God used to bring you to Christ. Was it someone you respected? Someone you trusted? Perhaps it was a chance encounter with someone you had never met, yet still there was something in her that told you that she had something worthwhile. You believed in *her,* so when she told you that the most important thing in life was the gospel of Jesus Christ, you were ready to listen.

That is why the greatest methodology of sharing the gospel is still personal evangelism. One-on-one, loving, intentional witnessing is our opportunity to be transparent and to let someone see what is at the very core of our being.

First Brain-Friendly

How, then, do we make friends with the gatekeeper—the first brain—so that our message can get through the gate? How do we become "first brain-friendly?"

By being natural. By being truly authentic—which is being freed up from inhibition so we are just ourselves. By learning to use naturally the energy, enthusiasm, motion, expression—all the multi-channel, nonverbal cues that God gave us to enable us to make emotional contact with the listener. By becoming looser and more spontaneous. By using all of those nine communication skills to give our message the credibility and impact that it deserves.

There are many Christians who know the *facts* of the Bible. Still many others know the *content* of the gospel. Why are some of them more effective teachers, preachers, and witnesses where so many others fail? Two people may have similar knowledge, education, and even a close walk with the Lord, yet one of them is more effective as a communicator. What makes the difference?

The great contrast is that—either intuitively or intentionally—great communicators have learned how to become "first brain-friendly." They know how to befriend the gatekeeper within their listeners—and thus they know how to get past the emotions so that people *really* hear them.

CHAPTER 13
The Essence of Energy

Spoken communication is so much more powerful than the written word because it delivers on so many more channels. The written word is like a black-and-white photograph, while spoken communication is high-definition color television!

Written words on a page communicate content well. Spoken words are better to create action. Spoken words carry more than just the face value of the words; they carry *passion*.

The written word tends to lie on the page, picked up by the passive but powerful eye. The spoken word captures the eye as well, but has to have energy behind it to stimulate the eye and reach the ear. Energy is a stimulus to the first brain. Whenever the first brain senses energy in communication, it swings the gate wide open. Important messages—the messages that can mean life or death—are usually delivered with great energy. Warnings of danger, the announcement of a birth, or a call to arms would be carried on waves of excitement and animation. Conversely, messages of relative unimportance almost always *lack* energy. No one gets excited about a comment about the weather—unless a tornado is on the way!

Imagine the impact this has on teaching, preaching, sharing the gospel, or coaching a Little League team! And imagine how ineffective you become when you ignore such a key.

The enthusiasm and passion of a speaker is contagious. When you think of the great teachers you have had, you probably will remember most that they were excited about their subject. Their teaching style made it abundantly clear that they were passionate about their subject; they *loved* it. These examples, along with hundreds of others from politics and popular culture, remind us that our information is more caught than taught.

Do not miss the point. We desire only to show you that history leads us to the inescapable conclusion that communicators are able to get people to see things their way. They get people to like and accept *them*, and then they have a platform for their *message*. Failure to communicate cannot be redeemed by brilliance, intelligence, sincerity, or even truth. No matter how great one's message, it cannot change those it does not reach.

DIVINE POWER AND HUMAN MEANS

In some ways there is a tension between our dependence on the inherent power of the Word and our need to communicate well. We dare not think that our skill and ability can save anyone or make him or her grow in grace. We must constantly check ourselves lest we lapse from a commitment to excellence into claiming a share of God's glory. But by the same token, if we excuse our own laziness and do not use every tool at our disposal, we presume on God. We might as well not study, improve our education, learn vocabulary, or concern ourselves with our appearance. Remember: the better we are at communicating, the less people notice *us* and the more they see *God*.

If we really understand the incredible power inherent in the gospel, and if we have experienced the power of the resurrection ourselves, how can we be unmoved and dispassionate about it?

Energy, passion, conviction—these are the *essential* ingredients of Christian communication. Enthusiasm

In my library are about a thousand volumes of biography—a rough calculation indicates that more of these deal with men who have talked themselves upward than with all the scientists, writers, saints and doers combined.

Talkers have always ruled.

They will continue to rule.

The smart thing is to join them.

BRUCE BARTON
(1886–1967)

and passion are not optional equipment; they are critically important because the treasure of truth we handle is worth it. No other message in the world deserves such excitement and intensity.

THE AFFECT-METER

"Affect" is a term used by psychologists to describe the "feelings" side of our human makeup—our emotions, moods, and temperament. The Affect-meter is a visual representation of physical and emotional energy and enthusiasm. To have "0 percent affect" is to have no emotional energy, to be completely unexpressive, flat, monotonous, colorless, and lifeless. To have "100 percent affect" is to be totally buoyant, exuberant, animated, and excited. The Affect-meter swings according to how much energy we feel free to express. For some of us, unfortunately, the pointer has gotten stuck somewhere during our emotional development.

From birth to two years old, a human being is at full affect (maximum emotional energy). He expresses himself with virtually no inhibition at all.

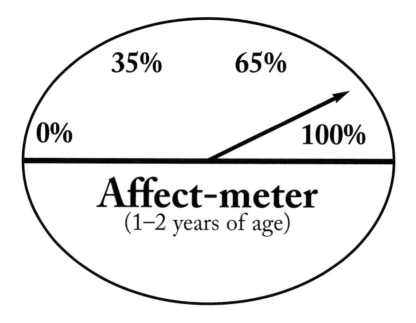

During the years from two to twelve, the momentum begins swinging to the left, toward narrow affect (minimum emotional energy). The natural exuberance of the child is gradually suppressed and deadened during the socialization process—a process that has both an up side and a down side. In most people, this process gets out of balance, the meter swinging way over toward low energy/affect. The result is repression and inhibition.

During the teenage years, thirteen to nineteen, even though actual stifling has usually stopped, the meter remains down at narrow affect, resulting in the phase I call "the unexpressed years." This is the last habit pattern the child experiences, and the unrelenting forces of adolescent peer

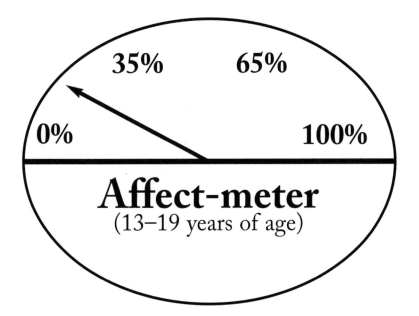

pressure reinforce this habit with a vengeance. Few teenagers escape the emotional pitfalls of the unexpressed years, and the adolescent patterns of awkwardness and shyness usually harden into inhibited adulthood.

It is the exceptional young adult who has both the strong self-image and natural energy to break through this shell of repression on his own. Our inhibiting habit patterns continue to form and harden during the years from twenty to thirty.

It's easy to see how we got the way we are. From our earliest years on into our twenties, thirties, and beyond, we have been subject to forces and pressures to conform, to fit in, to be correct. These are all inhibiting forces, pushing us deep into the pit of minimal emotional energy.

But we don't have to remain there. We *can* learn to push the meter back to where it belongs—indeed, where it has *always* belonged.

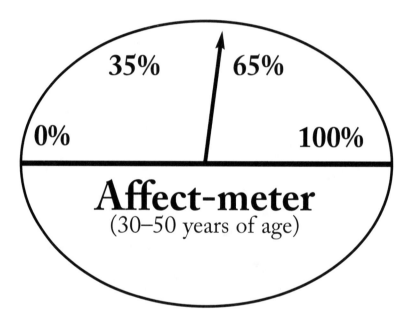

FULLY EXPRESSIVE COMMUNICATION

The most effective communicators are those who are expressive—yet fully in control. They are alive with energy, but they know boundaries. They consciously control the affect-meter in their own behavior. Very few of us have that kind of control. Instead, we are driven by unconscious habits laid down when we were children.

To become effective, we must *relearn* how to be fully expressive. We must *rediscover* the uninhibited state of the two-year-old, yet govern that expressiveness with the conscious control of a mature adult. We must consciously choose for the sake of our message to push that meter back to where it belongs.

The "Forward Lean" of Life

One of the simplest and easiest ways to communicate energetically and in a way that exudes confidence is to stand in what is called the "ready position." That simply means stand with your weight forward, your knees slightly flexed so that you can bounce on the balls of your feet. You feel like an athlete ready to move quickly and easily in any direction. With your weight forward like this it is impossible to slouch on one hip or to rock back on your heels.

This position is one of those subconscious triggers that tell your listeners you are excited and interested in what you are saying. The lack of energy and a posture that leans away signals just the opposite—apathy and disinterest. When you are speaking confidently from a self-assured stance and attitude, your energy is directed forward, both physically and psychologically, toward your listener.

The reason why we are introducing you to this bit of information is that we want this position to serve as a metaphor for your global attitude toward communication. Like the child who has great "affect," you are not inhibited, but excited. Your attitude about sharing the message God has given you is a forward lean! You are ready to flow rather than freeze. You are excited rather than nervous, anxious rather than reluctant. Everything about you must convey that, above all else, you *believe* in God's message and in your message. You are completely committed to the truth that you declare, whether it is sharing the gospel with a neighbor, teaching a lesson to your class, or telling your fourteen-year-old that you love her.

Sameness Is the Enemy

So for the Christian communicator, sameness is the enemy. If our message becomes mundane or has a routine tone, the natural mind can easily ignore it. In essence, the ears may hear it but it never goes any deeper. Some preachers preach loud all the time, even to the point of screaming, but it still has little impact because that is *all* they do. Others are monotone, while still others are very predictable; they *always* get loud at the same moments. Parishioners subconsciously learn to shut them out, just like the person who lives next to a railroad track never notices the train.

Preachers are not the only people with this problem. Many Christians feel a burden to share their faith, so they memorize a canned presentation. But relying on rote memory has made them sound unenthusiastic and uninterested. The result is that there are no waves of energy to carry the message. The first brain senses a conflicting signal and gives greater weight to the visual and vocal than to the verbal.

Physical movement and energy are important for the same reason. We always find listening to a speaker who moves much easier than giving our attention to someone who just stands there. The brain is designed to notice movement as opposed to stillness.

Imagine that you are looking at a room full of furniture. No people or animals are in the room—only furniture, drapes, carpet, and wall hangings. The only sound you hear is the ticking of a grandfather clock against the wall. You watch the room for several minutes, then your eye catches movement in one corner. A drape flutters in the wind, making only a slight noise, but the interruption in the visual field and in the slight noise from the same area draw your attention like a magnet. Your mind is drawn to the energy, the break in the sameness.

To speak with bold assurance, you have to exhibit energy so compelling that it will draw and hold the interest of your hearers. You need to speak with a passion that fits and highlights the great message God has given you. Get your information past the first brain so your listeners will *really see and hear* what you have to say.

Chapter 14

The Behavioral Skills

Effective communication is a wonderful balance between delivery and content, style and substance. Great communicators pay close attention to both elements. In addition, Christian communicators have the potential to become the greatest communicators in the world. If our message is biblical, then it is unquestionably true and has the inherent power of the Holy Spirit that transcends any human message or capacity. In addition, the confidence that comes from knowing we can do all things through Christ who strengthens us and our deep conviction of the truth of the Word of God gives us the bold assurance that is essential to connect with our hearers.

Such certainty should urge us into the "forward lean" that convinces our listeners of our excitement, passion, and conviction. We become a tool in God's hands that he uses to influence and persuade others that they need the assurance we exhibit. Never forget that a sovereign God has chosen the means of "the foolishness of preaching" as the primary means of sharing the Word of God and spreading the truth. It is a powerful method of spreading a powerful message.

A Word Worthy of Work

It would be a great sin to present God's message in an unworthy manner. God gave us the tools of communication so that we might *best* relay his message to others. This keeps us willing to work so we might give God's Word the presentation that befits its divine origin. An ambassador must convey the *content* of his sovereign; he must also convey the *character* and *temperament* of the one who sent him.

Most Christians would be shocked to discover how much God says in his Word about communicating. The common theme in almost all of those passages is *power*—complete confidence in *God's* power. Paul, for instance, reminded the Corinthian believers that he came to them "in weakness and fear, and with much trembling" (1 Cor. 2:3). But that was only how he *felt*, not how he came across. What they witnessed was that his "message and (his) preaching were not with wise and persuasive words, but with a demonstration of the Spirit's power." The result was that they believed because their faith rested on that demonstration of God's power conveyed through Paul's demeanor (1 Cor. 2:4–5).

Many people have used this very passage to teach exactly the opposite of what Paul is saying. They argue that since Paul seemed to be decrying the rhetoric and technique of his contemporaries, we should not use any type of human methodology. The power, they argue, rests solely in the *content* of the message, never in the *communication* of that message.

The question we must ask and answer, therefore, is what exactly *was* the demonstration of power to which Paul referred. If we really believed that *only* content matters, then we would have no need of anything but written communication. Pastors could merely mail manuscripts of messages to their members. The function of Sunday school teachers would be reduced to reading the lessons or the study guide. Sales personnel would never have to meet with potential customers; they could just e-mail them the appropriate information.

As important as content is—and it is essential and central to communication—it needs a conduit of communication, a method of transmitting it from one person to another. No one knew that better than those who heard the apostle Paul preach.

Picture what his first-century hearers witnessed. He must have been horribly scarred, having suffered beatings, flagellation, stoning, and the ravages of life on the road in an inhospitable environment. Tradition holds that he suffered near blindness. His life and freedom were threatened every time he opened his mouth to preach the gospel. They might scorn him or slight him, imprison or beat him, but he would not be intimidated into silence or retreat. No personal discomfort would diminish his passion. He was not afraid of any consequence except disobedience to the will of God.

This kind of fearlessness in the face of danger has always won an audience. People are moved by men and women who feel their message is worth the risk of death. *That* really is a demonstration of power!

To have the content and substance that gives our words power, we must saturate ourselves with the Word of God. We systematically and painstakingly study the Scriptures to learn life-giving and life-changing truth.

Improving our delivery and style so that we can best convey God's truth requires no less commitment. Just as a pastor must pay attention to his skill as an exegete and an expositor, so must all communicators learn how to develop the nine communication skills that make them most effective.

THE PARADOX OF PREACHING

Have you ever been in a worship service when someone sang a solo . . . who really *shouldn't* sing a solo? She rose nervously, bringing her sheet music with her. Hardly looking up from her music, she still botched the words. Her voice cracked as she tried in vain to hit the high notes. And to make matters worse, she was singing a Sandi Patti song that goes far into the upper register at the end—and you *dread* it coming!

Think back to that moment. How did you feel? Were you embarrassed for her? Did you twist in your seat a little bit? Were you anxious for the song to end? Did you pray for her, asking God to help her out of her misery, maybe even to endue her miraculously with a talent that she obviously did not have? You probably did all of these things. But we can almost guarantee what you did *not* do: you did not worship. It really didn't matter how great the song was, how true the lyrics, how beautiful the melody line. Her poor treatment of it robbed you of any chance to experience it as a time to worship the Lord—who was the subject of the song.

But contrast that with the times when you were in a service and someone who really knew what she was doing sang a solo. She did not rely on written music because she knew the song. With the first five seconds of the song, you felt at ease and not the least bit nervous for her because *she* was at ease and in control. Her face radiated peace and praise. You could really hear the words of the song because she sang so clearly and expressively. And after the first ten seconds of thinking, "Wow, is she good!" you really began to worship through the presentation of the song. It was as if she escorted you right into God's throne room.

Now shift your mind from singing to preaching. Can a congregation really hear the Word of God, can they worship, can they learn effectively if that message from God's Word is presented by someone who distracts them? *This* is the paradox of preaching. The better you are, the less people notice you. The greater your ability to present God's Word, the less you get in the way and the freer your listeners are to hear the message and to respond personally. And *that* is why we take the time to learn how to communicate better.

THE NINE COMMUNICATION SKILLS

Do you remember the nine skills that serve as the communicator's tools? These nine skills are the basis of good delivery and style that serve as the conduit for our message to reach the listener.

- Eye communication—the ability to make and maintain eye contact in a meaningful way.
- Gestures and facial expression—animation communicated through your face and body that corresponds with your message and conveys energy.
- Posture and movement—reflecting confidence and energy in your body position and movement.
- Dress and appearance—presenting yourself in a way that does not detract from the message you want your hearer to grasp.
- Voice and vocal variety—using pitch, volume, and vocal energy that will keep your listener engaged in the content of what you are saying.

- Words and fillers—using language that is replete with meaning, effective pauses, and devoid of "fillers"—those annoying "ums," "ahs," and meaningless phrases such as "whatever," "you know," "like," and "I mean."
- Humor—a healthy sense of humor about yourself and life in general that makes you approachable and likable.
- Listener involvement—involving yourself with your listeners in order to help them listen.
- The natural self—being *real*—using these communication parameters to let the real you come through without seeming stiff or phony.

If you want to develop your speaking ability, you must work on practicing these skills. In the following section you will learn each of these skills more fully as well as some practical exercises that will help you implement them.

These exercises are simple, but they are powerful. Beware of two responses that you might feel. First, "I already know that. I don't need to work on that." These exercises are designed to change what you do, not what you know. Even if you *know* them, you won't do them unless you consciously make yourself practice until you get to the place where you do them naturally and unconsciously.

The second response is "This feels silly. I don't think this will do anything." Almost anything feels silly the first time. Trust us—there is a disparity between how you feel and how you look! What really feels silly is when you have the opportunity to speak but you do it poorly because you have not learned to take control of these communication skills. The benefits you will experience almost immediately are worth any temporary discomfort you may feel.

These exercises are a new behavioral vocabulary for effective communicators. They develop a sensitivity and a control over your behavior as they help you learn how to open the first brain in your listeners so your content can get in. They may seem simple, even common sense, but if they are not executed you will never be as effective as you could be.

Skill 1: Eye Communication

> *"An eye can threaten like a loaded and leveled gun;*
> *or can insult like hissing and kicking;*
> *or in its altered mood by beams of kindness,*
> *make the heart dance with joy."*
> —RALPH WALDO EMERSON

Objective: To look at another person steadily and confidently

The primary skill for gaining credibility is the ability to make and to maintain eye contact. It has the greatest impact in both one-on-one communications and large group communications. Your eyes literally connect your mind to someone else's since your eyes are the only part of your central nervous system that are in direct contact with another human being. When your eyes meet the eyes of another person, you make a first-brain-to-first-brain connection. When you fail to make that connection, it matters little what you say.

Many people are not even aware that they do not use their eyes effectively. There are several common problems that we need to overcome or avoid.

What Others Do

Eye dart. Rhoda Bantry is a wonderful Christian mother who would like to have a greater impact in her church. But even in casual conversation after worship services, her eyes flit about like a child looking in a toy store. If she keeps them still at all, she usually looks at the person's shoulder rather than into her eyes. It gives others the feeling that she is hiding something. The minister of education won't ask her to teach a class because he knows how people feel when they speak with her. She fails to connect with the first brain, and people find her eye-dart distracting and annoying. Predictably, she has little impact even though she has great insight into the Scriptures.

Greener-grass gaze. John Loudon is a typical Type A personality. Full of energy and zest, he usually makes people feel unimportant and as though they are wasting his time. When he is talking to someone in the lobby before the service, he is always looking around at who is walking by, searching for people he has to connect with, and occasionally waving to a passing acquaintance while conversing with someone else. He gives obligatory nods to the people he is talking to, but they see him looking elsewhere.

Prayer eyes. Jerry Walker is a young pastor in a small church who has to do *everything,* including leading worship. Sometimes, when he is singing, he closes his eyes and tilts his head back as though looking upward. But often when he is preaching he will go into that same closed-eye mode. He will keep his eyes closed for as much as five seconds at a time between glances at the congregation. This habit carries over into his personal conversations too, and his parishioners tend to view him as cold and detached—the exact opposite of the way Jerry sees himself, and certainly not the way he wants to be perceived. Could it be that some of the tensions he feels around the church are not caused so much by any doctrinal differences, but by his undiagnosed "slo-blink?"

What You Can Do

Do you see yourself in one or more of these examples? If so, there's hope! These eye communication problems are curable. Don't assume that just making "eye contact" is enough. "Eye contact" implies a short glance will connect, but good eye communication means *really looking at an individual*—making a first-brain-to-first-brain connection.

Use involvement rather than intimidation or intimacy. When you look at a person for a long time, you are either staring down or gazing longingly. To look at someone for twenty or thirty uninterrupted seconds would make most listeners feel uncomfortable. But, quite frankly, few speakers struggle with looking at listeners too long. Most exhibit the opposite tendencies, even though most of our communications call for involvement.

Look for five seconds. How then can you achieve that appropriate level of eye communication? How can you be certain that you have looked at audience members enough, but not too much? The answer is to *count to five.*

A feeling of involvement requires about five seconds of steady eye contact, the time we normally take to complete a thought or a sentence. When we talk to another person and are excited, enthusiastic, and confident, we communicate best by looking at him or her for five to ten seconds. This is one way that a speaker before a large audience can still make each of them feel that they are individually important.

One warning is in order, however. If you are not accustomed to good eye communication, it will feel weird the first time you do it. Five seconds seems like an eternity. But the results are worth the temporary discomfort, so push beyond your comfort zone for longer eye communication. You'll get used to the change of habit.

Beware of eye dart and slo-blink. When we lack confidence or feel the pressure, our instinct is to avoid the eyes of our listener. We think we can hide our nervousness or lack of confidence, but the opposite is true. The listener can read our anxiety and it subconsciously undermines our message. Like a scared rabbit, we exude the "aroma" of fear.

In addition to eye dart, beware of slo-blink. Whenever a person closes his or her eyes for up to two or three seconds, the listener intuits that the message is unexciting and unimportant. Slo-blink communicates "I don't really want to be here. Even I am bored with what I am saying." Listeners don't require a lot of time to determine that they feel the same way.

Get on video. For all of these eye communication deficiencies, as well as for many other problems you will encounter, one exercise stands head and shoulders above the rest. The quickest and most effective cure can be found in getting *video feedback*. Make a video tape of yourself speaking and then watch it carefully, focusing especially on your eye movements. Notice your length of contact and the idiosyncrasies like eye dart or slo-blink. Before watching yourself on tape you may be unaware of your habits and movements, but the tape will not lie!

Practice, practice, practice. Another helpful exercise is to *practice one-on-one* at every opportunity. Ask a faithful friend to notice your eye movements during a normal conversation. Have him count the number of times you blink, shift your gaze, look away, or make eye contact. Get an average count of how long you tend to look at a person. Work at increasing your time until you can look at an individual for at least five seconds or more.

Even when you are alone, you can *practice with a paper audience.* By sticking Post-it notes with little happy faces on them around the room, you can get accustomed to looking at audience members for five seconds or more. Stick the notes on chairs, on the wall, or just around the room. Be certain that you put a face at the far fringes of the room, next to the corners so you learn to include the entire audience. As you make your presentation to your paper audience, focus on each individual, but work the whole room, corner to corner. As outlined below, you can also practice your movement with this exercise.

Even when you are watching television you can increase your awareness and "eye savvy" by noticing real people in pressure situations. Observe people being interviewed, conversing with someone on a talk show, or making extemporaneous political commentary. Watch those news shows where interviewers put the heat on and get their subjects on the defensive. Notice how you feel about the person based on his or her response. Do you notice more what he says, or *how* he says it? The first brain reveals itself primarily through eye communication. You can notice the unmistakable signs of fear, anger, confidence, credibility, or disbelief. Sensitize yourself to the importance of eye communication and how it enhances or betrays a speaker's credibility and general likability.

As you use these exercises and eye communication becomes habitual, you will notice that you feel less nervous and you appear confident. Remember that it is not a problem for you to *feel* nervous, only to *appear* nervous. As you gain experience, you learn how to convert that nervousness into a positive energy that propels you forward. This breeds confidence, focuses your thoughts, and motivates your audience. You convey the power of your message through your eyes more than through any other single avenue of communication, so it is worth all the effort and practice.

Skill 2: Gestures and Facial Expression

Objective: To be relaxed and natural—open and energetic

The first brain is always sizing up whether or not a speaker *really* believes his message. One of the primary measurements that it takes is the level of animation. To communicate successfully, you must be enthused, excited, and speak with conviction and passion. Your listener's first brain is automatically and immediately determining how you *feel* about what you are saying.

An open-armed gesture and a warm, open smile is welcoming. It invites the listener in as your smile dominates your listener's impression of you and of your message. A smile shows on your mouth and around your eyes. It demonstrates openness, amiability, and credibility. The first brain just naturally closes the shutters on a closed body and a face that is not smiling. It may even perceive the messenger as a threat.

The visual component of spoken communication is the most critical, and it is decided largely by your level of gesture and facial expression. These reveal our inner state and when active and open propel our message with energy and emotional force.

What Others Do

Convicting passion. Think of Billy Graham as he preaches. Hundreds of thousands of people who are otherwise hostile to the gospel still watch him on television or attend his crusades because they see in him a conviction and a passion. Even if they do not believe his message, many still listen because they know *he* believes it. His open gestures and his gentle and fatherly smile are convincing evidence that his message is genuine. No one—kings, presidents, or peasants—feels threatened by Billy Graham, even if they reject his message. Graham makes certain that his manner never gets in the way of his message, but enhances it

Wooden gestures. Although there are many variables to winning an election, the ability of a candidate to communicate is one of the most important. Former vice president Al Gore has had a very difficult time with this—almost solely due to his stiff posture, wooden gestures, and stoic facial expression.

What You Can Do

Find your nervous gesture. Video feedback may reveal that you suffer from one or more common gesture problems. Obviously one's message can easily get lost in the distraction that any nervous gesture causes! Find out what your nervous gesture is (we each have one) and do anything but that one.

In order to take your speaking to the next level, use video feedback to find your nervous gesture—and then stop making it. There is usually some place our hands seem to stray when we are speaking. Do you grip the pulpit? Do you tug at your sleeves? Do your hands slip into your pockets? Let your gestures arise naturally from your enthusiasm and emphasis. That cannot happen if your hands are locked in a habit.

Hands at your sides when not "in use." Often we feel awkward when we let our hands rest at our sides—but it looks composed and centered as a rest position. Watch to see how few people actually do that, and how effective it can be as a base for gesturing.

Remember that there is a principle of disparity at work. If you are basically introverted and unaccustomed to using gestures, the slightest hand movement may feel like you are making windmills with your arms. If you watch yourself on video, however, you will see that your movement is not exaggerated at all.

Express yourself. Escape the poverty caused by communications gridlock and express yourself freely in both gestures and facial expression.

Practice by exaggerating. Exaggerate your gestures and your facial expressions. Video yourself and see if you can go over the top. Can you gesture too much? Smile too much? Try it, then watch the video. You'll see that *you cannot over-exaggerate.* Not only will you learn that your gestures and smiles look good and are effective, but you will defuse your inhibitions and become less fearful. If you practice in situations where you can experiment and in which you feel no pressure, you will automatically be *bigger* without thinking about it when you are in a more critical situation.

One of the greatest methods of practice is to *imitate an "Expressor,"* someone who is an expressive role model. It doesn't even have to be someone you like, just someone you can have fun imitating in an uninhibited way. Try to get inside his skin. Watch a video of an expressive preacher like Adrian Rogers, and then pretend that you are him. Imitate his movement, his gestures, his expressive face. Maybe some secular comedian like Phyllis Diller, Robin Williams, or Mel Brooks would be a good exercise. Try to *become* that energetic, expressive person, and you will discover and unharness your own hidden energy.

Smile to become first brain-friendly. A person with a natural unsmiling face may, upon first trying to smile, feel that he is exhibiting the most toothsome grin in history. Others, watching the same event, may be thinking, "Why is he so grim?" In reality few people truly exaggerate their gestures or facial expressions, no matter how hard they try to do it. Remember the fact of disparity. Just video yourself trying to overdo it, and you will be stunned when you watch it. The gestures and expressions that seemed so over the top will look very natural and appropriate on video.

Another problem that undermines your message is neglecting to smile appropriately. You need not grin like a Cheshire cat to get your point across, but failing to smile when you are telling the Good News is unforgivable. Parents undermine their relationship with their children, employers harm their employees, and pastors lose their congregations when they fail to smile. If you think of the people you most enjoy being with, you will realize that most of them smile a lot.

Lift your apples. If you find that you have trouble smiling, think of the upper part of your cheeks as apples. Smiling is just "lifting your apples," but what a difference it makes in your communication.

Have you ever thought about why little children wanted to be around Jesus? Nothing attracts little children and makes them feel more secure than a smile. Very early they learn that smiling people comfort them, care for them, coddle them. People who don't smile tend to neglect them, scold them, even hurt them. For the rest of our lives we feel drawn to smiling people. It makes little sense to tell people that Jesus is the greatest man who ever lived, that he offers the greatest gift ever given, and that this is the best news they have ever heard— and to do it without a smile! Lift those apples!

> *"An unfriendly man pursues selfish ends; he defies all sound judgment."*
> PROVERBS 18:1

Your smile even affects you! It lifts your spirits. It generates more energy. You feel the smile throughout your whole body! But beware—phony smiles don't work. Quite frankly, they look phony. We aren't suggesting that you learn how to fake it. We are suggesting that you comprehend that your message is good news and that you let it give you a real smile.

You will find that good gestures and a smile will free you to share your thoughts fully. You will find a ready audience, because when you smile, the world smiles with you. Your gestures show your openness that people find inviting. The gestures you use naturally emphasize your most important points and concepts as your movement highlights your content. A warm smile and kinetic gestures go a long way toward demonstrating the bold assurance that God has given you through his Word.

SKILL 3: POSTURE AND MOVEMENT

> *"Stand tall. The difference between towering and cowering is totally a matter of inner posture. It's got nothing to do with height, it costs nothing and it's more fun."*
> —MALCOLM FORBES

Objective: To stand tall and move with an ease and confidence

Think of the best speakers you know. Preachers, politicians, or presidents may qualify. Are any of them "slumpers?" Can you imagine Ronald Reagan in Berlin, lazily *slouching* as he demands, "Mr. Gorbachev, tear down this wall!" There aren't many slumpers to be found among elite communicators, and for good reason. Confidence is expressed through good, upright posture. Your physical position reflects your mental readiness, and it is a decisive factor in how others see you and judge the credibility of your message.

A speaker with poor posture fails to appreciate that people make assumptions in the first few seconds they meet someone. They make assumptions about the speaker's level of confidence, competence, and credibility. Poor posture undermines the trust and openness of our listeners.

Tall people often hunch over because they grew fast or early and perhaps felt self-conscious. Height, however, was not the problem—consciousness was. Still others slump because of a related weakness; they stick their nose in a manuscript or notes, so they slouch over to read them.

What Others Do

The power of movement. Few pastors in America have had a greater impact on younger preachers than Adrian Rogers, pastor of the Bellevue Baptist Church in Memphis, Tennessee. From the moment he strides onto the platform until his exit after the last amen, Rogers's posture and movement communicates a readiness and attunement to the worship service that sets the tone for everyone in the 7,000-seat sanctuary. During the musical worship, Rogers sits directly facing the audience with back straight, sitting tall and erect, with both feet planted on the floor, looking as though he is ready to spring into action at any moment. When it's time for him to welcome guests, the pastor moves with excitement, confidence, and purpose. While preaching Rogers also moves resolutely about the platform. No one doubts that he *owns* that space.

Credibility slouches. Author and commentator William F. Buckley is one of America's brightest and most colorful personalities, but he is better read than watched. Often on television to expound his views, he slouches in his chair as though he can barely stay awake, occasionally widening his narrow eyes, stuttering through broken sentences, and rarely changing his tone. He has such a keen mind and wit, think of how powerful he could be if his posture matched the alertness of his intellect.

Acting the part. Jim was a bright seminarian, but he was terrified to stand in front of a crowd and teach a lesson or preach. He had finally resigned himself to becoming a military chaplain because he thought that would require little public speaking. The first time he preached in a seminary classroom he was frightened and his posture showed it. With coaching and feedback he learned to stand erect, to move confidently about the platform, and to use a forward lean. The more adept he became at *looking* confident, the more confident he actually became. By the end of the semester, Jim was an assured and accomplished speaker. Within a few months he became the pastor of a church where he had a great impact and grew to love the very thing that had once intimidated him.

What You Can Do

Stand tall. Posture and poise go together, so stand with your shoulders back and your stomach in. Stand straight and move naturally, knees slightly bent rather than locked and rigid.

Watch your lower body. You may limit your effectiveness and negate your energy if you rock back on one hip. This communicates that you really don't want to be there and distances you from your listeners, even in casual conversations. Common variations of this mistake are rocking from side to side or going forward and back from heel to toe.

"Forward lean" in thought and deed. Think of the concept of "forward lean" as not only something to do, but a way to be. This means that you always are in a state of readiness—leaning forward to volunteer, to do, to say. Physically you will lean slightly forward, knees somewhat flexed. Keep your weight on the balls of your feet. Like an athlete, you can get in the ready position. You are ready and able to move easily and quickly in any direction. Communication rides on energy, and your posture indicates either interest and energy and a "forward lean," or else it communicates apathy and disinterest and a laying back. Direct your energy forward, physically and psychologically, toward your listener. In this position you are always ready to communicate in any situation, formal or informal.

Move. No matter how strong the temptation to stay in one place, whether behind a pulpit or a lectern, resist that temptation! Get out and move, and you will make emotional contact with your listeners. You will convey excitement, enthusiasm, and confidence in your movement. Remove any physical obstacle between you and your audience—which is the traditional lectern or podium. They are great note holders, but also great energy blockers. Move to the side.

Be careful of pacing back and forth, but move in a natural and purposeful way. Let your eye communication motivate your movement so that you move toward the person you are looking at. Take at least two steps at a time rather than a single tentative step. If you normally stand behind a lectern, come out from behind it and push yourself to get at least two steps away. This forces you to direct your energy forward and to remove the barriers between you and your audience.

Practice an easy exercise. You can practice both posture and movement by standing straight against a wall, your heels, buttocks, and head all touching the wall. Now walk away from the wall, being careful to hold that erect posture. You may feel stiff, but rest assured that you look great. If you want to video yourself to see the disparity in how it feels and how it looks, then go ahead. You will be convinced. You *can* improve your posture.

Like the eye exercise, you can also *practice with a paper audience*. With Post-it notes stuck around the room, give your presentation and let your eye communication motivate your movement. Move to one side of the room, plant your feet in the ready position, make good eye communication with your paper audience, then move directly and purposefully to the other side and do the same thing there.

As always, *use video feedback to watch posture and movement.* While other people can give you feedback and share their opinions, they are subjective and may not notice some things. The video captures all and is objective. And as you push yourself to stand erect, focus forward on your audience and move out and connect with them, you will see that it looks great on video. You appear natural, relaxed, and confident. Bold assurance becomes the hallmark of your presentation because you feel taller, you look more confident, and your movement energizes both you and your audience.

SKILL 4: DRESS AND APPEARANCE

*"You never get a second chance
to make a good first impression."*
—JOHN MOLLOY

OBJECTIVE: TO BE APPROPRIATE TO YOUR ENVIRONMENT IN DRESS AND GROOMING

After posture, the most immediate visual impression we make on our listener's first brain is that of our dress and appearance. The impressions made in the first three seconds are so vivid that it takes another three minutes to add fifty percent more impression—whether negative or positive. Since those first three seconds are almost entirely visual, our appearance determines the immediate receptivity of our audience. So if we make a poor first impression, even before we open our mouth, it takes a long time and a lot of work to overcome it.

Our dress and appearance are a crucial part of communicating who we are—our values, our self-image, and our self-respect. Whether we sport a three-piece pin-striped suit or a green mohawk, we choose our look to communicate something about ourselves. We are sending a message. Our goal is not to impress our audience, but to make them feel comfortable and to have a sense of identification with us. Our dress should not only be appropriate to who we are, but it should also be consistent with our message as well.

What Others Do

Right coat in the right place. Ever since Joseph wore his coat of many colors, clothes and appearance have communicated a message. More than that, our appearance affects the way we feel about ourselves. Shawn Miller prided himself on his casual approach to ministry. He was convinced that he was going to be approachable, casual, and comfortable in the ministry, so he preached in jeans, flannel shirts, and he let his hair grow long. If Shawn had been pastoring in lumberjack country, his strategy may have worked. Unfortunately, his church was in a suburban, upscale community. Church members were so embarrassed by his appearance that they felt uncomfortable inviting others to church, even though his preaching was otherwise biblical and engaging. His dress was just too great an obstacle, however, and soon he found himself faced with losing half his church or his job.

Appropriate to the setting. In past years great preachers like W. A. Criswell of First Baptist Church, Dallas, Texas, or R. G. Lee of Bellevue Baptist in Memphis were identified by their bright white suits and fresh boutonnieres. Today pastors like Rick Warren of Saddleback Valley Community Church in Southern California or Bill Hybels of Willow Creek in Chicago can get away with golf shirts, no ties, and even Hawaiian shirts (in Warren's case). Corporate America has established casual dress as the norm on Fridays. Neither a white suit nor a Hawaiian shirt can fit all situations. What makes all of them successful is that they dressed *appropriately* for their own cultural context.

What You Can Do

Be appropriate for your audience. Dress, fashion, and style vary according to place and time, so there are no hard and fast rules about *what* to wear, but there are a few basic guidelines that help us keep our message central and avoid the mistakes that undermine its impact.

First, be appropriate. Such a rule presupposes that you know your audience. If you are speaking somewhere for the first time, be sure you investigate enough to determine what dress is appropriate. Most churches, for instance, develop their own ecclesiastical culture that includes a certain mode of dress. Even as corporate America has adopted a more casual dress code, so have many churches. Others staunchly maintain a traditional "Sunday-best" fashion requirement. The point to keep in mind is that fitting in is worth it.

The best speakers always get themselves out of the way. In the very same way that nervous habits distract a listener from the message, so sloppy dress or even flashy fashion can force the wrong focus. An appropriate style of clothing that fits in with the surrounding culture is always best because it does not draw attention to the wrong thing.

Be appropriate to yourself. But you should also be appropriate to *yourself.* Be certain that your dress makes you feel comfortable and at ease with yourself. If you wear a tie, for instance, don't wear a shirt whose collar is too tight and tempts you to tug at it while you speak (not to mention that a tight collar is terrible for your vocal chords). Bear in mind the norms of the group, the social setting, the time of day, and the weather.

Remember these dress and appearance tips:
- Conservative dress is usually better for a spiritual message.
- Dress and groom up, not down. Better to overdress than to underdress if you are unable to know the norms ahead of time.
- Dress and groom at the conscious level rather than just according to habit. Don't just dress the same way you always have or wear the same colors. Ask if your mode of dress is effective. Make choices at the conscious level, especially mindful of how it will appear to those you want to influence.
- Remember that the first appearance *instantly* communicates how you feel about yourself and even about your audience.
- Button your jacket when you are standing. Some women's jackets are tailored to be unbuttoned, but men's suits and jackets are tailored to be buttoned for a "smart" look. It communicates a sharp, neat, and organized feel.

Get people feedback. To make sure you always look your best in an appropriate way, get people feedback. It is one area where people feedback may be more important than video feedback because style is subjective. It pays to find out what *others* think about your appearance, and you do that by asking. Men need to ask about clothing, hair, beard, and moustache (if you have one), and jewelry. Women should ask about clothing and accents, haircut and hairstyle, makeup, and jewelry. Seek honest appraisals from a variety of people. Explain that you value their opinion and that you really want to know because dress and appearance are important factors in fulfilling God's plan for your life.

Observe those around you. In addition to the personal feedback you get from others, you should also be extra observant. Read current magazines on style. If you hear a great speaker, pay special attention to how his or her clothing contributes to your experience of him or her and your acceptance of the message. John Molloy's classic, *Dress for Success,* is a helpful, if opinionated, digest of extensive research on the subject. Above all, notice what others around you are wearing—but don't try to become a carbon copy of *anyone* else. Be yourself—but the best and smartest you possible!

As a result, you will feel confident in how you look. Eventually you will take less time in dressing and grooming because you will know what you are doing and why. Most important, you will make a positive and *lasting* impression that will add to your overall effectiveness.

The Visual Impact Skills

The above first four of the nine communication skills have one thing in common: they transform our *visual impact.* These are the skills that listeners will notice immediately, visually, and will cause them to let our message past the first brain. The next four are *energy skills,* which help us pack more energy into our message and help our listeners get involved with our message. As with the other skills, you will see how easy it is to put the energy factor into your communication and to experience the kind of impact you want when you speak.

SKILL 5: VOICE AND VOCAL VARIETY

*"The Devil hath not, in all his quiver's choice,
An arrow for the heart like a sweet voice."*
—BYRON

OBJECTIVE: TO USE YOUR VOICE AS A RICH, RESONANT INSTRUMENT

Your voice is a wonderfully expressive instrument, a tool with a range of ability with infinite possibility and precision. Few people stop to think about their voice, but great communicators pay special attention to their "instrument."

Your voice is the vehicle that carries your message. While some people treat it like an old truck, you should realize that it is a Porsche. You can push it, open it up, and let it soar. The voice is the primary means of transmitting the energy you have and infusing your message with a sense of direction and importance.

The first brain is finely attuned to the voice. It hears nuance and seeks meaning in volume, pitch, and especially, in tone. A single word can reveal volumes of information about you. If you are skeptical, just make a phone call to some people whom you know well. Listen to them as they say hello. Often you can tell if they are rushed, aggravated, disturbed by the interruption, in a good mood, or excited. How many arguments have married couples waged over the tone or volume of a single word? Parents often recognize the attitude of their teens by taking notice of their tone or speech pattern.

The human voice has an infinite variety and capacity to communicate meaning that goes far beyond the bare dictionary meaning of the words. You are undoubtedly aware of this capacity when you listen to others, but have you ever listened to your own voice on tape? Were you pleased or embarrassed? Perhaps you said something like, "That doesn't sound like me!" In reality, the voice on the tape is truer to your "real" voice than the one you hear as you speak. The voice on tape is carried by sound waves through the air, but the voice you hear in your head travels by vibration through the bones in your head.

What Others Do

A memorable voice from the past. Martin Luther King's "I Have a Dream" speech, given from the steps of the Lincoln memorial, is one of the greatest and most memorable speeches in American history. King's greatest tool was his voice. Every American who has heard that speech can still conjure up its clear echoes in memory. His lilting vibrato, the quickening pace of his words, the rise and fall of his pitch are forever recorded in the national consciousness. Can you imagine King's speech in a monotone?

A memorable voice from the present. During the impeachment trial of President Clinton, most Americans got their first glimpse of Lloyd John Ogilvie, chaplain of the United States Senate. Every day before the legal battle began, Ogilvie would stand beside the chief justice and lead in a prayer. Although the proceedings themselves attracted controversy, Ogilvie's voice, perhaps the deepest *basso profundo* ever heard on American television, received unanimity in comment by the pundits and observers. When he speaks, his voice filled the Senate chamber like God thundering from Mount Sinai or speaking from heaven.

What You Can Do

Record yourself. To hear ourselves as others hear us, we have to record ourselves—whether on the phone, in casual conversation, in a meeting, or giving a formal speech. Though you may find listening to yourself a bit uncomfortable at first, it is worth it because a recording is the only way you can really know how much energy you transmit when you speak. And if you really hear your voice, you'll be able to change your voice.

Make your voice naturally authoritative. Not everyone is blessed with a deep, resonant, and authoritative voice like James Earl Jones or Adrian Rogers, but everyone can learn how to speak in a lower register. With just a few minutes of practice and a conscious effort to speak in a lower voice, you can begin to develop a voice that more effectively gets and keeps attention.

Use the full range of your voice. God has given us an incredible vocal range, yet most people use only about 30 percent of that range when they speak. Treat your voice like a roller coaster. Let it change its pace and its pitch. Let it rise and fall with the meaning of your words. Make it express emotion and emphasize your message with appropriate changes in pitch. Remember that "sameness" is the enemy! A monotone voice, no matter how great the content, will put others to sleep. So lift that voice over the summit, then let it plummet. As you picture the roller coaster when you speak, it develops your range and makes you aware of your full vocal toolbox.

Be aware of your telephone voice. Remember Albert Mehrabian, whose research we cited earlier? Not only did he discover that the vocal and visual account for 93 percent of a person's appraisal of credibility, but he also found something important about the voice. His research indicates that your voice—intonation, resonance, and auditory delivery of your message—accounts for as much as *84 percent* of your emotional impact and believa-bility when people can't see you—such as on the phone or on an audiotape!

So the opinion a listener forms about the credibility or the level of importance of your message derives specifically from how you use your voice. Surprisingly, most people are less expressive and energetic on the phone than in person. Particularly in leaving voice mail messages, people tend to get "information heavy" and talk in a monotone. Your goal should be to use the kind of passion and energy on the phone that you would use in face-to-face situations.

Put a smile in your voice. Smile as you talk! Can't you hear a smile from happy people on the phone? Well, they can hear whether you are smiling or not, too. Smile as you practice with a tape recorder. You will be amazed at the difference you hear. As you become conscious of the emotional signals your voice sends, you become conscious of the importance of letting your voice show happiness, excitement, and enthusiasm.

Use voice mail. Many of us now have access to voice mail systems in our churches. It is growing fast in the home market too, so most people will be able to use it now, or soon, in a new way—to practice communication skills. Use it as a feedback tool. Send yourself a copy of a real message you are sending to a colleague or friend, and listen to the sound of your voice. Do it daily at first, then weekly. Begin experimenting with some of these concepts and hear your voice take on new life and give new meaning to your words.

SKILL 6: WORDS AND FILLERS

> *"Perhaps of all the creations of man,*
> *language is the most astonishing."*
> —LYTTON STRACHEY

OBJECTIVE: TO USE WORDS WELL, AND TO USE THE POWER OF THE PAUSE

To say that *words* are powerful and a great way to infuse our message may seem obvious. Yet a common way to undermine that power and to suck the life out of those words is through the use of what we call *fillers*—those words and nonwords that have no real meaning.

Let's take a moment to reflect on both of these and their respective effects. Selecting the right words for the right situation, understanding and using the right nuance and connotations of words, is what makes the difference between giving a speech and being a communicator. A rich, varied vocabulary and the ability to use it appropriately makes the difference between "good enough" and "great!"

Yet so many conversations, speeches, and sermons are filled with the ugly nonword fillers like "uhm" and "and" and "you know" and in the teenage world "whatever." Although uhm's and ah's are the most common, there are dozens of different non-words, but the debilitating fact is their monotonous repetition—their verbal redundancy. So choose your words, and pauses, well.

"A word fitly spoken," says Proverbs 25:11, "is like apples of gold in pictures of silver" (KJV).

What Others Do

Words in print. Some of the most memorable sermons ever preached remain powerful, even years later and left only in print, because they use powerful, picturesque words to represent God's message of truth. Jonathan Edwards's classic, "Sinners in the Hands of an Angry God" still reverberates with incredible emotional power and effect after two hundred years. R. G. Lee's "Payday Someday" is another fine example of an excellent vocabulary used to maximum effect and yet never at the expense of comprehension and accessibility.

Words that overcome. David Miller, a Southern Baptist evangelist from Arkansas, likes to call himself "just a country preacher," but his self-effacing title belies the tremendous reputation he has as a great communicator of God's Word. In addition to the typical difficulties inherent in full-time evangelism, David has to contend with the additional problems associated with the crippling and mysterious disease of muscular dystrophy. Suffering from this debilitating disease since he was fifteen, David is now confined to a wheelchair and unable to move and gesture when he preaches.

Just as he has faced and conquered the physical challenges of everyday life, so he has learned to compensate for those communication skills he cannot use because of his handicap. Preaching from a wheelchair, David is unable to move on the platform or even to gesture with his hands. He cannot hold a Bible or look at notes. A gifted expositor of God's Word, David understands that he still needs to infuse his message with energy and passion that will keep his audience involved with his message. So how does he do it?

David uses the most vivid facial expressions and picturesque language imaginable. His words are precise yet always comprehensible to his audience. He makes an emotional connection, through words, that carries the biblical content to the hearts and minds of his audience. If anyone doubts the power of language, he need look no further than a communicator like David Miller to see just how potent a rich vocabulary can be.

Watch the professionals. Nothing gets attention as easily and yet as effectively as a pause. It interrupts the barrage of sound and indicates a thoughtful deliberation. The pause indicates that what is to follow is momentous, is worth listening to, is weighty. If you watch videos of great comedians and communicators, not only will you notice that they pause frequently, but you can even notice that you can usually count three between setup and delivery, between question and answer, between joke and punch line. Bill Cosby, for instance, is a master of the pause, using it to let comedic expectation and laughter build while he makes a funny face or allows the humor to sink in.

What You Can Do

Build your vocabulary. The English language is a powerful tool, loaded with extra attachments and gadgets called "synonyms." Because of the wealth of synonyms in our language, we can take a single thought and express it in hundreds of ways. With a well-stocked vocabulary at our disposal, we can speak with precision, with subtle shades of meaning, with evocative imagery, and most of all with *energy*.

This does not mean that we have to know and use a lot of "big words," but we should have at our disposal the power to communicate in a variety of ways. We should have an entire warehouse of words immediately available. We should know how to say "meticulous" instead of "careful," "conundrum" instead of "riddle," "pivotal" instead of "crucial," "endow" instead of "give," "disciple" instead of "follower," "rebuff" instead of "refuse," and "*ad infinitum*" (or *even "ad nauseum"*) instead of "and so on and so forth," or worse yet, "yada yada yada."

With a little effort and intention, it's easy to stretch your vocabulary. Just try to use one new word a day. If you come across a new word while you're reading a book or a magazine, jot it down, look it up in a dictionary, start using it in conversation, and make it your own. Your purpose is not to show off, but to communicate effectively. A strong vocabulary is a powerful tool in your communication toolbox. Continually be on the lookout for new words that can help you communicate in the clearest, most colorful, most interesting way for every situation.

Paint word pictures. Language can do a lot more for our message than merely give us multiple ways of expressing an idea. Language can pack the energy factor into our communication by enabling us to paint intense, colorful word pictures. We can lend the energy of both *motion* and *emotion* to our speech by the use of metaphors and vivid expressions.

With a little imaginative language, the night sky becomes a "sparkling cosmic ocean." An F-16 fighter bomber becomes a "screaming bird of prey." A freeway at night becomes "a river of glowing red coals." The stock market didn't just go down; it "plummeted."

These are not "big words" used to impress other people with how smart we are. They are fairly simple words, but put together in ways that create memorable, exciting images that make vivid impressions on the first brain of our listener. Our goal is not to impress, but *to make an impression.* A rich and varied language can be one of the best tools at our command for getting our point across with energy and impact.

Beware of jargon. Christianity has its own language, so be careful! Among insiders, jargon can be a convenient form of shorthand communication. Maybe other mature believers know what "washed in the blood of the lamb" or "concupiscence" or "propitiation" means, but does your audience? Make sure that your audience actually understands what you are saying. Technical terms that they don't understand soon slam their first brains shut.

Find your level of fillers. Video yourself in conversation, teaching a class, or preaching a sermon. We can't overemphasize the power of feedback to uncover your communicating weaknesses so you can deal with them. As you listen or watch yourself on tape, count the fillers you use. You will probably wince a lot as you listen—but you'll also become more aware. That awareness will help you control the nonword habit.

Replace your nonwords with something more powerful. You're probably thinking, "But what if I can't live without my fillers? What happens if there's a big silent *gap* in my sentence while I'm thinking of the next phrase? Don't I need to fill those gaps with some sort of sound?" *No!* You fill those gaps with something *infinitely more powerful* than meaningless sounds. You fill those gaps with something that gives energy and drama to your message: *the pause.*

Use the "power of the pause." Did you know that the pause can be one of your most dynamic communicating tools? You can pause for as long as three or four seconds, right in the middle of a sentence—and it will not only seem perfectly natural to your listener; it will give extra punch to your message.

The problem with pausing is that most of us have never tried it. We are afraid of silence in our communication. We're not used to pausing, so we rush to fill the silence with inane and meaningless sound—sound which dampens our energy factor and blunts the point of our message.

Following are some basic exercises you can use to practice the pause.

(1) *Record yourself.* Use video or audio taping regularly to practice leaving pauses, and to sensitize yourself to your patterns of filler uses. It won't take long for you to sharpen your ear to those irritants. In fact, you'll soon begin catching yourself *before* the filler comes out of your mouth! You'll replace it with a pause. Being conscious of fillers is the first step to eliminating them.

(2) *Use voice mail.* Use your voice mail system as a feedback tool. Send yourself a copy of a real message you are sending to a colleague or friend, and listen to your pauses, or fillers. Do it daily at first.

(3) *Practice with a buddy.* Have a friend listen while you give an impromptu talk. Ask him or her to say your name instantly every time you use a filler. For some of us, the filler habit is so ingrained that we will not even notice it when it is pointed out to us. We may even feel picked on unfairly: "I did *not* say 'Uhh'!" It helps to work with a friend who is trying to get rid of his or her own filler habit so you can trade off.

When you feel tempted to lapse into a filler, just *pause*—three, four, five, six seconds or even more—while you gather your thoughts for the next sentence. Push your pauses to the limit. Then get feedback on your pauses: Did they seem forced or natural? Did they heighten the drama of your message and grab your listeners' attention? Remember the disparity that you will feel. It is valuable to get this experience of disparity many times over. You'll be surprised to discover how natural and confident you sound when you have learned the power of the pause.

Skill 7: Humor

*"The one who causes them to laugh,
gains more votes for the measure
than the one who forces them to think."*
—MALCOLM DE CHAZALL

Objective: To use humor to create a bond with your listeners

Humor creates a special bond between you and your listeners. It's virtually impossible to dislike someone who makes us laugh, who helps us enjoy ourselves. We are more able to accept tough truths and even correction when they are presented with a light touch. We not only tend to like to be around those people with a sense of humor who can laugh at themselves and the world around them; we tend to trust them more than the grim and serious. A sense of humor—whether sharp and explosive or dry and witty—makes you appear more genial, warmer, and more likable. And the strong, pleasurable emotions people associate with good fun and high spirits make your message enjoyable to listen to—and *memorable.*

One of the greatest examples of humor in action comes from American political history. In 1984, running for a second term in the White House against Walter Mondale, 76-year-old Ronald Reagan knew that age was a concern in the campaign. If reelected, he would be the oldest president in American history. A fumbling performance against Mondale in the first debate had already created the impression that Reagan was getting a little foggy, if not senile. So when a reporter served up the age question to Reagan during the second debate, the President was ready for it. "I will not make age an issue in this campaign," he replied with a mischievous glint in his eye. "I am not going to exploit for political purposes my opponent's youth and inexperience."

The press and the audience howled. Mondale himself could not repress an unexpected laugh—even though his fate was perhaps sealed at that moment. The age issue never came up again during the rest of the campaign—and that one exchange was the most remembered event of the debate, arguably of the entire campaign.

Humor can be a powerful tool for packing positive energy into your communication. Your goal and the effect of humor is to *make the formal informal.* No matter how sticky the situation, humor can turn the tide and make the most reluctant listeners open to your point of view. Though it doesn't come easily, developing an appropriate sense of humor is definitely worth working on.

What Others Do

One of the great challenges for a somewhat legalistic and staid Kentucky congregation was that the sanctuary had no air conditioning to combat the stifling summer heat. Finally the pastor broached the subject during the church business meeting and advocated getting central air installed. The old-timers rose up in arms. This was ungodly, so far as they were concerned, because it was using "worldly enticements" to get people to come to church. The pastor allowed a slight grin to creep across his face. "Then let's take out the furnace," he said. Suddenly the whole church began to laugh, even those who had been so zealous to protect their tradition. The air conditioner was installed shortly thereafter.

What You Can Do

Don't tell jokes. First and surprisingly, we strongly say *don't tell jokes!* Leave comedy to the comedians. Not many people are really good joke-tellers— perhaps one person in a hundred—and unfortunately, about ten times that many *think* they are good joke-tellers. If your joke falls flat, you'll go down with it. Everyone in the room feels uncomfortable and embarrassed when a speaker's joke does the old lead zeppelin. First brains snap shut. Persuasion screeches to a halt. Your listeners notice your technique—or lack thereof—

rather than your subject matter. Unless you are in that rare 1 percent who can actually tell a joke successfully—with timing, delivery, and flair—*don't.*

Second, understand that *fun is better than funny.* Your goal is not comedy but *connection*—creating an atmosphere of fun, friendliness, and openness. You want to put your listeners at ease, not develop a comedy routine for a night at the Improv.

Find the form of humor that works for you. So if jokes won't work for you, what will? Perhaps you can use stories and anecdotes. Or perhaps a slightly skewed outlook on life. Of course, a warm, genuine smile *always* works. Seeing the absurdity of your own world is a good start. What's your sense of humor like? A dry, subtle wit? The ability to poke gentle fun at yourself, to not take yourself too seriously? A unique outlook on everyday life? Do you find unexpected amusement in the things that happen around your home or the office? What kinds of things do you do and say in private conversations that make people laugh—and how can you work them into your talk, teaching, preaching, or presentations? Do you have a gift for seeing the humor and the opportunity in a crisis? Use what God has given you—because he has given all of us a sense of humor with different ways to apply it.

Use the humor in language. The right emphasis of a single word can provoke a laugh and cement the connection between you and your listener. Example: the speaker who defined "ageism" as "prejudice against the aged by the *temporarily* young." The great African-American pastor Shadrach Meshach Lockridge jokes that his mother did not give him the name of the third of the Hebrew children, Abednego, because in those days before improved civil rights she feared that someone might mistakenly call him "A bad Negro."

Think funny. How do you develop humor for your communication? Humor is the hardest communication skill to exercise, and the best exercise is actually working at a mind-set. Think funny, and you will begin to not only see the humor around you, but you will begin to use humor in your communications. Look for the humor in the serious; it is almost always there. There is even appropriate laughter and warm memories at funerals. Because people like to laugh. They like to be with people who are light-hearted. So do you.

Look at those who make you laugh or feel light-hearted, and emulate them. Think funny.

Think friendly. This is also a mind-set, and you can exercise your attitude on this one. The next person you see, think of being friendly, rather than judging or advocating or questioning or however you might set your attitude. With this mind-set, humor and humanization are much more likely to occur, and it will become a habit.

> "Laughter is the shortest distance between two people."
> —VICTOR BORGE

Keep a humor notebook. Keep a journal or diary of observations and funny quotations, anecdotes, and stories—especially those stories that happen to you. When keeping a story diary, don't write the entire story down—just a few trigger words to bring it back to mind when you're preparing your talk. Review it regularly, and it will add to your mind-set of thinking funny.

SKILL 8: LISTENER INVOLVEMENT

> "Your listeners won't care how much you know until they know how much you care."
> —ANONYMOUS

OBJECTIVE: TO MAINTAIN INTEREST AND INVOLVEMENT OF EACH PERSON TO WHOM YOU ARE COMMUNICATING

Books dispense information, but human beings communicate. There's a big difference. The question is: Are you a human being—or a book? Every time you communicate with another human being through the spoken word, you are doing much more than just imparting information. You are revealing ideas, opinions, and emotions. As a Christian communicator committed to sharing the Word of God, your subject matter and intent is even more significant. You are attempting to move that person to action, or to persuade that person to submit to God's Word. In other words, you are trying to *involve* your listener. If all you want to do is impart information, you might as well be a book!

Right now, we are coming to you in the form of a book. You can read *us*, but we can't read *you*. Are you bored? Fascinated? Irritated? Yawning? Excited? Are you smiling? Frowning? Giving half your attention to the TV? Are you sitting in a comfortable chair? Lying down? Do you sit at a desk and study this book intently—or is it bathroom reading? We don't know! We can't see you and adjust our message to better involve you! At this moment in your life, we are nothing but words on paper!

But if we were sitting together in conversation in your living room, or if you were in our audience—even if you were just one face in a sea of faces—we could *involve* you in a conversation. We could see if you are falling asleep or leaning forward in anticipation—and we could adjust the message and our behavior accordingly. We could change strategy to keep your first brain open to the flow of the message.

What Others Do

Contrast. Elisabeth Elliot addressed a group of college students at a gathering sponsored by a well-known campus ministry. Though separated by a generation and years of painful experience, her passionate delivery and "in-your-face" challenge to the tens of thousands of young adults was right on the mark. "Have the courage," she said slowly and deliberately, "to stay . . . out . . . of bed." At one point in the speech she involved her audience by taking the tone of a "valley girl" and offering feeble excuses like an ambivalent teen might propose. The effect was electric! Through identifying with her listeners, she had involved them and made them really hear her message.

Dramatic volume. John Rogers was asked to give a talk to a church group. His subject was "Conflict." As he stood up in front of the group, the babble of various conversations continued from different portions of the audience. "Shut up!" John shouted at the top of his lungs. "I'm tired of listening to you! From now on I talk and *you* listen!" At that moment, all eyes—some of them as big as saucers—were looking at John. You could have heard a snowflake drop. John went on: "The man who shouted those words in my face was about six feet tall and two hundred pounds. At that moment, I knew I was in for a heap of conflict." The tension broke—but John's listeners stayed quietly, attentively involved for the rest of his talk.

Using another medium. Rick Warren is the only pastor that Saddleback Valley Community Church has ever had. Taking the church from its inception to its current location and membership of over 15,000 has been largely due to his emphasis on application in his teaching. Warren was and is consistent in using one simple method of getting his congregation involved in his messages: he includes fill-in-the-blank outlines in the church bulletin. As Warren preaches, his parishioners fill in the key words that complete the application points Warren sees in the biblical text. This simple involving technique is a great tool for learning—and listening.

People as props. Adrian Rogers wanted every member of Bellevue Baptist Church to understand their mission, so right in the middle of his sermon he invited four men from the congregation to come to the platform with him. He placed one at the far left of the platform, one at the far right, and one in the middle, keeping the fourth man by his side. He explained that the man on the left represented the worst sinner who ever lived. Taking advantage of the obvious humor in bestowing such a title on one of his church members, Rogers explained that the apostle Paul said that was his place, as the "chief of sinners." The man on the far right represented the best Christian in the world. After having a little fun with that, the pastor then explained that the man in the middle represented Jesus Christ. He went on to remind the church that everyone they meet is somewhere in that continuum, somewhere between the worst and the best, and more importantly, on one side of Christ or the other.

Then taking the fourth man, Rogers placed him between the "worst" and "Jesus." He told the members, "You may not be able to get this man to Jesus, but through your smile and influence, your words and witness, maybe you can move him a step closer. Then one day," he continued, "he comes to know Christ," and with that he moved the subject to the other side of "Jesus," toward the "best man." Then, looking quizzically at the audience he asked, "Are we through with him now?" The entire congregation answered in unison a vibrant "No!" "No we aren't!" he assured them. "We want to move him on up the line. That is what discipleship and Bible study are all about!"

What You Can Do

Here are some of the many ideas to involve your audience. Some of them are behaviors we talked about before—here with an added reason for mastery. Use your creativity to mix and combine these in your communication. It takes practice and *confidence* to risk implementing these, but the reward in your impact is worth every bit of it.

Use drama. You can immediately involve your listener with a strong opening. Start with a striking statement, a dramatic story, or a question that forces the listener to focus on your message. Make your message visual and energetic with the use of action and motion. Use your voice to create drama: vocal tone or pitch variation, dramatic pauses, and strong emotional content (anger, sorrow, joy, laughter). Close your talk with a motivational call to specific action, or with a memorable quotation.

Maintain eye communication. Don't look over the heads of your audience; *meet them in the eye!* Survey your listeners for a few moments before you begin speaking. Maintain three to six seconds of eye contact with as many individuals as possible. Don't forget to include people in the "fringes" at either end of the audience or conference table. Read the eye contact they give back to you. Gauge whether your listeners are bored, wary, hostile, interested, or enthusiastic—and *adjust* your approach accordingly.

Move. Don't nail your shoes to the carpet—*move!* Avoid using a lectern or hiding behind a pulpit. If a lectern is provided, move out from behind it. Make your movements purposeful and authoritative. Never back away from your audience; it makes you look intimidated. In fact, at both the beginning and end of your talk, it lends force to your message to take a few steps *toward* your listeners.

Use visuals. In addition to making your own presence as interesting as possible, give your listeners something visual. Make your communication memorable with the use of bold, striking graphic aids, props, overheads, flip charts, or other sensory enhancements if possible and appropriate. Mix assorted kinds of media (for example, use both overheads and video clips) in order to keep the visual dimension varied and interesting. Rehearse the visual part of your presentation so that transitions will be fluid rather than fumbling. Involve your listeners with your visuals; for example, ask questions of your audience and briefly tabulate their answers on an overhead transparency.

Ask questions. Rhetorical questions will keep your listeners thinking and focused. Asking for a volunteer is even more involving. You actually feel a surge of intensity go through an audience, and you can read the thoughts of many of your listeners right on their faces: "Should I answer that question?" Asking for a show of hands also generates involvement—and it gives you a quick gauge of your audience's mood and opinions.

Use demonstrations. Plan and time every step or procedure. Have a volunteer from the audience assist in the demonstration. Above all, make sure your demonstration *works.* Once a pastor wanted to illustrate the incredible pressure on marriages and how one small matter can bring the whole marriage down. He had seen teenage boys stand on empty pop cans in the parking lot, amazed that they would hold the entire weight of a two-hundred pound man standing flat-footed on top of the can. Then someone else would take a pen or some small object and lightly touch the side of the can bearing the human weight. The can would then be crushed flat beneath the load it was bearing.

Thinking it a fitting illustration, the pastor asked for a volunteer from the audience to come to the platform, intending to use the subject to illustrate his point. He had never tried the scenario on the platform, however, and did not realize that a spongy carpeted surface made it impossible to distribute weight flatly on top. His volunteer crushed the can immediately, even before he could touch the side with a pen or explain his point. He did not even have a backup can for a clumsy second effort. People would not remember his point, but his embarrassment. The lesson is simple: When you demonstrate a concept for your listeners, make sure the demonstration doesn't backfire!

Use samples and gimmicks. Have fun with your listeners. If appropriate to your subject matter, have samples or small gifts available to give as rewards for volunteer participants. Be creative with using gimmicks—but be careful.

Gimmicks can backfire, so proceed with caution. When they work well, they work very well. But when they bomb, they explode with a big bang.

Create interest. Remember that your listeners have a short attention span. Pace your various involvement techniques to keep the level of interest high. Use eye contact to gauge your listeners' involvement.

Most of all, keep your own interest level high, even if you are giving a familiar sermon, lesson, or speech for the thousandth time. Change the order, change techniques, vary the stories you use. If you demonstrate genuine enthusiasm for your message, your emotional involvement and energy will be infectious!

SKILL 9: THE NATURAL SELF OBJECTIVE:
TO BE AUTHENTIC, LEARNING NEW SKILLS SO THEY
BECOME NATURAL

> *"When we encounter a natural style*
> *we are always surprised and delighted,*
> *for we thought to see an author,*
> *and found a man."*
> —PASCAL

The natural self is a paradox. It is the most simple "skill." Just to be yourself is easy and it is obviously natural. Yet so often we are unconscious about how that "self" comes across to others. Often that self is *not* natural, but is nervous or uncomfortable and not the way God intended us to be. And we usually don't know it. So the difficult part comes from gaining conscious awareness of how we come across and then learning new skills so we can have *conscious choice* about our impact on others.

Being our natural self is being authentic, and gaining the skills of communication so they become part of us. It is moving from the stage of unconscious incompetence to unconscious competence (see Maslow's stages of learning later in this section.) It is taking a look at our natural and unnatural habits, and getting a choice about them.

What You Can Do

Use habits wisely. God made us to use habits constructively. We have literally hundreds, even thousands of habits that help us daily, so that we do not have to live by bringing everything up to conscious thought. We can dress, drive, and dine without thinking. Can you imagine what it would be like if you had to think of what arm to put in your shirt first when you dress, or how to lift your leg to apply the brakes when you drive, or what you need to do to put your fork into a piece of food? We need to do many things at the unconscious level, but we do not need to communicate at the unconscious level. We are creatures of habits in our communications as well, and the purpose of this book is to bring those habits to the conscious level so we can have some choice about our communication habits. Because you are not born with your communication habits; they develop.

In his book *Psycho-Cybernetics,* Maxwell Maltz said that it takes twenty-one days to change a habit, and our experience shows that he is about right. There are hundreds of interpersonal communication habits that we have, both positive and negative. Most are in the nine communication skill areas covered in this book. Changing habits takes practice—framing, forming, and molding our minds to do certain physical behaviors that are repeated over and over again.

Change habits that are not working. To make a forward lean and increase your habit-changing skills, change one communication habit a day. Make it a campaign to work on them regularly. Today, concentrate on eye communication—looking at people for five seconds at a time. Tomorrow concentrate on leaving pauses—replacing nonwords with a pause. Use audio feedback with your voice mail. Then one day try to consciously "overdo" your gestures. (You probably can't.) Or "roller coaster" your voice.

Consider the four stages of learning. This is a good concept to hold around your practice at changing habits. The psychologist who gave us the "Hierarchy of Needs," Abraham Maslow has also given us a valuable framework to understand how we learn things:

1. *Unconscious incompetence.* We *don't know* that we don't know.

Most of us who have never had extensive feedback about our interpersonal skills are at this state of unconscious incompetence. We simply are not aware of our interpersonal communication habits.

2. *Conscious incompetence.* We *know* that we don't know.

Here we learn that we are not competent at something. This often comes as a rude awakening, usually through feedback. Video feedback is particularly valuable in moving us from stage 1 to stage 2.

3. *Conscious competence.* We *consciously work* at what we don't know.

Here we consciously make an effort to learn a new skill. Practice, drill, and repetition are at the forefront. This is where most learning takes place. It takes effort and work.

4. *Unconscious competence.* We *don't have to think* about knowing it.

Here the skill set happens automatically at an unconscious level. A speaker with a distracting habit who has learned to overcome it through practice doesn't have to concentrate on *not* doing the distracting habit.

Consider the juggler. Every juggler first learned by starting with one ball, just to get the rhythm, then added another to practice with both hands working together. Finally, a third ball was added, and more, until the juggler juggled proficiently. Becoming an expert in interpersonal communications is much like juggling. You master one skill at a time, and add to them once they become a habit.

Start by acknowledging your natural strengths and be thankful you don't have to learn them from scratch, for many others do. You may have an easy, natural smile, where others may have to work at lightening themselves up in their interpersonal communications. On the other hand, you may find it difficult to gesture naturally, where another might have been born more effusive. Acknowledge strengths and work to improve and capitalize on them.

Then work on your weaknesses, one at a time, until they become strengths. Take your weakest area first and concentrate on improving it every day for a week. Using uhm's and ah's may be a difficulty for you. Put your conscious mental energy into leaving pauses each day for a week or two—with no nonwords! Then move to another skill. Continue that process until you have gone through the many parts of all nine skills.

Remember that communicating well is a lifetime process. We are not born effective communicators. God gave us certain potentials and abilities, and much room to learn and to change. He gave us habits to help us in all things, and particularly in our communication. We always find new unwanted habits that pop up, as well as old undesirable habits that creep back. We also find new strengths that occur as we mature and as we experiment with various behavioral skills. Often synergy occurs where a new-found habit will work to improve an old habit. Or two habits work together to form an effective new behavior.

For example, movement and extended eye communication can breed confidence that allows somebody to maintain excellent eye communication with an individual and even allow perhaps a reaching out and touching the arm of the listener.

Conclusion

You can probably find at least as many ways to preach God's Word as there are different types of literature in the Bible. And while we acknowledge that you can preach effectively using a different approach than what we advocate, we are also convinced that following this methodology is a sure way to give your people a strategic grasp of the Scriptures and a steady spiritual diet that motivates them to action. While you may have occasion to deviate, make certain that you never move away from giving them the meaning and challenging them with the application of the Scripture.

As you practice the various elements of attention to text, sermon, and delivery, you will certainly develop your own style and modifications on the things we teach here. We certainly hope so. In the limited scope of a single book of this size, we can only scratch the surface, so you have lots of room to learn, to grow, and to develop your own nuances.

But beware letting your preaching become routine or mundane, even to you. Ironically, the better preacher you are, the more you have to consciously realize your dependence on the Lord. May God protect you from operating in the realm of talent rather than of the Spirit. God help you if you let a system—even *our* system—lead you away from his heart and into a coldly efficient, powerless preaching that people mistake for the anointed blessing of the Holy Spirit.

Never forget what a privilege God has given you. You speak for God! You are an ambassador of heaven, a bearer of the best news that people could ever hear. That responsibility demands and deserves your best. You must not change or dilute the King's message. You dare not confuse the people whose lives depend on it by presenting the life-giving word in a dreary and routine manner. And if you are blessed enough to become proficient as a communicator, you must never succumb to the temptation to stop building God's kingdom and start building your own.

No matter what anyone says, the greatest need of the twenty-first century is the gospel. And the greatest need of the gospel is a generation of passionate and convicted preachers who will stand and preach God's Word with bold assurance. When preaching such as that thunders from the pulpits of our churches, evangelistic fervor and holy devotion will emanate from the pews.

Endnotes

1. The concept of these five commitments originated with Duane Litfin, currently president of Wheaton College. He shared these with a doctoral seminar in which one of the authors was enrolled at Mid-America Baptist Theological Seminary in 1989. At this writing Litfin has not yet published these, yet he graciously allowed us to include them here. The wording is slightly changed from Litfin's, but the ideas are distinctly and originally his and have been adapted here.

2. Haddon W. Robinson, *Biblical Preaching: The Development and Delivery of Expository Messages* (Grand Rapids: Baker Book House, 1980), 20.

3. Haddon W. Robinson, *Biblical Preaching: The Development and Delivery of Expository Messages* (Grand Rapids, Baker Book House, 1980), 31.

4. For more detailed instruction in diagramming, consult Walt Kaiser's classic *Toward an Exegetical Theology* (Grand Rapids: Baker Book House, 1981). For a much more grammatical method of diagramming, see Thomas Schreiner's *Interpreting the Pauline Epistles* (Grand Rapids: Baker Book House, 1990).

5. This inelegant, woodenly literal translation is York's own. By preserving the syntax of the Greek sentence, the importance and method of diagramming can be more clearly demonstrated.

6. The authors are indebted to Rick Melick of Golden Gate Baptist Theological Seminary for these helpful categories. Much of what follows is adapted from his "Exegetical Method Overview" that he shared in the

"Preaching from the Greek New Testament" class he taught at Mid-America Baptist Theological Seminary when one of the authors was his student.

7. For a helpful understanding of issues related to genre and hermeneutics, see Robert Stein's excellent book, _A Basic Guide to Interpreting the Bible: Playing by the Rules_ (Grand Rapids: Baker Book House, 1997).

8. We could add a fourth category, textual analysis, but feel that such a technical discussion as textual criticism warrants would take us further afield than we want to go. Suffice it to say that a good expositor, especially one who works from the original Greek or Hebrew, needs to be aware of the textual variants and reach a settled conclusion about what the original text actually is. We recommend Bruce Metzger's _Textual Commentary on the Greek New Testament_ (Philadelphia: Fortress Press, 2002) and _The Text of the New Testament: Its Transmission, Corruption, and Restoration_ (London: Oxford University Press, 1992); Kurt and Barbara Aland's _The Text of the New Testament: an Introduction to the Critical Editions and to the Theory and Practice of Modern Textual Criticism_ (Grand Rapids: Wm. B. Eerdmans, 1995); and J. Harold Greenlee's _Introduction to New Testament Textual Criticism_ (Peabody, Mass.: Hendrickson Publishers, 1995) or (on the popular level) _Scribes, Scrolls, and Scriptures_ (Grand Rapids: Wm. B. Eerdmans, 1985). Emanuel Tov's _Textual Criticism of the Hebrew Bible_ (Philadelphia: Fortress Press, 2001) is the standard for Old Testament textual criticism. These books describe the process of textual criticism and how the student can have confidence in the text of the Bible, and the basis on which one judges textual variants.

9. The UBS text actually divides the sentence into three sentences, but since they do so at the relative pronouns "in whom," most scholars agree that Paul wrote it as one single sentence.

10. Just as the UBS editors put two extra periods in the sentence, so did the translators of the KJV, and they did it at the same places. Since the two additional sentences begin with the relative pronoun "in whom" we can still safely say that Paul just wrote one sentence that begins in verse three and lasts through verse fourteen.

11. The Greek word order is explicit. "Son" is the first word of the quote and also the last.

12. See Kenneth E. Bailey, *Poet and Peasant Through Peasant Eyes* (Grand Rapids: Wm. B. Eerdmans, 1983).

13. Haddon Robinson, "The Heresy of Application," *Leadership* (Fall 1997), 21-27.

14. Ibid., pp. 23-24.

15. The authors are again indebted to Rick Melick for much of this process. His lectures in his class, "Preaching from the Greek New Testament," at Mid-America Baptist Theological Seminary had a profound impact on one of the authors who has adapted and advocated this methodology for years.

16. Details of this story were taken from *Ghosts of Everest: The Search for Mallory and Irvine* by Jochen Hemmleb, Larry A. Johnson, Eric R. Simonson, Will Northdurft, and Clare Millikan (Seattle: Mountaineers Books, 1999).

17. Jon Krakauer, *Into Thin Air: A Personal Account of the Mt. Everest Disaster* (New York: Villard, 1997).

18. Duane A. Litfin, *Public Speaking: A Handbook for Christians* (Grand Rapids: Baker Book House, 1992), 46-47.

19. Charles Panati, *Panati's Extraordinary Endings of Practically Everything and Everybody* (New York: Harper & Row, 1989), 346.

20. Ibid., p. 398.

21. Ibid., p. 361.

22. Solomon Stoddard, *The Defects of Preachers Reproved.* Preached at Northampton, Massachusetts, May 19, 1723. Punctuation has been edited for clarity.

23. John E. Smith, ed., *Works of Jonathan Edwards, Volume 2: Religious Affections* (New Haven: Yale University Press, 1959), 121.

24. Richard A. Bailey, "Driven by Passion: Jonathan Edwards and the Art of Preaching," in *The Legacy of Jonathan Edwards: American Religion and the Evangelical Tradition.* Edited by D.G. Hart, Sean Michael Lucas, Stephen J. Nichols. Grand Rapids, MI: Baker Book House, forthcoming 2003.

25. John A. Broadus, *A Treatise on the Preparation and Delivery of Sermons* (Philadelphia: Smith, English and Co., 1870), 18.

Sample Sermon

How to Have the Compassion
to Confront

1 Corinthians 5:1–13

In 1974 I was fourteen years old and very vulnerable, at an easily impressionable stage of adolescence. Before that time, my life was very tranquil. I enjoyed a happy home and a wonderful relationship with my Christian parents. But then a man came into my life who heaped all kinds of abuse on me. Every day after school I would go see this man before I went home, and he would subject me to the most intense forms of physical torture and verbal abuse imaginable. By the time I left a few hours later, my body was wracked with pain and indescribable feelings of inferiority because of the torturous physical and verbal punishment he heaped on me. Yet, strange as it may seem, I always went back to him. You see, that man was my wrestling coach; and he helped me understand that if I went through this kind of physical torture, if I learned to negotiate the rigors of his practices, then I would ultimately be a better wrestler. I would be disciplined.

I invite you now to a different scene in my life. I am no longer fourteen, but forty-three, married to a wonderful wife and blessed to be the father of two teenage sons. If you could be an unseen guest in our home, you would be able to see us sitting at the table around a meal and engaging in happy banter, relational repartee, sometimes finding ourselves lost in laughter, sometimes sharing those moments that seem insignificant though they define the direction of one's life or home. You might also witness one of those times when we delight in one another more than I could possibly describe. On the other hand, you might happen to glance in and see us when things are tense, when my sons have violated the will of their father and they are experiencing the tough side of love. You might hear me speak in animated voice and unhappy tones. Listen closely, and you might hear them being grounded or lectured. Had you come when they were younger, you might even see them being spanked. But if you stayed long enough you would eventually notice that the rare times when we administer discipline is what liberates and frees our home for the peace, harmony, and mutual delight that usually reigns.

Like every father, I love my sons. There has never been a time where I've had to discipline them that I enjoyed it (contrary to what I make them believe). I've never said to them, "This hurts me worse than it hurts you." I tell them, "It's going to hurt you a lot worse than it hurts me." That is, after all, the point! But recently I received a card from one of my sons that read: "You took center stage in my thoughts today, and my heart gave you a standing ovation. I appreciate you so much. Dad, I love you so, so much that not a day goes by when I don't thank God for your wonderful heart for God and your desire to raise Michael and me to be great people. I know it's no special occasion or anything, but you're a special dad, so I just wanted to say thanks. I love you and mom bunches. Seth." Some might be incredulous that a son whom I have spanked and grounded, lectured and rebuked, would write me a card like that, but these two things are connected.

And that's not only true in our physical family, but that's true in God's family as well. It is the discipline that he imposes on us that keeps our hearts close to his and in fellowship with him. The correction that he offers us through the body of Christ—through our fellow believers and church members, keeps us in love with his people—in love with his heart—in love with his way.

The apostle Paul wrote to the church at Corinth about just such an event. A brother in the church had fallen into gross sin. Paul wrote to the Corinthians in 1 Corinthians 5:1-3: " *It is actually reported that there is immorality among you, and immorality of such a kind as does not even exist among the Gentiles, that someone has his father's wife. And you have become arrogant, and have not mourned instead, in order that the one who had done this deed might be removed from your midst. For I, on my part, though absent in body but present in spirit, have already judged him who has so committed this, as though I were present. In the name of our Lord Jesus, when you are assembled, and I with you in spirit, with the power of our Lord Jesus, I have decided to deliver such a one to Satan for the destruction of his flesh, that his spirit may be saved in the day of the Lord Jesus. Your boasting is not good. Do you not know that a little leaven leavens the whole lump of dough? Clean out the old leaven, that you may be a new lump, just as you are in fact unleavened. For Christ our Passover also has been sacrificed. Let us therefore celebrate the feast, not with old leaven, or with the leaven of malice and wickedness, but with the unleavened bread of sincerity and truth. I wrote you in my letter not to associate with immoral people; I did not at all mean with immoral people of this world, or with the covetous and swindlers, or with idolaters; for then you would have to go out of the world. But actually, I wrote to you not to associate with any so-called brother if he should be an immoral person, or covetous, or an idolater, or a reviler, or a drunkard, or a swindler—not even to eat with such a one. For what have I to do with judging outsiders? Do you not judge those who are within the church? But those who are outside, God judges. Remove the wicked man from among yourselves"* (NASB).

Individuals and churches usually commit one of two errors when they think about discipline. On the one hand, some say, "Well, this is such a private matter, we have no business interfering in people's lives. After all, we are all sinners. Who are we to judge one sin worse than another?" and therefore, they exercise no discipline. And where there is no discipline, there is no security, and ultimately there is no fellowship. On the other hand, some take it to the opposite extreme and think that the purpose of discipline is merely to censor, to be harsh, and to keep the church rolls clean. They ignore or forget its redemptive purpose and settle for an enforced conformity that never penetrates to the heart. But one can't argue against something based on its abuse. Otherwise we would have to argue against marriage because some men beat their wives. We would have to oppose disciplining our children because some people abuse theirs. No, the proper argument is against the abuse of the thing and not the thing itself. Clearly in Scripture, and in this chapter, we see unequivocally that discipline is commanded in the church of the Lord Jesus. The apostle makes it obligatory, not optional.

Proposition: *Every church should practice loving church discipline to keep its members from the path of sin.*

Transitional sentence: Fortunately the Bible states three reasons to practice compassionate discipline, as well as the way to do it.

I. DISCIPLINE BECAUSE OF SIN'S EFFECT (1–5)

A. Sin has a witness to the world (1).

1. Not every sin makes a church member the object of church discipline.

2. What qualities made this sin worthy of such an extraordinary step?

  a. It is public: actually reported.

  b. It is gross immorality: such a kind that even unbelievers know that Christians don't do that!

    (1) The Lord gives the world the right to judge us!

      (a) By our love—"By this all men will know that you are my disciples" (John 13:35).

      (b) and by our holiness.

    (2) even the world knows that this is what Christians should be.

  c. Other categories of sin mentioned in Scripture that call for church discipline are:

    (1) doctrinal heresy, is taught in Romans 16:17-18: "I urge you, brothers, to watch out for those who cause divisions and put obstacles in your way that are contrary to the teaching you have learned. Keep away from them. For such people are not serving our Lord Christ, but their own appetites. By smooth talk and flattery they deceive the minds of naive people."

      (a) If anyone in the church insists on teaching contrary to the clear doctrine of the Bible in a cardinal area, then that person must be marked, set aside.

      (b) *Illustration:* Once at my church we had a man who persisted in trying to persuade everyone that all people were going to heaven. He put flyers on their cars, in mail boxes, and in every conversation. He was lovingly confronted, warned a first and second time, and when he would not repent of his error and stop teaching it, he was removed from the fellowship of the church creating division. This is taught in Titus 3:9-11: *But avoid foolish controversies and genealogies and arguments and quarrels about the law, because these are unprofitable and useless. Warn a divisive person once, and then warn him a second time.*

After that, have nothing to do with him. You may be sure that such a man is warped and sinful; he is self-condemned." In this passage it is not speaking of doctrinal conformity but of spiritual immaturity that manifests itself in an argumentative spirit. Some churches cannot progress until they deal with those members who are always arguing over the inane and the inconsequential. They should be rebuked privately and, then, if they will not hear and repent, they should be disciplined.

    (a)   *Illustration:* A man caused division and rebuked my staff member publicly while I was out of the country. And I rebuked him publicly.

    (b)   This is not for honest disagreement, but for a divisive spirit.

(2)   And *the sin of an elder:* If an elder sins—a pastor or one of the leaders of the church—should be rebuked before the entire church, even if he repents. 1 Timothy 5:19–21 states, *"Do not entertain an accusation against an elder unless it is brought by two or three witnesses. Those who sin are to be rebuked publicly, so that the others may take warning. I charge you, in the sight of God and Christ Jesus and the elect angels, to keep these instructions without partiality, and to do nothing out of favoritism."* I know of one of the largest churches in America where recently the pastor brought a staff member before the church who had experienced a moral failure in his life. Even though he was repentant, the pastor rebuked him before the entire church so that the church members would know the seriousness and the heartache of sin.

B. Sin has an effect on the church (2).

  1. It made them "puffed up" rather than mourn

    a. Not puffed up in that they enjoyed the sin

    b. But rather than they prided themselves on their tolerance, on leaving him alone, even though he would not repent!

  2. They became "desensitized" to sin. Why should we go to such lengths? First of all, because the *Bible is clear* about it and commands it. Believe

me, it is much easier in the short term to sweep it under the rug and
ignore it, but then the *church preaches a subtle message that sin is not
so serious* and that the rules change. Furthermore, there is no incentive
for repentance. *Trying to take the shame out of sin is a dangerous enterprise.*

C. The church should have an effect on sin (3–5).

1. The result of their mourning should be obvious that

    a. one who has done these things should be removed.

    b. *Note:* Paul does not in this text mention forgiveness.

        (1) Based on other passages, it is proper to infer that this brother
            was unrepentant and was persisting in the sin.

        (2) The opportunity for repentance had been refused.

    c. *Jesus himself* laid out the procedure in Matthew 18

        (1) Private confrontation

        (2) Small group confrontation

        (3) Church confrontation

        (4) Treat him as a heathen and a publican outcast

    d. Pastors must rigidly enforce this procedure

        (1) Don't let anyone skip a step!

        (2) Make them go to one another.

        (3) Have the church adopt the procedure, relying heavily on the
            Scripture.

2. Paul did not have to make a judgment.

    a. The judgment had already been made.

    b. If the facts are clear, the sin is evident, and the guilty party
       unrepentant, then that person must be put out of the church.

        (1) Praise God, often they repent at when confronted,
            but if they do not, they must be handed "over to Satan for the
            destruction of the flesh."

            (a) This means they are put out from under the supernatural
                protection afforded to those in the Lord's church.

            (b) One of two things will happen:
                i) they will hurt so badly that they repent,
                ii) or their continuation in sin will prove that they were
                    never saved.

            (c) Note how closely Paul's apostolic words parallel the

words of Jesus himself in Matthew 18:15–20.

    (1)   Where two or three are gathered together in my name, there am I in the midst of them—that means church discipline!

    (2)   Here Paul says that he will be with them in spirit as they do what they must do.

    (3)   *Always treat sin like sin would treat you!*

    (4)   Beware sin's effect and realize it for the serious problem it is.

Transitional sentence: But with sin's effect on the one who did it, there was an inherent effect on the church as well, so Paul not only identifies sin's effect, but he also tells us to

II. DISCIPLINE BECAUSE OF SALVATION'S EXPECTATION (6–8)

A. Don't treat sin lightly.

1. The church had a problem with sin as did the perpetrator
2. Their great problem was that they did not see sin as the serious offense against God that it is
3. They thought that a "little sin" would not be a problem
4. But Paul reminds them that a little leaven leavens the whole lump and results in
   a. Members who are a little guilty
   b. Unmarried girls who are a little pregnant
   c. Little bigots who are a little racist
   d. Men who commit a little adultery
   e. Churches that have little impact!
5. Do some spiritual housecleaning
   a. Purge out that old leaven
   b. Renew the church's commitment to purity

B. Don't treat the atonement lightly.

1. Notice the connection Paul makes between the way we view sin and the way we view the atonement.
   a. Ultimately, a light view of sin means a light view of what Jesus did.

    b. Paul reminds us that Jesus is our Passover lamb, sacrificed for us because of our sins.

    c. Once the Passover lamb was slain, the feast of unleavened bread began

        (1)   No leaven was allowed in the meal

        (2)   or even in the house!

        (3)   That leaven represents sin.

    d. We eat the Passover feast, but it is a different kind of feast.

    e. For the Christian, it is always Passover.

        (1)   Our lamb has been sacrificed,

        (2)   and now we must rid ourselves of leaven, sin, because our Lamb has been slain!

        (3)   Notice the order:

            (a)   first, the sacrifice

            (b)   and then the purging.

            (c)   It is the atonement that demands holiness!

                i) not in order to earn it

                ii) but in order to honor it!

        (4)   We get rid of the leaven of malice and evil

        (5)   And feast on sincerity and truth!

        (6)   *Illustration:* Once when our church disciplined a young lady, she repented. But her action was then a model for another young lady in the church who was scheduled for an abortion, but when she saw the loving way the church dealt with sin, she confessed her sin and kept her baby.

  2. A high commitment to sincerity and truth means a high commitment to get rid of sin

Transitional Sentence: But if we do as the apostle says and put an unrepentant person out of the fellowship of the church, how should we treat him?

III. DISCIPLINE IN HOPE OF A SINNER'S RESTORATION (9–13)

A. Practice biblical separation.

  1. You can't separate from lost sinners.

   2. You must separate from those in sin who claim to be saved!

   3. Don't eat with them.

      a. Does this mean the Lord's Supper,

      b. or does this mean to shun them altogether?

B. Don't judge those outside the church.

   1. They are only acting like what they are.

   2. They are consistent with their character.

C. You must judge those within the church.

   1. 1 Peter 4:17: *"For it is time for judgment to begin with the family of God; and if it begins with us, what will the outcome be for those who do not obey the gospel of God?"*

   2. Although most churches do not practice scriptural discipline, even those who attempt it seldom understand its purpose. It is meant to win back the erring brother. In Jesus' first sermon on the church in Matthew 18, he talked about discipline and said that often, when done right, "You have gained your brother." The whole purpose is to get that brother back in line with sound teaching, sound practice.

   3. But sometimes that brother must first be disfellowshipped that he might feel the loneliness and isolation that sin brings before he will ever repent.

CONCLUSION: Some years ago I received a letter from a lady member of the first church that I pastored. She told me that Robert, who had been my chairman of deacons, our church's greatest soulwinner, and my closest friend in the church had left his wife and was living with another woman. To say that I was shocked would be a gross understatement. I called Dora, his wife and asked what had happened. Confirming my worst fears she said, "It's true. He's left me. We're not even divorced but he's already living with another woman." I said, "Give me the phone number at the house where he is staying." She gave it to me, and I called. Robert's illicit lover answered and I asked for him. She said, "Yes, may I tell him who is calling?" I said, "Yes, tell him this is his friend and former pastor, Hershael York." As I heard her relay those words to him I could hear a gurgling, choking sound coming from his throat as he decided whether to even take the phone.

   "Hello," he managed to sheepishly say. My voice betraying the fervency of my disappointment and my righteous indignation, I said, "Robert, what are you doing?

What are you thinking?" Mustering his defense, he answered, "Well, I just got tired of being the only one making the effort. What do you do when you give and give and get nothing in return? What do you do when you try to express love, and she won't give any back? What do you do when you sacrifice everything for her, and she never even says thank you?" In a moment of insight supplied by the Holy Spirit, I said, "Here's what you do, Robert. You make a cold, hard, rational decision to obey God anyway. That's exactly what you do."

When the hard truth I offered received no further excuses, I continued, "Now you listen to me—I want you to pack your things right now and go home to your wife. I want you to get her, and I want the two of you to drive all the way up here to my home, and I want you to spend the weekend with me and Tanya."

I can't exactly explain what happened. Either God gave me the boldness to confront him, or he gave him the grace to be compliant, but Robert did exactly what I told him to do. He went home and got his wife, and they came up to our house and, during that whole weekend, Tanya and I just ministered to them from the Word. Three days later they went back home committed to make their marriage work. Three weeks later they came back to Lexington with their two children and said, "We want to repeat our vows and start fresh and new." Years have passed since that time, and they are both serving the Lord. Robert reports that he has been used of God to win hundreds of teenagers to Christ in the past four years. Recently I called and asked, "Dora, how's it going?" With her voice cracking from grateful emotion she answered, "If anyone had ever told me marriage and life could be this good, I would have never have believed it."

The cruelest thing you can ever do to a brother or sister in Christ is to find them in sin and leave them there.